David Lampe
May '91

12⁹⁵

MEDIEVAL

LITERARY CRITICISM

W9-ANN-943

MEDIEVAL
LITERARY CRITICISM

Translations and Interpretations

EDITED BY

O. B. HARDISON, JR.

ALEX PREMINGER

KEVIN KERRANE

LEON GOLDEN

FREDERICK UNGAR PUBLISHING CO.

NEW YORK

Copyright © 1974 by Frederick Ungar Publishing Co., Inc.
Printed in the United States of America
Designed by Irving Perkins

Library of Congress Cataloging in Publication Data
Main entry under title:

Medieval literary criticism.

Abridged ed. of: Classical and medieval literary
criticism. 1974.
  Bibliography: p.
  Includes index.
  1. Criticism, Medieval.   I. Preminger, Alex.
II. Hardison, O. B.   III. Kerrane, Kevin.
IV. Classical and medieval literary criticism.
PN88.M43   1985   801'.95'0902   84-28011
ISBN 0-8044-6665-3

ACKNOWLEDGMENTS

Acknowledgment is gratefully made to the following who have granted permission to use copyrighted material.

Duke University Press, for O.B. Hardison's "The Place of Averroes' Commentary on the *Poetics* in the History of Medieval Criticism" in *Medieval and Renaissance Studies*, no. 4., ed. by John Lievsay, copyright 1970 Duke University Press and reprinted here in abridged and modified form.

Pontifical Institute of Mediaeval Studies, for selections from *The Poetria Nova* of Geoffrey of Vinsauf, tr. by Margaret F. Nims and reprinted by permission of the translator of and the President of the Pontifical Institute.

CONTENTS

PREFACE

The history of criticism is one of the liveliest areas of current literary studies. Within the last decade it has grown in importance as a direct consequence of interest in structuralism, poststructuralism, and semiotics, all new fields that are rooted in earlier attempts to formulate rigorous critical methods.

The available histories and anthologies of criticism are adequate for the classical and postmedieval periods, up to and including the criticism of the 1960s and 1970s. There is, however, a yawning gap in the histories and anthologies for the millennium between the fourth and the fifteenth centuries. This gap is understandable but—since the publication of E. R. Curtius's *European Literature and the Latin Middle Ages*—inexcusable. It creates a distorted, if not totally false idea of the relationship between ancient and Renaissance literary aesthetics. It also renders unintelligible to all but the best-informed readers the significance of such apparently eccentric but, in fact, intensely serious treatments of literature as Christoforo Landino's reading of the *Aeneid* in his *Camaldulensian Disputations* and Edmund Spenser's outline of his concept of epic in the famous "Letter to Raleigh," which prefaced the second (1594) edition of *The Faerie Queene*.

The present book is intended to fill the gap in the history of criticism in three ways. In the first place, it provides a representative selection of medieval critical texts, many of them translated into English for the first time here, and most of them inaccessible or difficult to locate. In the second, it offers an extensive introductory essay outlining the main types and periods of medieval criticism, and there are also detailed introductions to each author. And in the third place it contains a bibliography of important works in a field that is often blurred to the point of unintelligibility by being combined with related but distinct fields such as rhetoric, biblical exegesis, and stylistics.

It is hoped that the present work will be useful to advanced students of the field, and also to teachers of courses in medieval literature, medieval culture, and the history of criticism.

Sincere thanks for assistance in the creation of the present volume are extended to Alex Preminger, Kevin Kerrane, and Leon Golden, all of whom offered useful advice and proposals for improvement. As in the past, my debt to my wife Marifrances is so great that it can be acknowledged but never repaid.

O. B. Hardison, Jr.
Washington, D.C.
November 14, 1984

MEDIEVAL
LITERARY CRITICISM

O. B. Hardison, Jr.

GENERAL INTRODUCTION

There is at present no authoritative work on the history of medieval criticism. The explanation is first, doubtless, that scholars have not thought it worth the effort. Few people read medieval poetry and fewer still are interested in the critical theories that lie behind it. But there is another reason than lack of general interest. The subject is particularly difficult to define. Studies tend either to be too narrow and hence to distort by exclusiveness, or too inclusive and hence to lose focus. First and foremost, medieval literature is international, not national. Yet, outside of departments of comparative literature, the orientation of modern literary studies is strongly nationalistic. One of the standard treatments of medieval criticism in use today is J. W. H. Atkins' *English Literary Criticism: The Medieval Phase* (1952). Atkins' approach is not merely biased, it is fatal to the subject. The habit of dividing literary subjects along national lines leads Atkins to treat Bede and Alcuin in detail, while ignoring the late classical authors who were their primary sources; to treat John of Salisbury and John of Garland while ignoring Bernard Silvestris, Hugh of St. Victor, Conrad of Hirsau, and Gervase of Melcheley, among others.

Again, literary criticism is related to, but different from the history of aesthetics and the history of style. Medieval aesthetics has been treated by Edgar de Bruyne, while stylistics has been analyzed by Hans Glunz. Neither de Bruyne nor Glunz, however, had any intention of writing a history of criticism. De Bruyne is interested in the idea of beauty and its manifestation in medieval architecture, music, painting, and sculpture, as well as literature. Plotinus and St. Thomas are key figures in his study, although they are secondary in the history of medieval criticism. Again, Glunz's analysis of medieval stylistics takes him beyond the limits of treatises on literary theory and into analysis of the verbal texture of medieval poems.

Finally, it cannot be stressed too often that rhetoric and poetic are two different disciplines during the Middle Ages. C. S. Baldwin's *Medieval Rhetoric and Poetic* (1928), heavily indebted to Edmond Faral, is perhaps our closest approximation to a modern history of medieval criticism. Baldwin rightly points out that rhetorical doctrine was absorbed wholesale in many critical documents and had a pervasive influence on others. This leads him to the assumption that medieval poetic is merely a variant of medieval rhetoric, an assumption that

3

is simply not valid. Baldwin's treatment of the *artes poeticae* of the twelfth and thirteenth centuries is a useful summary of their debt to rhetoric, particularly to the pseudo-Ciceronian *Rhetorica ad Herennium*. But it distorts the *artes* by ignoring the central fact that the rhetorical content has been adapted to artistic purposes. In other words, far from illustrating a confusion of rhetoric with poetic, the *artes* reveal a lively consciousness of the differences between them. The rhetorical approach also commits Baldwin to extended treatment of documents that are not primarily critical, like Alcuin's *Rhetoric,* while causing him to neglect such large and important segments of medieval criticism as allegory, the *accessus* (or list of authors), and scholastic treatises on poetry.

For present purposes, we will define literary criticism as a group of texts dealing with the history and theory of literature (in its narrower sense as against general discussions of art, the beautiful, and the like), literary creation, and the analysis of specific literary works. Biblical exegesis is an enormous subject in its own right. It will be mentioned from time to time simply because it is too large to be ignored. Certain challenges that it posed for criticism—for example, the assimilation of Hebrew literary forms into Graeco-Roman tradition and the extension of literary chronology to periods earlier than Homer—have a direct bearing on specific late classical developments. Others—whether a Christian should study pagan authors, the relation of biblical to secular allegory, and the concept of inspiration—provided standard critical topics throughout the whole period from Augustine to Boccaccio and gave rise to different responses at different times. But as a subject biblical exegesis is not literary criticism, and a history of medieval criticism must avoid the tendency to become excessively involved in the area covered so well by Henri de Lubac's *Exégèse médiévale.*

If we limit the topic successfully, we still have to come to terms with several problems. For example, what is the dividing line between "medieval" and "classical"? To select a historical date such as the conversion of Constantine is wholly unsatisfactory, for certain types of criticism that are generally considered typically medieval were commonplace before Plato. Allegorical criticism, for example, began with Theagenes of Rhegium in the sixth century B.C. and has a continuous history throughout the classical period. Alexandrian critical theory as exemplified in the works of Philo Judaeus, Clement of Alexandria, and Origen extends from the first century B.C. to the second century A.D., a period roughly coincident with the golden and silver ages of Roman literature. When we move to the Latin west, a still more curious situation presents itself. If Statius is "classical," is Tertullian "medieval"? If Augustine and Jerome are "medieval," are Servius, Donatus, and Macrobius "classical"? To ask questions like these is to call attention to the fact that the terms "classical" and "medieval" refer less to chronology than to cultural perspective.

Certain elements of the classical tradition were absorbed easily and naturally by medieval authors, while others—classical drama, for example—were intractable and were either neglected or had to be modified profoundly before being assimilated. Macrobius and Boethius are in the first category. They were read easily throughout the Middle Ages. At the same time, both were conscious of the whole body of classical tradition. They can be considered either "classical" or "medieval" with equal validity. On the other hand, Vergil and Ovid are un-ambiguously classical. They were read universally during the Middle Ages, but— as we know from Fulgentius, Bernard Silvestris, Bercorius and Boccaccio—their work was only admitted to the canon of medieval classics after it had been dis-torted almost beyond recognition. This process of assimilation by distortion was quite conscious.

In his *Clerical Institute* Rabanus Maurus advised, "If we wish to read the poems and books of the gentiles because of their flowers of eloquence, we must take as our type the captive woman in Deuteronomy . . . If an Israelite should want her as a wife, he should shave her head, cut off her nails, and pluck her eyebrows. When she has been made clean, he can then embrace her as a husband. By the same token, we customarily do this when a book of secular learn-ing comes into our hands. If we find anything useful in it we absorb it into our teaching. If there is anything superfluous concerning idols, love, or purely secular affairs, we reject it. We shave the head of some books, we cut the nails of others with razor-sharp scissors." This expresses quite accurately the process whereby much pagan literature was assimilated by medieval culture. It could be called assimilation by selection and—in many cases—by distortion.

Second, there is the problem of systems of classification. The late classical period was fascinated to the point of obsession with terminology. Rhetoric was particularly fruitful of systems and terms. It bequeathed to the Middle Ages the system of the three (or four) styles, the division of figures into schemes and tropes, figures of amplification, figures of thought, and figures of words, the debate over the importance of talent in comparison to art, the doctrine of imita-tion in the sense of copying the masterpieces, the distinction between matter (*res*) and language (*verba*), the concept of decorum in terms of age, sex, and status, and the formulas for compositions such as encomium, epithalamium, and epicede, to name only a few of the more prominent topics. Poets assimilated most of these and added many schemata derived from poetics rather than rhetoric: the division of a critical essay into sections on *poesis* (general questions of poetry), *poema* (types of poetry), and *poeta* (the character and education of the poet), the system of genres, the conventions of classical prosody, the concept of imitation as "making," the question of whether poetry lies, the instruct and delight formula, and many others.

Allegory is a topic in itself. At least five distinct systems were common-place by the fifth century: allegory as etymology, allegory as euhemerism (the theory that mythological figures are based on historical persons), allegory as doctrine related to science, ethics, or religion, and allegory as divinely inspired truth concealed under the veil of fiction either to protect it from the eyes of the unenlightened or because transcendent vision can only be expressed in symbols and metaphors. To these systems Christian writers beginning, apparently, with John Cassian (360–435), added a sixth, the idea that scripture (and eventually, secular poetry) has four levels of meaning: literal, allegorical, moral, and anagogical (spiritual).

The fact that during the Middle Ages certain terms and categories were isolated, analyzed, and defined through standardized formulas is demonstration of their central relevance to medieval critical theory. They run continuously through critical treatises from the fourth to the seventeenth century. They can be examined individually, and when approached in this way they emerge as critical themes which can be used as evidence of the continuity of medieval thought. Their deeper significance, however, is not their persistence as *topoi*, but their specific implications in different periods and different contexts, and it is this deeper significance which constitutes their chief interest here.

Christopher Caudwell once observed that the practice of criticism is something like carving a chicken. There are any number of ways in which the job can be done but there is only one right way and that is along the joints. In medieval criticism the joints are the classifications used at various times during the period for different kinds of knowledge. For most of the Middle Ages this means classifications based on the divisions in the trivium of grammar, rhetoric, and logic, and the quadrivium of arithmetic, geometry, music, and astronomy. If, for example, we take the trivium as our point of reference, we find that poetic can be considered a part of grammar or of rhetoric or of logic. Each placement results in distinctive forms of criticism related to the function which the placement implies. At the same time, subject matter frequently overlaps categories. To take the most obvious example, one finds the "colors of rhetoric"—that is, rhetorical imagery—included in both grammatical and rhetorical treatises of the late classical period. Their appearance in grammatical treatises doubtless reflects the exigencies of pedagogy: as the student was introduced to literary texts in the grammar curriculum it was only natural to begin teaching him the stylistic techniques that he would study, in more detail, as a part of rhetoric. The overlap is not the result of positive theory but of convenience. As the treatises collected by Heinrich Keil in his *Grammatici Latini* (1897–1923) and Carolus Halm in his *Rhetores Latini Minores* (1863) amply demonstrate, when late classical authors wrote as professional grammarians and rhetoricians they generally had a very clear sense of the difference between the two disciplines.

POETRY AND GRAMMAR

The most traditional and enduring "placement" of medieval poetic is in the grammar curriculum. Quintilian provided the basic formula relating poetic to grammar in his definition of grammar as "the science of correct speaking and the reading of the poets" (*Institutio Oratoria* I.iv.2). Book X of the *Institute* begins with an outline of the most elaborate formal literary curriculum that we possess from antiquity. It is a list of Greek and Roman authors to be studied for their eloquence and imitated in composition exercises involving translation and paraphrase as well as in original essays on set topics. The list in the *Institute* is the forerunner of the medieval *accessus* and a precedent for the emphasis on imitation and composition that formed a key element in the curriculum of the Cathedral schools of the twelfth century.

The association of grammar with "reading of the poets" can be traced through late classical treatises such as *De Arte Grammatica* of Victorinus, which follows Quintilian in defining grammar as "the science of interpreting the poets and historians and the method of correct speaking and writing," through discussions of the trivium by Cassiodorus and Rabanus Maurus. John of Salisbury sums up the matter for the twelfth century by observing that "poetry belongs to grammar, which is the mother and source of its study." It is no accident, then, that throughout the Middle Ages grammatical tradition preserves a strong attachment to pagan literature and a vivid memory of the commonplaces of classical criticism. This is to say that the grammar curriculum is the chief vehicle of medieval humanism. Although displaced in the thirteenth century in the wake of the so-called "battle of the liberal arts," grammar re-emerged in the fourteenth and fifteenth centuries in the treatises of humanist educators like Vittorino da Feltre, Guarino da Verona, and Erasmus, all of whom believed that the study of literature —and "reading the poets"—should be the center of the humanistic curriculum.

The association of poetry with grammar gave rise to three characteristic types of treatise. The first is the commentary or gloss. This sort of commentary is not an essay. Although a medieval gloss generally begins with a brief, generalized discussion of the life of the author whose works are being explained, followed by comments on the form and style of the works themselves—as exemplified by the commentaries of Donatus on Terence and Servius on Vergil—it consists chiefly of notes on individual words and lines of the text. These notes have a practical purpose. The poets were not read for aesthetic reasons but to develop eloquence, or, among Christian writers like Bede, Cassiodorus, and Rabanus Maurus, as preparation for interpreting scripture. Obviously, before the student can make use of the poets he must understand them. The grammatical commentary defines unfamiliar expressions, explains hard constructions, points out striking rhetorical figures, and may, on occasion, draw moral lessons or provide allegorical explanations of mythological allusions. The major extant commentaries date, with one exception, from the late classical period. They are the commentaries of Servius on Vergil, Aelius Donatus on Terence, and Arcon and Porphyrion on Horace. Typical of the numerous later commentaries in the same tradition are those by Remigius of Auxerre and Scotus Erigena on Martianus Capella, and the so-called *Scholia Recentiora,* dated after the eleventh century, on Terence. The exception to the rule that the major commentaries are pre-Carolingian is the twelfth century *Glossa Ordinaria* of Nicholas of Lyra, the standard high medieval commentary on the Bible.

A second specialized type of criticism created by the association of poetry with grammar is the *ars metrica*. Classical grammar involved the study of spelling, syllabification, and vowel quantities. Typically, a full-scale treatment of grammar required three books. In the third book, treatment of vowel quantities broadened out into a discussion of prosody. These discussions served a double purpose. They illustrated the quantities of various syllables together with such practices as elision and poetic license. And they prepared the student for "reading the poets" by introducing him to the standard poetic forms. The basic literary theory shared by the treatises on *ars metrica* is that poetry is not a matter of content or method but of versification. Poetry is to be distinguished not from history but from prose. In this system function follows form. That is, a work is "heroic" as much because it uses heroic meter (dactylic hexameter) as for its content. Beyond this, the typical *ars metrica* gives formulas for nine (or eight or ten) basic meters, usually beginning with dactylic and including anapest, troche, iamb, choriamb and the like. The meters are usually treated in detail; thirty-two "figures" are recognized as appropriate for heroic meter. Further instruction is given in such stanzaic forms as Sapphic, Alcaic, and Anacreontic.

The major late classical essays on the *ars metrica* are collected in Volume VI of Keil's *Grammatici Latini*. Bede's *De Arte Metrica*, which is in Keil's seventh volume, is of special interest on two counts. It consistently balances Christian, including biblical works, against their pagan counterparts. And it contains one of the earliest formal discussions of accentual prosody, which is "composition determined not by metrical practice, but by the number of syllables as determined by their sound [*iudicium aurium*] as in the songs of the popular poets."

Bede's treatise is the forerunner of a group of Latin treatises written between the eleventh and fourteenth centuries with the generic title *ars rhythmica*, as well as one of the true masterpieces of medieval criticism, Dante's *De Vulgari Eloquentia* (ca. 1304–07). The same tradition is evident in vernacular treatments of prosody, beginning with Eustace Deschamps' *L'art de dictier* (1392) and moving through the essays of the *seconde rhetorique* to Renaissance treatises on prosody including Trissino's *Poetica*, Du Bellay's *Deffence et illustration de la langue françoyse*, and George Gascoigne's *Certain Notes of Instruction*.

The list of curriculum authors in Book X of Quintilian's *Institute* establishes a precedent for medieval lists of *auctores* (standard authors). The critical interest of such lists comes from the fact that from the very beginning the tradition was comparative. Quintilian's list of Greek and Roman authors is, as has been noted, a precedent for the formal rhetorical comparison of a Roman work to the Greek work that is imitated. Plutarch compares Terence and Menander; Aulus Gellius, Vergil and Pindar; and Macrobius, whose *Saturnalia* provides the most elaborate examples of poetic (as against rhetorical) comparison, sets Vergil against Homer, Theocritus, and Hesiod among the Greeks, and Livius Andronicus and Ennius among the Romans. When the tradition was assimilated by the Christian authors, comparisons were drawn between Latin and Hebrew authors. Jerome was fond of such comparisons. "David" he remarked, "is our Simonides, our Pindar, our Horace," and it is to Jerome that Latin tradition owes its conception of Job as a tragedy, Pentateuch as heroic poem, and Ecclesiastes as an elegy. Bede, as we have seen, takes the same approach. Job to him is an heroic poem, while Deuteronomy and Psalms 118 and 119 are elegies. The Song of Songs is a biblical drama; Ecclesiastes is the biblical equivalent of the "narrative" form illustrated in antiquity by the *Georgics* and the *De Rerum Natura*; and Job is an example of the "mixed" form used by Homer in the *Iliad* and Vergil in the *Aeneid*.

Beginning in the early eleventh century, perhaps much earlier, the tradition of lists of authors was formalized in a group of treatises with the generic title *accessus ad auctores*. The earliest extant example of the type is an *accessus* by Bernard of Utrecht to the *Eclogue* of Theodulus, evidently the sole survivor of a large number of similar works. The formula for the *accessus* is given in the most complete example of the form that we possess, the *Dialogus Super Auctores, Sive Didascalon* of Conrad of Hirsau (ca. 1070–1150). Conrad explains: "You should not overlook that in explaining books, the ancients considered seven topics: author, title, type of poem, intention of the writer, order, number of books, and explanation [of the text]." The proximate source for this form of treatment—and presumably one of the "ancients" whom Conrad had in mind—is Servius; but behind Servius we can detect the influence of sophistic rhetoric.

What is important is that in order to provide the necessary information Conrad runs through a whole series of classical distinctions and definitions: the meaning of prose, rhythm, and meter; the definition of poet ("he is called a maker of fictions or a creator because he says false things instead of true or mixes the false with the true"); the difference between *poema, poesis,* and *poeta* (or *"poetria"*); the nature of bucolic, comic, tragic, and satiric poetry; the three styles; and so forth. This is followed by discussions of the *auctores* themselves, who are arranged from easy to difficult. The final subject is scripture—a reminder that according to Augustine, Cassiodorus, and Rabanus Maurus, the chief justification for the study of secular letters was as preparation for interpreting the Bible. The list is: Donatus (the *Ars Minor*), Cato (the *Distichs*), Aesop, Avianus, Sedulius, Juvencus, Prosper of Aquitaine, Theodulus, Arator, Prudentius, Cicero (*De Amicitia, De Senectute*), Sallust, Boethius, Lucan, Horace, Ovid, Vergil (incomplete), and scripture. While there is no attempt at pairing or contrasting Christian and pagan authors, the differences between Christian and pagan outlooks, and the dangers of paganism, are regularly stressed.

As Bruno Sandkühler has shown, the *accessus* tradition lies behind Dante's

Epistle to Can Grande della Scala. The *accessus* supplements the other two treatise types produced by the association of poetry with grammar—the commentary-gloss and the *ars metrica*—as a vehicle for medieval humanism. It is a precedent for, if not an influence on, the new "canon of the classics" developed for the Renaissance curriculum. A trace of the *accessus* tendency to include Christian along with pagan classics is found in John Colet's regulations for St. Paul's School, which stipulate that the schoolboys be introduced to classical eloquence not through Cicero but through Lactantius, a safe Christian author believed by early humanists like John Colet to have attained a near-Ciceronian eloquence.

RHETORIC AND POETIC

The typical forms of medieval grammatical criticism are clearly defined. The case is by no means so plain for medieval rhetorical criticism. In some ways, rhetoric and poetic are more closely interrelated during the classical period than during the Middle Ages. As the classical section of this volume shows, only one ancient document, Aristotle's *Poetics*, treats poetry without drawing heavily on rhetoric. Much of what passes for classical literary criticism—the work of Dionysius of Halicarnassus, Demetrius *On Style*, and Longinus *On the Sublime*, for example—is really oratorical criticism which is applicable to poetry. Horace's *Ars Poetica* draws in part on Alexandrian poetic theory (itself deeply influenced by rhetoric), but its debt to Roman rhetoric is pervasive. The topics of imitation, of the training of the poet, of talent (*physis*) versus experience (*episteme*) and learning (*melete*), of decorum of character, of the three styles and their correlative faults, and of the dual function of poetry to instruct and delight all have close parallels in Ciceronian rhetoric, from which they were probably taken. We know further that the Gorgian figures so important in sophistic rhetoric were thought in antiquity to have been derived from the poets and that this same sophistic tradition later produced formulas for epideictic orations like the encomium and epithalamium that were copied in occasional poetry. Classical rhetorical manuals regularly quote poetry to illustrate effective expression, while a major purpose of "reading the poets" in the grammar curriculum was to acquaint the student with the rhetorical figures that he would later use in prose orations.

This overlap is symptomatic of confusion only if we insist that poetic and rhetoric must be kept absolutely separate. The concept of an absolute separation of the two disciplines was not even generally available until the sixteenth century, when the *Poetics* again became current; but even if it had been, the practical and didactic temper of classical criticism would have insured its rejection. The same is true of late classical and early medieval criticism, with the ironic qualification that the closest approximation to a theory of art for art's sake during the period under consideration was the flowering of epideictic oratory and literary

Asianism during the late classical period. Both of these developments were stimulated by rhetorical rather than poetic theory.

Throughout the Middle Ages rhetorical theory impinges on critical thought. This is most obvious in the case of the rhetorical figures which were known through the *Ad Herennium*, the *De Inventione*, late classical essays on the rhetorical colors, and grammatical treatises like the *Ars Grammatica* of Donatus. We also hear frequent echoes in medieval criticism of some of the larger issues of rhetoric. The system of the three styles, for example, was adopted by Augustine in the *De Doctrina* and recurs in the *Scholia Vindobonensia* on Horace, Conrad of Hirsau's *Didascalon*, Geoffrey of Vinsauf's *Documentum de Arte Dictandi et Versificandi*, John of Garland's *Poetria*, John of Salisbury's *Metalogicon*, and elsewhere.

On the other hand, not all rhetorical treatises are directly relevant to medieval poetic theory. Works like Bede's *De Schematibus et Tropis*, Alcuin's *Rhetoric*, and Geoffrey of Vinsauf's *De Coloribus Rhetoricis* are purely rhetorical, referring to prose rather than poetic composition. This is true also of the *artes dictaminis* (treatises on letter-writing) and the *artes praedicandi* (arts of preaching) of the high Middle Ages. In the history of criticism such works are significant for the light they frequently throw on literary topics rather than as primary documents.

In terms of sources, the primary document for rhetorical criticism *qua* criticism throughout the Middle Ages was Horace's *Ars Poetica*. This work was evidently regarded by medieval scholars as part of grammar rather than rhetoric. Horace was one of the standard *auctores,* and the *Ars Poetica* was used in conjunction with "reading the poets." Thus, on the basis of classification we would have to regard treatises influenced by the *Ars Poetica* as part of the tradition of grammatical rather than rhetorical criticism, in spite of their heavy debt to formal rhetoric.

During the late classical period three documents illustrate formal and self-conscious rhetorical criticism. The first of these is the incomplete treatise *On the Sublime*, which is traditionally assigned to "Longinus." The essay is of great interest as an assertion of the claims of genius over training and skill, and of the primacy of imagery over arrangement. Each of these questions was debated in ancient rhetoric, and each is touched on in Horace's *Ars Poetica*. The position which "Longinus" takes on each of these topics is the opposite to that taken by Horace, and by and large the anti-Horatian stance would have been congenial to Latin authors after the Silver Age. However, *On the Sublime* had no discernible influence during the Middle Ages, and it was not translated into Latin until the 16th century. If it is a third-century document and its author was indeed, as tradition once had him, a pupil of Plotinus, it illustrates the late classical Neoplatonic aesthetic which also appears to have encouraged late classical Asianism. But until the matter of dating is settled this remains wholly conjectural.

The two late classical examples of rhetorical criticism which were unquestionably available, at least sporadically, to medieval readers are the *Interpretationes Vergilianae* of Tiberius Claudius Donatus and the lengthy discussion of Vergil in Books V and VI of Macrobius' *Saturnalia*. Both of these are fourth-century works. The *Interpretationes* begins with a prologue in the form of a letter from Donatus to his son. In it the father complains that the grammarians cannot appreciate Vergil. They are concerned with elementary matters fit only for school boys. Vergil was a master of all departments of rhetoric and therefore only an orator can appreciate his achievement. This prelude does not lead, as we might expect, to Vergil's use of schemes and tropes. Donatus was a good Ciceronian, and was able to consider the larger questions implicit in his approach. The resulting analysis is a wide-ranging, often philosophical treatise with something of the sophistication, if not the artistry, of Cicero's *De Oratore*. Vergil, we learn, had a dual purpose—to celebrate the early history of Rome and to praise the *Gens Julia* (the house to which Julius Caesar belonged). He was deeply learned, particularly in moral philosophy, and his work can be read as a guide to the conduct of life as well as a repository of much useful knowledge (*doctrina*). Donatus frequently notices Vergil's use of figurative language, and contends that he was a master in this department as well as in arrangement and invention, but the discussion never becomes a list of "colors." The result is not a grammatical commentary-gloss but a series of intelligent, informed essays covering all twelve books of the *Aeneid*. If the criticism is somewhat arid to modern tastes, this is because rhetoric itself is out of favor today and not because of the author's inadequacy.

The *Saturnalia* is quite different, in some ways more conventional. During the Silver Age, the question "Is Vergil an orator or a poet?" was sufficiently commonplace to become a standard topic for school exercises, called *controversiae*. The *Saturnalia* is an extended dialogue covering a large variety of subjects in the manner of Aulus Gellius' *Attic Nights*. In Book IV Symmachus, one of the speakers, discusses Vergil's use of the rules of rhetoric. His command of language is illustrated by citations of the numerous appeals to emotion and figures woven into the *Aeneid*. In Book V and Book VI the *controversia* topic is revived. Vergil's ability to use the four styles of oratory is demonstrated, with the conclusion that he combines the virtues of the ten Attic orators. The discussion then turns to Vergil as an imitator, in the rhetorical sense of one who follows great models. Homer, of course, comes first, but Roman authors are also cited—principally Ennius. Innumerable examples are given of passages in which Vergil parallels his sources closely. Although there are similar comparative treatments of poetry in "Longinus," Plutarch, and Aulus Gellius, no other classical or late classical work treats imitation so extensively.

As we move from the late classical to the Carolingian period and beyond, the tradition of purely rhetorical criticism disappears. In its place, we have grammatical treatises which draw most of their substance from rhetoric. The *artes poeticae* of the twelfth and thirteenth centuries rely heavily on the *Rhetorica ad Herennium* and variously contain brief sections on arrangement, memory, delivery, the three styles, imitation, art versus talent, and the like. They have been treated by Faral and Baldwin as prime examples of rhetorical criticism and as illustrations of the medieval confusion of rhetoric and poetic. On the other hand, there was a lively debate during the twelfth and thirteenth centuries concerning the relative importance of the disciplines of the trivium, and this debate reflects the very opposite of confusion. It shows that the authors involved had a very acute understanding of the subjects appropriate for the three departments of the trivium. They disagreed because of their recognition of the implications inherent in the available alternatives. The debate is summarized by John of Salisbury in the *Metalogicon*. It does not concern the relation of poetic to rhetoric but the claim that poetry is an art independent of both disciplines:

> Poetry stays so close to the things of nature that many have refused
> to include it in grammar, asserting that it is an art in its own right
> and is no more related to grammar than to rhetoric, though it is
> related to both and has precepts in common.

John of Salisbury emphatically believed that, in spite of its relation to rhetoric, poetry belongs with grammar, and it is most likely that the authors of the *artes poeticae* agreed with him. We know from the *Metalogicon* that the Cathedral schools required imitation as well as passive reading of the *auctores*. The *artes poeticae* were textbooks designed for this curriculum, and therefore—in spite of their rhetorical content—they must be considered part of grammar rather than rhetoric. True rhetorical criticism along the line of Donatus and Macrobius did not reappear in Europe until the educational reforms and the controversy over imitation in the fifteenth century.

LOGIC AND POETRY

When we move from rhetoric to logic, the third of the disciplines of the trivium, we enter a clearly defined area associated with a specific period of medieval history. The link between poetry and logic was made by late classical commentators on Aristotle, most notably Alexander of Aphrodisias. The option of associating poetry with logic had no attraction for the early Middle Ages. We have hints of it during the twelfth century in the explanations of Bernard of Utrecht and Conrad of Hirsau of the relation of the *accessus* formula to Aristotle's four causes, and in the thirteenth century in the preference of Gervase of Melcheley for a logical rather than a rhetorical system of classifying figures. Further indications of a new view of poetry are evident in the debate over the liberal arts, in which the Cathedral schools stood by grammar and the *auctores,* while the *avant garde* representing the newly-emergent universities insisted that logic should be the queen of the trivium. To quote *The Battle of the Seven Arts* of Henri d'Andeli (ca. 1250):

> Paris and Orleans are at odds.
> It is a great loss and a great sorrow,
> That they do not agree.
> Do you know the reason for this discord?
> It is because they differ about learning;
> For logic, who is always wrangling,
> Calls the *auctores* authorlings
> And the students of Orleans mere grammar-boys . . .
> However logic has the students
> Whereas grammar is reduced in numbers.

The main impulse for a revaluation of the placing of poetry in the curriculum came from Arabic Spain. The question of "the division of the sciences" had been treated by al-Farabi (d. 950) and Averroes (1126–98), who taught that Aristotle considered poetic a part of the *Organon.* The revival of Aristotelian philosophy which is intimately associated with scholasticism was made possible initially by wholesale translation into Latin of Arabic commentaries and translations, and the concept of poetic as a part of logic was one of the ideas that accompanied them. Since this placing was apparently an authoritative Aristotelian doctrine, it had considerable prestige. Its implications, however, were anti-humanistic. To make poetic a part of logic is to assert that it is an "instrument" or "faculty" without content—a technique for manipulating symbols like demonstrative logic, dialectic, and sophistic—rather than a "science" like politics or astronomy. The theory is developed in several scholastic treatises—in the Latin translation of al-Farabi's *Catalogue of the Sciences* by Gerard of Cremona, in the treatise *On the Division of the Sciences* by Dominicus Gundissalinus, and in the translation by Hermannus Alemannus of Averroes' *Commentary on the Poetics of Aristotle.*

The problem is that to define poetic as a "faculty" rather than a "science" is to deny its immemorial claim to providing instruction as well as delight. Throughout the Middle Ages one of the standard defenses of reading the *auctores* had been that they provided useful *doctrina* (general knowledge) and, above all, moral instruction through examples. This didactic bias is as common in the *accessus* tradition as it is to allegorical readings of Vergil and Ovid. The moral utility of Christian poetry, was, of course, obvious. That of the ethnic writers was considered "Egyptian gold," as Augustine put it, which Christians could use for their own profit, just as the Hebrews were allowed to take the gold of their heathen masters on their departure from Egypt. But to deny that poetry is a "science" is to deny that it has any ethical content. According to Gundissalinus, it is merely the technique of creating illusions. The implication is that poetry may well be a pleasant recreation, but it is essentially trivial. This is a challenge to the whole rationale of medieval humanism. In particular, it is a direct attack on the humanism of Chartres.

Echoes of the debate which the logical "placing" of poetry stimulated can be heard in St. Thomas and Roger Bacon, who are willing to concede that poetry has a dual place in the system of the sciences—as a technique it is part of logic; as an activity it is a kind of ethical teaching or a method of creating moral examples. More radical responses are evident in Dante, whose *Epistle to Can Grande della Scala* explicitly states that the *Divine Comedy* is a part of moral philosophy, and who interprets three of his *canzoni* in the *Convivio* as allegories of the ennobling effect of love, the value of philosophical studies, and the nature of true nobility, respectively. Mussato and Boccaccio agree with Dante that poetry teaches virtue. They add the considerably more audacious claim, based on Aristotle's *Metaphysics,* that poetry is allied to theology. That the controversy was a bitter one is evident from Petrarch's *Invective Against a Physician* and Boccaccio's defense of poetry in the *Genealogy of the Gentile Gods,* both of which record the bitter attacks of clerics against the new concepts. The revival of Platonism in the fifteenth century, it may be added, intensified the debate by providing fresh arguments in the running battle between humanists like Landino and Politian and Thomistic conservatives like Savonarola. It passed into the sixteenth century as a standard topic—the placement of poetry among the sciences—to be dealt with at the beginning of any full-scale critical essay.

POETRY AND THE QUADRIVIUM

Beyond grammar, rhetoric, and logic are the sciences of the quadrivium. There is no medieval treatise on poetry and arithmetic although we know that "numerical composition" was regarded as a legitimate device for imitating the divine numbers which are the basis of creation. St. Augustine's *De Musica* contains a lengthy analysis of the relation between musical rhythms and classical meters. Again, however, no medieval treatise exists which deals specifically with poetry and music, unless the theoretically rather barren treatises on the *ars rhythmica* are included in this category. The sense of the real and symbolic importance of harmony in poetry may be assumed from de Bruyne's treatment of twelfth-century aesthetics and is obviously relevant to such developments as the trope and the sequence. Dante treats the relation of music to the *canzone, ballata,* and other vernacular verse forms in Book II of the *De Vulgari Eloquentia,* but his treatment is technical, with nothing to offer concerning an underlying theory.

In fact, the first critical treatise to pay serious attention to the relation of poetry to music is Book I of Coluccio Salutati's *De Laboribus Herculis,* which belongs to the fifteenth century.

In medieval criticism the major "type" created by placement of poetry outside the trivium is the result of considering poetry a part of philosophy or theology. To do justice to this concept it would be necessary to refer to anthropology. We know that primitive poetry is often considered prophecy or revelation, and that, in fact, it embodies a world-view which is the primitive equivalent of formal philosophy. In this sense medieval critics who found inspired revelations in texts like the Bible, the *Hermetica,* Ovid's *Metamorphoses,* and Vergil's *Aeneid* may have been nearer the truth than nineteenth-century philologists.

The tradition of allegorical criticism is diffuse and was so even in antiquity. The practice of classifying the kinds of wisdom derived from the poets into scientific ("natural" or "physical"), ethical, and religious (or "rational") knowledge has been traced to Theagenes of Rhegium in the sixth century B.C. It was associated with Stoicism in antiquity and is evident, for example, in Cicero's *De Natura Deorum.* The standard Roman formulation is by Varro, and it is commonplace in late classical criticism. Macrobius writes at the conclusion of the commentary of the *Somnium Scipionis:*

> There are three branches of the whole field of philosophy—
> moral, physical, and rational. Moral philosophy is a guide to
> the highest perfection in moral conduct, physical philosophy is
> concerned with the physical part of the divine order, and ra-
> tional philosophy discusses incorporealities, matter apprehended
> only by the mind . . .

As is clear from Macrobius, the allegorical approach is based on the assumption that poetry is not a part of grammar, rhetoric, or logic, but of philosophy proper. "I must declare," he writes in his commentary on the *Somnium Scipionis,* "that there is nothing more complete than this work which embraces the entire body of philosophy." Equally well developed in antiquity is the practice of using etymologies as a key to allegorical intentions. Plato's *Cratylus* and *Republic* furnish instances. The best ancient example of sustained allegorizing is the *Questiones Homericae* by Heraclitus, probably written in the first century A.D., which treats the *Iliad* and the *Odyssey* in detail, frequently using etymology and extracting all of the standard types of *doctrina* from the two works.

The techniques and commonplaces of Stoic criticism were absorbed by the late classical period, but the philosophical point of view to which they were subservient changed to Neoplatonic. This is reflected in emphasis on religious as against scientific and moral allegory, and in the strong insistence of critics on the importance of inspiration. For late classical and medieval critics allegory is not simply disguised textbook lore, but divinely revealed truth which is not available to discursive reason.

The extensive influence of Platonic thought on late classical authors and the persistence of a Platonic tradition throughout the Middle Ages has been documented, most notably by Raymond Klibansky in *The Continuity of the Platonic Tradition in the Middle Ages* (1939). This influence is based in part on the remarkable achievement of pagan Neoplatonists beginning with Plotinus (205–269/70), and in part on Alexandrian authors—Philo Judaeus, Clement of Alexandria, and Origen. A few Platonic texts, most notably Calcidius' translation of the *Timaeus,* were continually available in the West after the decline of Greek studies, but the major vehicles for Latin Neoplatonic tradition were Latin works which had themselves been influenced by Neoplatonism. Servius, Macrobius, and Boethius are especially important among the secular writers in this regard, while Augustine is the chief Latin patristic source for medieval Neoplatonism.

The assumptions on which Neoplatonic critical theory is based are spelled out by Proclus (ca. 410–85) in his discussion of the poetic questions in the *Republic*. As his citations of the *Phaedrus* and *Ion* show, the precedent for his theory is to be found in Plato himself. The theory begins, however, with an idea that Plato explicitly denies in the *Republic*. For Proclus, poetry is a higher version of truth than is available through contemplation of the visible world. This sort of poetry is not an imitation of nature, or, to use a common medieval analogy, a "mirror of custom." It is possible because the poet draws on a mental faculty that goes beyond reason. This faculty, the "intellect" or *mens,* is intuitive. It does not observe or reason things out but responds directly to inspiration. Consequently the deepest truths in poetry are transcendent, having the quality of revelation. Being transcendent they are necessarily obscure. To draw on a concept familiar in Alexandrian biblical criticism, they are "accommodated" to the limits of human understanding by being expressed as symbols and analogies. Because they are realities, they are supremely valuable. At the same time, precisely because they are a kind of revelation, they carry with them a radiance, a supernatural beauty, which is objectified through exquisite imagery and language. Of course, the fact that poetry can express these truths does not mean that they are the only truths with which it is concerned. In addition to divine wisdom, poets also present the truths of reason—of science, and ethics. This level of truth is important, and Proclus places special emphasis on the ethical lessons in poetry. Finally, there is an element in poetry that depends on appearance—the subrational faculties associated with sensation. This kind of poetry is the least valuable sort, but it has its uses. Since it directly reproduces sensory information, even when such information is faulty, it corresponds to the Socratic category of imitative poetry in the tenth Book of the *Republic*. The complex of ideas offered by Proclus, then, includes poetry as revelation, the poet as inspired seer, the poetic faculty as supra-rational, allegory as a veil or as an accommodation, with ornamentation and adornment correlative to the inner beauty of the work, and ethical teaching as an important but subsidiary poetic function.

Similar ideas can be found in varying combinations in the commentary of Philo Judaeus on Genesis, the commentary of Porphyry on the cave of the nymphs episode in Homer, the essay of Plutarch on the Isis and Osiris myth (*Moralia* V.1) and the commentary of Macrobius on the *Somnium Scipionis*. Related texts, which stress the ethical utility of poetry without going into its "mystical" aspects, are the two essays on Homer in Maximus Tyrius' *Dissertations* and Plutarch's "How a Young Man Should Study the Poets" (*Moralia* I.2).

The medieval continuation of this tradition involves the new question of whether pagans can ever have been inspired and what the source of inspiration really is. It was difficult throughout the whole history of allegorical criticism for Christians to answer these questions without appearing to undermine the unique authority of scripture. By and large, they accepted the idea that the Holy Spirit had, indeed, inspired the pagans; and by and large they incurred the hostility of more conservative clerics for this suspiciously deistic teaching. The doctrine is Alexandrian. It is most evident in the *Miscellanies* (*Stromata*) of Clement of Alexandria and various essays by Origen. The prime example and probably the most convincing proof of its validity—for Latin critics—was Vergil's sixth ("Messianic") eclogue, which was universally considered an inspired prophecy of the birth of Christ. That many other teachings of Vergil were considered anticipations of Christian truth is evident from the *De Continentia Vergiliana* of Fulgentius. Cassiodorus uses the metaphor of planting for this idea: "In the origin of spiritual wisdom, as it were, evidences of these matters were sown abroad in the manner of seeds, which instructors in secular letters later most usually transferred to their own rules." The corollary of this point of view is that pagan mythology can be a veil for higher truth. Fulgentius wrote a much-used compendium of allegories of the ancient pantheon, the *Mythologiarum Libri Tres*. The tradition reached its medieval culmination in the works *Epître d'Othéa* of Christine de Pisan, the *Ovidius Moralizatus* of Bercorius, and Boccaccio's *Genealogy of the Gentile Gods*.

Much medieval biblical criticism and much of the thought of high medieval mysticism echoes the same theory which justifies allegorical reading of pagan literature. For present purposes, the earliest critical document to have a more or less continuous influence on medieval criticism is the commentary on the *Somnium Scipionis* of Macrobius. Here the Platonic influence is everywhere apparent. The "dream" itself, which formed the concluding section of Cicero's *De Republica,* is an imitation of the "Vision of Er" episode that closes Plato's *Republic*. In it the elder Scipio appears to his son in a dream to disclose the secrets of the after-life. The text is thus a precedent for a favorite medieval genre, the dream allegory, as well as for the convention, used by Fulgentius, of presenting allegedly inspired truths through a superhuman agent. The commentary proper is an extended analysis of these truths. Although its debts are manifold, it relies especially heavily on a lost *Commentary on the Timaeus* by Porphyry.

In the second chapter of Book I, Macrobius defends the right of philosophy to use fictions. Here, and again in the conclusion of Book II, it is clear that he considers his text allegorized philosophy. Menander, Apuleius, and Petronius, he observes, used fables to delight, while Aesop used them to teach. Philosophers use them to present natural, physical, and rational (i.e., incorporeal) truths. They do this because Nature herself veils her secrets. In a particularly interesting passage, Macrobius offers what amounts to his own theory of accommodation. He observes that fables can be used in reference to the soul and divine matters, but that "similes and analogies are frequently used for the highest, most difficult truths such as the nature of the highest good and the divine intellect." The comment which follows deals with a miscellany of topics suggested by the text. There are chapters on numerology (I.6, II.2), prophecy (I.7), the cardinal virtues (I.8–9), the Zodiac (I.12), astronomy (I.15–22), the earth (II.5–9), and the soul (II.12–17). In short, all three kinds of philosophy are shown to be present in the text. Of particular interest, because it is recurrent in the allegorical tradition throughout its history, is the evident predilection for cosmological allegory. This is present in the *Timaeus* itself. It recurs in Philo Judaeus, who reads Genesis as a kind of Christian *Timaeus;* in Porphyry's essay *On the Cave of the Nymphs;* in Augustine's commentary on Genesis; and in such Renaissance works as Pico's *Heptaplus* and John Colet's *Letters to Radulphus on the Mosaic Account of Creation.*

The purely critical tradition next reappears after Macrobius in *The Exposition of the Content of Vergil According to Moral Philosophy* of Fulgentius, written in the late fifth or sixth century. This work has no obvious source. At times it seems to echo Heraclitus' discussion of the *Odyssey* in his *Questiones Homericae,* at times Servius, and, at least in its use of Vergil's ghost to expound his philosophy, the *Somnium Scipionis.* Any echoes, however, must be at two or three removes. A modest Platonic coloring is given by references to Plato, Porphyrius, and the late classical Latin poem *On the God of Socrates;* but the citations are all minor and appear to be from a handbook rather than the authors themselves.

As the title of the work announces, it treats poetry as philosophy with the emphasis on moral philosophy. We learn that Aeneas represents mankind. The *Aeneid* is an allegory of human life from birth to maturity. Each of its episodes is exemplary, and the characters typically represent virtues to be imitated or vices to be shunned. The Cyclops is vanity, Dido lust, Deiphobus cowardice,

Turnus rage, Anchises parental authority, the golden bough knowledge, Lavinia "the path of labor," and so on. When he has completed the *Aeneid,* the reader has a full knowledge of the virtuous life.

The strong moral bias of the *Exposition* resembles that found in ancient Stoic allegories, but, as we have seen from Proclus, it is perfectly compatible with the Platonic tradition as well. It is qualified in two important ways. First, Fulgentius makes it perfectly clear that Vergil "included the secrets of almost every art" in his works. Fulgentius states that he has avoided most of these secrets because they are "more dangerous than praiseworthy" for the age—that is, they are not suitable for Christians. We are reminded of the comparison of pagan literature to the gentile woman whose nails and hair must be trimmed before she can be married to an Israelite. It is evident from the list of secrets Fulgentius will not reveal that many of them are related to "rational" or "divine" philosophy. Second, Fulgentius often remarks that Vergil's teachings correspond to those revealed to Christians by the Holy Spirit. At one point he quotes the first Psalm, "Blessed is he who walks not in the counsel of the ungodly" to illustrate the parallel. Vergil replies, "I rejoice . . . at these sentiments. Athough I did not know the full truth concerning the nature of the righteous life, still, truth sprinkled its sparks in my darkened mind with a kind of blind favor." Thus, in addition to being a compendium of moral philosophy, the *Aeneid* contains adumbrations of Christian revelation. Its more abstruse doctrines remain mysterious, even dangerous, but they are there for the reader who is bold enough to lift the veil of Vergil's fiction.

The continuity of allegorical interpretation during the Carolingian period is obvious from biblical commentaries and allegorical interpretations of liturgy, especially the *Liber Officialis* of Amalarius of Metz. Theodolphus of Orleans touches on secular allegorizing in a reference to "books which I used to read and how the fables of the poets are mystically employed by philosophers." He mentions Vergil, Ovid, and Prudentius, adding "in their writings although there are many frivolities, a great many truths are hidden under the veil of falsehood. The pen of the poets gives us falsehood, of the Stoics, truth. But the poets often turn their falsehoods to truth. Thus Proteus symbolizes truth, Virgo justice, Hercules virtue, and Cacus crime." The next full-scale critical essay in the Fulgentian tradition, however, is the commentary on the first six books of the *Aeneid* by Bernard Silvestris, written in the twelfth century. Bernard's first sentence asserts, with a bow to Macrobius, that "Vergil was concerned with two kinds of doctrine in the *Aeneid*—. . . he both taught the truth of philosophy and did not neglect poetic fable." He continues with comment on the dual function of the poet to teach and instruct and with the observation that poems can follow a natural or artificial order. The latter point is important to Vergil because, "His procedure is this. Under the veil of fable he described what the human soul placed in a human body in the temporal world should do or endure. And in writing this he followed the natural order, and thus he used both kinds of narrative order—as a poet he used the artificial, and as a philosopher the natural."

All of this represents a considerable advance in sophistication beyond Fulgentius. The commentary proper, while far more copious, is in a less involuted style than Fulgentius. The first Book of the *Aeneid* is an allegory of infancy, the second of childhood, the third of adolescence, the fourth of youth, and the fifth of young manhood. The sixth occupies four-fifths of Bernard's commentary. It contains Vergil's most profound philosophic lore, and Bernard provides an almost word-for-word gloss, drawing heavily on Macrobius for its strategies and Boethius for many of its generalizations. The basic concept, however, remains Fulgentian. The episode in the underworld summarizes all human experience, and the descent of Aeneas, like that of Orpheus and Hercules, is an allegory of the wise man studying human experience, "so that recognizing its fragility and turning away from it, he may concern himself with higher things (*invisibilia*) and recognize the Creator more readily from knowledge of his creations."

Bernard's sources are Fulgentius and Macrobius, with supplementary debts to Boethius, Calcidius (commentary on the *Timaeus*), and a miscellany of less frequently cited writers—Horace, Ovid, Servius, and others. It seems unlikely, however, that Bernard would have made the effort if he had not been deeply involved in the Neoplatonic revival that followed in the wake of Scotus Erigena's translation of the works of Dionysius the pseudo-Areopagite at the end of the tenth century. We can follow the influence of this movement on secular poetry in Bernard's *Microcosmus* and *Megacosmus* and Alanus de Insulis' *De Planctu Naturae* and *Anticlaudianus*. If this is a valid suggestion, Bernard's interest in allegory is connected directly with Platonism through Dionysius, as well as indirectly through Macrobius, Calcidius, and Fulgentius.

During the fourteenth century the allegorical tradition continued to flourish. In France it is evident in the allegorical mythology of Christine de Pisan and Peter Bercorius. In Italy it appears in Dante's *Convivio*, which uses the tradition of biblical, rather than classical allegorizing to draw truths concerning the psychology of love, the importance of philosophy, and the nature of true nobility from three of Dante's *canzoni*. In general, the *Convivio* concentrates on truth available to reason, and Dante is careful to distinguish between "poet's allegory" and theological allegory of the sort elicited from scripture. The *Divine Comedy* is said in the *Epistle to Can Grande della Scala* to belong to the category of moral philosophy, and Dante's Fulgentian tour of the underworld consists largely in *exempla* of the vices. The *Paradiso*, however, begins with a retelling of the fable of Marsyas flayed after his singing contest with Apollo interpreted as an allegory of the departure of the soul from the body during flights of inspiration. It treats those highest mysteries that Macrobius said could only be presented through "similes and analogies." All human agencies—Beatrice and eventually even St. Bernard—finally leave Dante as he ascends the levels of a Dionysian heaven toward a final, transcendent vision which can only be expressed in terms of the imagery of light.

If Dante writes a poem justifying the claim of the poets to divine inspiration, Albertino Mussato and Boccaccio translate Dante's achievement into critical theory. In both of them the claim emerges in the form of an assertion: the poets are not only teachers of ethics, they are also—perhaps primarily—theologians. The only thing new about this claim, which goes back to Aristotle's *Metaphysics,* is the explicitness with which it is made. The critics are quite conscious of what they are doing. "Cavillers," as Boccaccio calls them, assert that poetry is a tissue of lies, that it is idolatrous, that it is morally depraved, and that it should be banished from a Christian society even as Plato banished it from his *Republic.* The mythological interpretations of the *Genealogy of the Gentile Gods* (Books I-XIII) answer the charge by showing that ancient myths are allegories of moral truth, and, on occasion, adumbrations of Christian revelation. Books XIV and IV defend Boccaccio's critical position. The early poets—the *prisci poetae*—were theologians writing directly from divine inspiration. Rightly understood, the fables of the poets are wholly edifying. Although sacred allegory is obviously distinct from secular allegory, at least one modern poet—Dante—has demonstrated that poetry can be a vehicle for the deepest of theological truths. Petrarch, Boccaccio's friend and mentor, has many of the same points to make about poetry in his letters and his *Invective Against a Physician,* on which Boccaccio leaned heavily in Book XIV of the *Genealogy.* However, in the context of Petrarch's work, the claims for supernatural vision and the importance of allegory are less pronounced than in Boccaccio. Petrarch admits the importance of both, but he seems more interested as a critic in eloquence, imitation, and moral instruction. His humanism tends to be conservative, classical, civic, while Boccaccio's is more radical and anticipates the work of the Florentine Neoplatonists of the fifteenth century—Ficino, Landino, Pico, and Politian.

To summarize, the four "placings" of poetry which are most important during the Middle Ages are as a part of grammar, of rhetoric, of logic, and of philosophy. The grammatical placement is the most persistent and is the vehicle of medieval humanism, if that term is understood as referring to the continuity of the classical tradition. Rhetorical placement seems to disappear after the late classical period, although, as we have seen, much rhetorical lore was absorbed by treatises on poetry and the *artes poeticae* were used in the grammar curriculum. Logical placement is associated specifically with scholasticism. Philosophical placement, like grammatical placement, is continuous from the late classical period through the Renaissance. It is associated with Platonism and its orthodoxy frequently tends to be suspect because it purports to find evidence of divine inspiration and adumbrations of Christian truth in secular works.

PERIODS OF MEDIEVAL CRITICISM

The placing of poetry among the disciplines of the trivium and quadrivium provides the threads that connect different periods of criticism from the fourth to the fourteenth century. Medieval criticism, however, is anything but continuous. At times a given tradition is dominant, at times it is muted, and at times it may simply disappear.

It is useful to think of medieval criticism as divided into five periods, the first and last of which are transitional. The periods are:

     I.   Late Classical (1st c. B.C. to 7th c. A.D.)
    II.   Carolingian (8th c. to 10th c.)
  III.   High Medieval (11th c. to 13th c.)
  IV.   Scholastic (13th c. to 14th c.)
   V.   Humanist (14th c. to 16th c.)

The last three of these periods overlap one another. During the twelfth century the Platonizing humanism of Chartres was already in conflict with the scholasticism of Paris. Later, in spite of the triumph of humanism, scholasticism continued to be important in criticism throughout the Renaissance, as numerous essays on the relation of poetry to logic testify. There is also a question of whether the humanism of Petrarch and Boccaccio is a new movement or merely a new phase of twelfth-century humanism. Burckhardt's emphasis on the novelty of the Renaissance is to be balanced against increasingly conspicuous evidence emphasized by Paul Kristeller and Eugenio Garin, among others, of its ties with the past. As Richard Schoeck recently observed of medieval rhetoric, "One may feel secure in holding the conclusion that from the late thirteenth century to the end of the fifteenth, for all of the changes and developments, there is an essential continuity."

LATE CLASSICAL PERIOD

The late classical period is the most various of those to be considered. This is not surprising. Pretty much the full range of the classical tradition was available in the Latin West through the end of the fourth century. The critical works of Heraclitus, Plotinus, Prophyry, and Proclus were not translated, but the ideas which they had to offer were assimilated by Latin writers. Philo Judaeus, Clement, and Origen were thoroughly digested by the Latin fathers, especially Ambrose and Augustine. The rhetorical treatises of Cicero and Quintilian were available both directly and in digest in the treatises reprinted in Halm's

Rhetores Latini Minores and in Christian adaptations, of which Augustine's *De Doctrina Christiana* is the most important. Horace was known and read continuously. In general, however, the late classical works most important for medieval criticism are the redactions, commentaries, and collections written between the fourth and seventh centuries.

If we look back on this body of material, we can perhaps gain a sense of why parts of it were valuable and parts simply ignored. To say that a new culture was emerging is not quite adequate. Early Christians were not drifting unwittingly in a new direction. They were fully aware of being the Chosen People, and to a large extent the new culture was conscious fabrication intended to fit the New Dispensation. It is hard to find a Christian work that deals with pagan thought between Tertullian and Cassiodorus that does not reveal a full awareness of this fact.

From the point of view of the New Dispensation the problem was one of assimilation. Pagan culture, said Augustine in the *De Doctrina,* is like the gold that the prudent Hebrews took with them on their flight to Egypt. It was too valuable to discard but, being pagan, it was suspect. This is particularly true of pagan poetry and its corollary, pagan mythology. Tertullian rejected ancient drama in the *De Spectaculis* as depraved and idolotrous. Jerome was taunted in a dream for being more of a Ciceronian than a Christian and once called secular poetry "the wine of demons." St. Augustine, former rhetor and author of a treatise *On the Apt and the Beautiful,* recalled in the *Confessions* how he used to weep over the death of Dido in the *Aeneid,* while Lactantius suggested that the classical gods are fallen angels in disguise.

Given many different shades of opinion, the first and most basic justification for literary study was practical. Poetry had been included in the classical grammar curriculum to teach eloquence, not for aesthetic reasons. It could be used to teach the same skill to Christians, who needed linguistic skill both to wage the wars of truth and to interpret scripture. St. Augustine's *De Doctrina Christiana* is a highly intelligent adaptation of Cicero and "the rules of Tychonius" to the teaching of scriptural exegesis and preaching. The *Institutes of Divine and Secular Letters* of Cassiodorus is more comprehensive than the *De Doctrina* but has the same object. Knowledge of the liberal arts "as it seemed to our Fathers, is useful . . . since one finds this knowledge diffused everywhere in sacred literature." The same argument was used by Gratian in *The Concord of Discordant Causes* to justify secular literature in the twelfth century:

> We read that Moses and Daniel were learned in *all* the wisdom of the Egyptians and Chaldeans. We read that our Lord ordered the children of Israel to spoil the Egyptians of their gold and silver: the moral interpretation of this teaches that should we find

in the poets either the gold of wisdom or the silver of eloquence, we should turn it to the profit of salutary learning. In Leviticus we also are ordered to offer up to the Lord the first fruits of honey, that is, the sweetness of human eloquence.

The dominant mode of early medieval criticism was therefore practical. The key pagan documents were those useful in the grammar curriculum—the commentaries of Servius on Vergil and Donatus on Terence, Horace's *Ars Poetica,* treatises on the *ars metrica,* and summaries of critical doctrine in grammar texts, such as Diomedes' *Ars Grammatica.* This material was easily assimilated by writers who were self-consciously Christian. Christian poets like Prudentius, Sedulius, and Juvencus used the forms and style of ancient poetry for scriptural and devotional subjects. Isidore of Seville derived a considerable miscellany of information about poetry from Diomedes, Evanthius, Donatus, and other sources, which he duly passed along to the later Middle Ages in his *Encyclopedia.* Bede restated the commonplaces on classical prosody in his *De Arte Metrica,* adding examples from Christian poetry and a chapter on the new rhythmic versification. His summary of the rhetorical figures in *De Schematibus et Tropis* is propadeutic to biblical studies and uses illustrations from scripture.

Medieval assimilation of pagan tradition created special problems in the area of literary history. The list of authors in Book X of Quintilian's *Institute* is limited to Greece and Rome, as are the comments on literary history in works like Horace's *Ars Poetica,* Evanthius' *De Fabula,* and Diomedes' *Ars Grammatica.* Christians, however, found themselves committed to a radical enlargement of the curriculum to include Old Testament authors on the one hand, and a rapidly growing body of Christian literature on the other. This had three results. First, the chronology of world literature was revised. With this revision the classical assumption that classical literature is self-contained and self-influenced was called into question. Being older than Greek literature, Hebrew literature may have influenced classical works. Second, the forms of Hebrew literature had to be described. The possibility of Hebrew influence on the classics encouraged speculation that much of the Old Testament is in forms analogous to those used by the Greeks and Romans. At the very least, however, the suggestion that the Song of Songs is a pastoral or an epithalamium and Job a tragedy implies a significant broadening of classical genre concepts. Third, a list of curriculum authors is also a canon of the classics. As Christian authors were added to the list and Greek authors disappeared, the concept of the classical tradition itself began to change. This change was accelerated by allegorical distortions of true classical authors like Vergil and Ovid, and by the ornate style of the literary parts of the Old Testament, which reinforced the widespread early medieval taste for Asiatic style.

It is impossible to do justice here to these developments. For chronology (and its corollary the indebtedness of Greek to Hebrew literature) the important precedents are the *History of the Jews* by Josephus, Philo's commentary on Genesis, the *Chronicle* of Eusebius, and the *Miscellanies* of Clement of Alexandria. Jerome's translation of Eusebius provided the Latin West with a system of dates beginning with the Creation which allowed Greek and Roman history to be plotted against Hebrew history. A looser system, used by Augustine in *The City of God,* divided history into six ages—from Creation to Noah, from Noah to Moses, from Moses to David, from David to the prophets, from the prophets to Christ, and from Christ to the Last Judgment. Greek civilization does not emerge in this system until the third age.

On the basis of the enlarged chronology, Jerome asserted that Hebrew literature influenced the classics and that the Old Testament anticipates classical forms. The Psalms are in iambics, Alcaics, and Sapphics, while Deuteronomy, Isaiah, and Job are in mixed pentameters and hexameters. Isidore wavers, but his *Encyclopedia* asserts that Moses used heroic verse in Deuteronomy long before Homer, and "it is apparent that the study of poetry was much older among the Hebrews than among the Gentiles." Bede's *De Arte Metrica* incorporates these ideas into formal criticism. In addition to repeating the commonplaces concerning the use of classical prosody in scripture, he notes that Hebrew poets anticipated the three classical manners of imitation. The pure mimetic, or dramatic, manner is used in the Song of Songs; the pure narrative in Ecclesiastes, and the "mixed"—the manner used by Homer and Vergil—in the Book of Job. The *De Arte Metrica* also illustrates the new canon of the classics by adding Prudentius, Arator, Sedulius, and Ambrose to the list of classical poets.

If grammar is the dominant mode of late classical criticism, Neoplatonism is its sub-dominant mode. The Greek background includes Philo Judaeus, Clement, and Origen in the Hebraeo-Christian tradition, and Plotinus, Iamblicus, Porphyry, and Proclus among the pagans. The basic Latin critical documents are Macrobius on the *Somnium Scipionis* and Fulgentius' *Exposition* of the *Aeneid.* These documents are supplemented by a general late classical interest in Neoplatonism evident in Augustine and Boethius, in Calcidius' commentary on the *Timaeus,* in the fashion of scriptural allegory, and in two much-admired allegorical poems, the *Psychomachia* of Prudentius and the *Marriage of Philology and Mercury* by Martianus Capella. The commentary of Servius on the *Aeneid* demonstrates that grammatical criticism could take on a Neoplatonic coloring. In general, however, grammatical criticism is conservative. It concentrates on practical matters which aid understanding and imitation, and secondarily on the moral values of literature. Neoplatonic criticism recognizes the moral utility of literature, but its interest is centered on the esoteric wisdom which poets conceal in their fables. If the grammatical and Neoplatonic traditions are not separate in the late classical period, they tend to diverge.

THE CAROLINGIAN PERIOD

The Carolingian period saw a flowering of poetry comparable to a "revival of classical antiquity" in little. Manitius records an impressive number of commentaries on classical, late classical, and Christian authors including works by Rabanus Maurus, Lupus of Ferrières, Remigius of Auxerre, and Scotus Erigena. In his commentary on Prician and in his *Clerical Institute* Rabanus repeats the grammatical commonplaces on poetry and offers a standard defense of reading pagan literature. We know from Theodolphus of Orleans that the pagan poets were read and regularly allegorized, and the *Liber Officialis* by Amalarius of Metz, an interpretation of Gregorian liturgy, illustrates how far the allegorical method could be taken. Rhetorical theory of the period is summarized in Alcuin's *Rhetoric*. This work is of particular interest in the history of medieval style. It is Ciceronian in scope and is evidently intended as a corrective to late classical emphasis on the oratory of display and the "rhetorical colors"—the lists of figures which were supposed to make the display impressive. De Bruyne therefore considers Alcuin a central figure in the history of the conflict between Attic and Asiatic ideals of style.

It is disappointing to find that in spite of all this literary activity there is only one purely critical document from the Carolingian period. This is the *Scholia Vindobonensia* on Horace's *Ars Poetica*. Although the work was attributed to Alcuin by Zechmeister, its nineteenth century editor, it is clearly much later.

In spite of its title the *Scholia* is more than a gloss on the model of Servius. It follows Horace line-by-line, but the result is more of a running discussion of critical theory—a kind of "close reading"—than a series of footnotes. It offers a considerable body of information concerning classical poetic theory along with a good deal of misinformation. In general, it is conservative, and we are probably not wrong in assuming that it was intended as an aid to the reading of Horace in the grammar curriculum. Its chief sources other than the *Ars Poetica* itself are the commentaries of Porphyrion and Arcon on Horace and of Servius on Vergil, the *Ad Herennium* and the rhetoric of Victorinus, Hyginus on mythology, the poetry of Ovid and Vergil, and (evidently) the *Rhetoric* and *Dialectic* of Alcuin.

At the beginning, poetic art is defined as "the art of making [*fingendi* —probably in the sense of 'making fictions'] and composing; Greek *poesis* means 'artifact' [*figmentum*] in Latin." The species of poetry are defined as "humble, middle, and serious" and are related to characteristic stylistic errors. The comment is based on the discussion of the three styles of oratory and their related vices in the *Ad Herennium* (IV. 8–12), which the scholiast attributes to Cicero. Line 45 of the *Ars Poetica* leads to a discussion of artificial and natural

order. Later (1. 46), we learn that an author should strive for *facundia*—
"beautiful and moderate expression" which is attained by restrained and careful use of language. This is supplemented by the observation (1. 87) that
rhetorical "colors" distinguish and ornament the subject treated and make it
"sweeter" (*dulcior*, 1. 99). The comment obviously refers to the rhetorical
figures (*colores rhetoricae*), but it is quite different in tone from the high
medieval *artes poeticae*, in which the "colors" are of central importance. Character depends (1. 114 ff.) on nation, age, and status, a point illustrated by a list
of types including the old man, the hero, the pious man, the matron, the
prostitute, the merchant, and the farmer.

The discussion of drama (11. 182 ff.) reveals the confusion that developed after the decline of the classical theatre. The scholiast correctly defines the
varieties of classical drama, the *togata* (based on Roman life), *palliata* (Greek
inspired), and *praetextata* (based on history), but he shows no understanding
whatever of terms that relate to performance. The five act convention is explained as follows: "The first act is for the old men, the second for youths, the
third for matrons, the fourth for the servant and maid, and the fifth is for the
pimp and the prostitute." The chorus is not part of the action but a group of
well-wishers who listen to the dramatic recitation (1. 195). A curious passage
explaining the convention of action offstage (1. 182: *res aut agitur in scenis*)
is interpreted by Zechmeister as a statement that biblical plays—specifically, a
play about Herod's feast—were being performed at the time the commentary
was written. Actually, it is at the most a reference to a literary recitation, which
is evidently what the scholiast understood by drama. One point which the
scholiast gets right is verisimilitude. Here and later (1. 340) he warns against
impossible and unbelievable episodes. De Bruyne considers this a key feature of
Scholia since it is an implicit criticism of the exotic style and subject matter of
early medieval allegory.

Once past drama, the scholiast is back on reasonably firm ground. He
sides with Horace in minimizing the value of genius. Poetry is nourished by
grammar, rhetoric, and logic, and its content is ethics and the sciences of the
quadrivium. Poems profit by offering moral instruction and arousing patriotism,
and they delight through fables and comedies.

In sum, the *Scholia* gives us what we would expect from a scholar following the tradition of Alcuin. It intelligently supplements Horace by drawing
on rhetoric, it subordinates genius to learning, and it recognizes both the moral
and recreative aspects of poetry. Its key doctrines are stylistic restraint and
verisimilitude. The misinformation is a by-product of the age rather than a
failure on the part of the scholiast. In view of the poetic fashions of the late
classical period its omissions are as significant as what it contains. There is no
direct mention of allegory. There is no special pleading for classical poets and
no statement that they anticipate Christian truths. Even Horace's assertion that

it is pointless to try to save a man bent on suicide (1. 467) is allowed to pass without moralizing. Finally, the scholiast is as conservative as Alcuin himself on the subject of style. He points out that there are three styles but does not express preference for the grave (or elevated) variety. He does not list rhetorical figures or show marked enthusiasm for rhetorical ornament. If anything, his comments on *facundia* indicate a bias in favor of stylistic restraint. In all of these respects the *Scholia Vindobonensia* is a poetic cousin of Alcuin's *Rhetoric.* It is not "representative" of the Carolingian period since we know that other kinds of criticism continued to flourish, but it represents an important, perhaps temporarily dominant current of critical thought.

THE HIGH MIDDLE AGES

As we move toward the twelfth century, the critical texts become more numerous and the problem of understanding the factors that influenced them more complex. In one way or another the intellectual ferment caused by a reawakened interest in Neoplatonism underlies the most significant intellectual developments of the period. A major cause of this ferment was the translation by Scotus Erigena of the works of Dionysius the pseudo-Areopagite at the end of the tenth century. Dionysius offers a Christian theology completely dominated by the metaphysics of Plotinus. He had a special claim to authority during the Middle Ages since he was believed to be the Dionysius who conversed with St. Paul on the Areopagus. Supplemented by a miscellany of late classical works— especially the commentary of Calcidius on the *Timaeus,* Macrobius on the *Somnium Scipionis* and Boethius *On the Consolation of Philosophy*—Dionysius provided the basis for an articulated form of mysticism involving the concept of a "negative theology" and a distinct process (the *scala perfectionis*) whereby one moves from the material world to a vision of God. We see this mysticism in the works of Bernard of Clairvaux and St. Bonaventura. Its corollary is a renewed emphasis on the supra-rational, on inspiration, on the intellect (*mens*) as against the reason, and on visionary experiences which can only be communicated through symbols. The treatises of Dionysius *On the Heavenly Hierarchy* and *On the Ecclesiastical Hierarchy* provided a new geography of heaven and a new sense of the ways in which the visible world is a shadow of the invisible one. His symbolism pointed the way to a new interest in the transcendent and new ways of expressing transcendent experience. His God is an architect or a geometer making a world from numbers, or, alternately, a musician creating harmonies out of the discord of matter. As experienced by the Dionysian mystic, God is also light, an emanation from the source of light, and a radiance that shines in the beauty of the created world.

Dionysius is not the unique source of the various ramifications of high medieval Platonism, but many of them find precedent in his work, and the stimulus which it provided led to more energetic exploration of complementary works and more daring speculation by medieval authors themselves—a daring particularly evident in the *Megacosmus* and *Microcosmus* of Bernard Silvestris and in his *Commentary on the First Six Books of the Aeneid*. Its influence is also evident in the revival of grammatical humanism in the twelfth century as reflected in the series of *artes poeticae* that begins with Matthew of Vendôme's *Ars Versificatoria* composed at Orleans around 1175 and extends to Gervase of Melcheley's *Ars Poetica* of around 1215. There is evidence that Bernard Silvestris influenced the *ars poetica* tradition strongly. Matthew of Vendôme was his student at Orleans, and Gervase of Melcheley refers to a lost treatise on poetry by Bernard on which he drew for his own work. If such a treatise existed, it was in all probability the parent of the *ars poetica* tradition. In view of Bernard's keen interest in Platonic philosophy, which often gives his work a pagan or naturalistic tone, this text would undoubtedly be of great interest.

Indirect evidence of the Platonic influence on the *artes poeticae* is provided by Geoffrey of Vinsauf's *Poetria Nova*. Like all of the authors in the tradition, Geoffrey drew heavily on the figures in the *Rhetorica ad Herennium*. But he was not content simply to list figures. Throughout his treatise he emphasizes the inward, intellectual element in art. Geoffrey says nothing about imagination; the *Poetria* is a textbook and it naturally concentrates on what can be taught. While Geoffrey recognizes the importance of genius, he insists that experience and judgment are essential to the poet. In this he is closer to Cicero and Horace than to pagan Neoplatonists. In place of imagination, Geoffrey stresses the shaping power of the mind:

> If a man has a house to build, his impetuous hand does not rush into action. The measuring line of his mind first lays out the work, and he mentally outlines the successive steps in a definite order. The mind's hand shapes the entire house before the body's hand builds it. Its mode of being is archetypal before it is actual. Poetic art may see in this analogy the law to be given to poets . . . let the mind's interior compass first circle the whole extent of the material . . . When due order has arranged the material in the hidden chamber of the mind, let poetic art come forward to clothe the matter with words.

The images of the poet as architect, of planning a work by circling it with the compass of the mind, and of language as "clothing" for the poetic conception —all have their parallels in twelfth century poems, including Bernard Silvestris' *Megacosmus* and *Microcosmus,* which describe the creative activities of God. The theme of inwardness extends in the *Poetria* to language and imagery. The inner meaning of words is more important than their appearance—that is, in

Geoffrey's terms, their sound. By the same token, intention has precedence over ornament. Ornament is essential, and Geoffrey devotes over two-thirds of the *Poetria* to an extended treatment of figures, but ornament should always be appropriate. It is consistently described in terms of light imagery. The figures are "colors" or many-colored "flowers," and they are the outward expression of an inward "radiance."

The title *Poetria Nova* calls attention to the fact that the work differs from the *Ars Poetica. Poetria* was a common title for the *Ars Poetica* during the Middle Ages. Geoffrey's *Documentum de Mode et Arte Dictandi et Versificandi,* which is usually considered simply a prose version of the *Poetria Nova,* quotes the *Ars Poetica* extensively. The verse essay, however, contains no quotations from Horace, and does not even refer to him by name. The reason is plain. The *Poetria Nova* is a new poetic, not a redaction of Horace. Its novelty is its philosophy of art: the artist as creator, the superiority of mind to the materials of poetry, and ornament as the objectification of inner radiance.

If the philosophical background of the *artes poeticae* is Platonic, their immediate purpose was educational. John of Salisbury describes the teaching methods of the twelfth-century grammar curriculum in a famous tribute to Bernard of Chartres:

> Bernard of Chartres, the richest fountain of literary learning in modern times, taught the authors in this way: he pointed out what was simple and what conformed to rule; he called attention to grammatical figures, rhetorical colors, and sophistic fallacies; he showed where a given text was related to other disciplines . . . He expounded the poets and orators to those of his students who were assigned as preliminary exercises the imitation of works in prose or verse. Pointing out skillful connections between words and elegant closing rhythms, he would urge his students to follow in the steps of the authors . . . He bade them reproduce the very image of the author, and succeeded in making a student who imitated the great writers himself worthy of posterity's imitation. He also taught, among his first lessons, the merits of economy and the laudable adornment of thought and expression. (*Metalogicon* I.24)

The *artes poeticae* are manuals for the "preliminary exercises" involving "imitation of works in prose or verse." This explains their conservative tendencies— their heavy cargo of the figures which produce "laudable adornment," their careful illustration of each figure given, and their emphasis on the practical aspects of criticism rather than imagination, arcane philosophy and allegory.

The *accessus* tradition of the High Middle Ages is equally practical. Insofar as Platonism created a generally liberal intellectual climate and encouraged the emphasis of the Cathedral schools on the *auctores,* it encouraged the *accessus* tradition, but the works themselves are compendia and lack the larger philosophical interest which we find, for example, in the *Poetria Nova.*

A medieval *accessus* is a formal introduction to one or more of the curriculum authors. The earliest example of the form is the introduction by Bernard of Utrecht to the *Eclogue* of Theodulus, a much admired Christian imitation of Vergil composed in the tenth century. There is every reason to believe that the tradition was well established when Bernard began writing. Father Quain considers Servius an important precedent and traces the basic formula of the *accessus* to Hellenistic logic. According to this formula, a proper introduction to a work must include author, title, genre, intention, arrangement, number of books, and explanation. The best example of the type to survive is, as has been noted, the *Didascalon* of Conrad of Hirsau, written in the early twelfth century.

Conrad begins the *Didascalon* with a brief survey of standard poetic topics such as *poeta, poema, poesis,* the major genres, occasional forms like panegyric and epitaph, poetic arguments (which are explained in terms of Cicero's *Topics*), natural and artificial order, allegory, and the three styles as illustrated by Vergil's *Bucolics, Georgics,* and *Aeneid.* Much of Conrad's material is taken from Bernard of Utrecht. Directly or indirectly it goes back to late classical compendia like Diomedes' *Ars Grammatica* and Isidore's *Encyclopedia.*

This general survey is followed by introductions to the "authors" themselves. They are arranged from easy to difficult beginning with Donatus, whose *Ars Minor* provides a concise introduction to grammatical concepts and who is especially authoritative because he was a teacher of St. Jerome. The *Distichs* of Cato come next. They are filled with useful moral sentiments (*sententiae*) and are part of ethical as distinguished from natural philosophy. Two more pagans, Aesop and Avianus, are followed by Sedulius. Pagans, Conrad observes, sometimes experience bits of the truth, but Sedulius versified scripture and wrote expressly to lure readers away from seductive pagan poetry. Five more Christians are listed: Juvencus, Prosper of Aquitaine, Theodulus, Arator, and Prudentius. Conrad mentions the hymns of Prudentius but concentrates on the *Psychomachia* which shows how to avoid vice and is based on the technique of personification. We then return to the ancients and prose: Cicero, with emphasis on the *De Amicitia* and *De Senectute,* and Sallust's *Catiline's Conspiracy.* The *Consolation of Philosophy* teaches patience, and Boethius himself is a superb stylist as well as the best of all authorities on the seven liberal arts.

Lucan and Horace come next. The *Ars Poetica* is intended to correct bad poets and help those in need of advice. Curiously, Conrad believes its normal medieval title, *Poetria,* means "a woman studious of poetry" (*mulier carminis studens*). His explanation is that Horace began with the image of a woman beautiful above but a fish below, showing that he thought of poetry as feminine. Horace's odes are more suspect, and many of them are immoral (*viciosa*). This leads to comments on the dubious character of other pagan poets. Ovid is particularly dangerous. He teaches idolatry in the *Metamorphoses* and depicts the gods as animals. St. Paul has warned us about this sort of thing in his Epistle to the Romans (1:18–23). Terence, Juvenal, Statius, Persius, Homer, and Vergil are less dangerous. They are full of valid moral sentiments and have often been used by Christian authors. St. Paul quoted Menander and Augustine drew on Horace and Vergil.

The introductions to Juvenal, Homer, Persius, and Statius follow. They are incomplete. Vergil is given fuller treatment. The notion that in the *Bucolics* and *Georgics* "the poet included a full review of the liberal arts" is an echo of the Fulgentian tradition if not of the *Exposition* itself. Most of Conrad's discussion of the *Aeneid* has been lost. It is followed by comments on reading scripture. The disciplines of the trivium help us with the literal sense; those of the quadrivium are useful for its allegorical senses. Near the end, secular knowledge is defended in the venerable Augustinian way as Egyptian gold.

Conrad's list gives us an idea of the canon of the classics for the Cathedral schools. It includes Christian as well as pagan authors, and prose alternates with poetry. In general the selection is stylistically conservative—Martianus Capella is conspicuous by his absence. Interpretation is heavily and explicitly didactic. Equally important is the idea of imitation. Conrad asserts that all the great authors practiced imitation: Terence followed Menander; Horace, Lucinius (i.e., Lucilius); Sallust, Livy; Statius, Vergil; Boethius, Martianus Capella; and Theodulus, Vergil's *Bucolics*. Clearly the *accessus* is intended for the curriculum described by John of Salisbury. It provides historical and critical information which complements the practical instruction of the *artes poeticae*. The list of *auctores* is crowned by scripture. We are reminded that the basic justification for reading the poets was the preparation they provided for reading the Bible.

The twelfth-century Renaissance stimulated the writing of several general surveys of knowledge following the "Institute" tradition of Quintilian, Cassiodorus, and Rabanus Maurus. Hugh of St. Victor's *Didascalicon* has little to say about grammar and rhetoric and nothing about poetry. It concentrates almost entirely on biblical studies. Conversely, John of Salisbury's *Metalogicon* is extremely important for both its description of the grammar curriculum and its use of the *auctores,* and for the light it casts on the controversy between advocates of literary studies, generally associated with the Cathedral schools, and advocates of logic, generally associated with the University of Paris. John of Salisbury complains bitterly over the scornful attitude of the *avant garde* toward the older curriculum: "Poets who related history were considered reprobates, and if anyone applied himself to studying the ancients, he became a marked man and a laughing-stock to all."

The same controversy recurs in the literature of "the battle of the liberal arts," which raged during the thirteenth century and which derives its title from a poem on the subject by Henri d'Andeli, written around 1250. Paris, Henri d'Andeli tells us, stands for logic. The university men ridicule the study of the *auctores* and the emphasis on grammar of the Cathedral school of Orleans.

Evidently, humanists were fully conscious of themselves as a party united by a shared set of assumptions. Grammar and the *auctores* were the vehicles for the movement, and they were, as we have seen, intimately related. Consequently the controversy between the humanists and the scholastics tended to settle around two topics: the value of grammar in comparison to dialectic, and the value of reading the *auctores* in comparison with more technical studies. Although *Metalogicon* is primarily a work on dialectic, John of Salisbury insists that logic by itself is "bloodless and barren, nor does it quicken the soul to yield fruit of philosophy." Furthermore, poetry is essential to the grammar curriculum, and grammar is "the mother and nurse of its study."

Gervase of Melcheley's *Ars Poetica* (ca. 1215–16) may illustrate a compromise between the older and newer points of view. In content and presumably in its place in the curriculum it belongs with the *artes poeticae* of the Cathedral schools. In form, however, it is scholastic. It abandons the rhetorical division of the figures used by Matthew of Vendôme and Geoffrey of Vinsauf in favor of a logical division into figures of identity, similitude, and contrarity— i.e., figures in which the words are proper to their subject, figures which depend on resemblance, and figures, like allegory and irony, which depend on differences.

SCHOLASTIC PERIOD

With Gervase we have already entered the scholastic phase of medieval criticism. This phase is characterized by the application of logical theory to poetry. Its dominant mode is Aristotelian, with most of the Aristotle coming second-hand from translations of Arabic texts and commentaries.

When we see twelfth-century humanism from a scholastic point of view, we understand why it appeared superficial. It is not analytic. It looks backward rather than forward, and it wastes its energies on grammar when the intricacies of logic and (by the middle of the thirteenth century) the whole of Aristotle's *Organon* offer both a challenge to the mature man and an exciting new method for solving the major problems of the Christian faith. As for poetry, it is essentially a diversion. At its best it teaches moral lessons through *exampla,* but those who are seriously interested in morality will consult Aristotle's *Ethics* rather than the *Aeneid.*

This does not mean that the scholastics ignored poetry. Following al-Farabi, they dutifully included chapters on poetry in treatises explaining the system of the sciences. In such works, poetry is placed within logic as the last of the treatises of the *Organon*. This placement makes it a "faculty" rather than a "science"—that is, a technique for manipulating language rather than a subject with its own content like physics or ethics. As a "faculty" it has a distinctive function—illusion—as against rhetoric, for example, which seeks to persuade, or dialectic, which seeks "probable demonstration." Along with this function it had a distinctive instrument paralleling the enthymeme (a syllogism in which one premise is unexpressed) of rhetoric and the "probable syllogism" of dialectic. The strictest (and most opaque) definition of the poetic instrument is "imaginative syllogism," a phrase used by Dominicus Gundissalinus in his treatise *On the Division of the Sciences*. By and large, the later scholastics were inclined to be more generous. Roger Bacon and St. Thomas were willing to regard poetry as both a faculty and a branch of moral philosophy with a definite "content." For St. Thomas, the characteristic instrument of poetry is example, which is a logical form that can be used to teach lessons in ethics.

The most important theoretical statement of the scholastic period is the *Commentary of Averroes on the Poetics of Aristotle* translated into Latin in 1256 by Hermannus Alemannus. Medieval readers learned from this work that Aristotle considered poetry a branch of logic and that metaphor is its characteristic instrument. They could also learn, and in considerably more detail, that poetry concerns "matters of choice." In this sense, it is a kind of praise or blame. It uses praise to "heighten" the virtues of good men and thereby stimulates the reader to emulation. Through blame poetry exposes vice to ridicule and thus causes the reader to shun it. The praise and blame formula and the logical placement of poetry coexist in the treatise. If Averroes realized their incompatibility, he made no attempt to reconcile them. The Arab commentary thus nicely complements the scholastic conclusion that poetry has a dual allegiance to logic and ethics.

The best illustration of practical criticism along scholastic lines is Dante's *Epistle to Can Grande della Scala*. As Bruno Sandkühler has shown, the Epistle follows the *accessus* pattern. Its distinctive feature is not its content but its conscious emphasis on exact definitions and logical distinctions, an emphasis that is a by-product of the scholastic habit of mind. It is so stylized, in fact, that its authenticity has been questioned. No matter who wrote it, however, its relation to the *accessus* is established firmly by Dante's list of topics to be covered: "There are six things to be inquired about at the beginning of any work, to wit, the subject, the author, the form, the end, the title of the work, and the genus of its philosophy." A brief résumé follows of the four levels of theological allegory. Dante then moves to the *accessus* topics. The placement of the *Divine Comedy* in ethical philosophy is typically scholastic in its precision: "The genus of philosophy under which the work proceeds in its whole and in part is moral activity or ethics, for the whole and the part are devised not for the sake of speculation but of possible action. For if in any place or passage the method of discussion is that of speculative thought, it is not for the sake of speculative thought but for the sake of practical activity, since, as the Philosopher says in the second of the *Metaphysics,* 'practical men now and then speculate on something or other'."

HUMANISTIC PERIOD

The last period of medieval criticism is fourteenth century humanism. The documents begin with Dante's *De Vulgari Eloquentia,* the first self-conscious treatment of the vernacular as a medium for great poetry. Dante's immediate successors, Petrarch, Mussato, and Boccaccio, can be seen either as the end of the medieval tradition or the beginning of the Renaissance. Both points of view are valid, but in a survey of medieval criticism, their link to the past must receive major emphasis. This link is evident in their reliance on traditional medieval sources and in the fact that they frequently repeat, though with greater vehemence and broader knowledge of classical literature, the arguments for liberal studies that we encounter in the twelfth century. Finally, all three authors were driven to write defenses of poetry because of attacks against it. Their opponents were conservative. Just as the humanists of Orleans were eclipsed in the thirteenth century by the logicians of Paris, the logicians, in turn, were beginning to feel threatened by the humanists of Florence, and they reacted violently. Many of their arguments against poetry are based on scholastic theory, and these arguments largely determine the content of the defenses.

Contemporary with the revival of humanism in Italy a group of French works appear which are best understood as a continuation of twelfth-century humanism untouched by the "new learning." The tradition of the *artes poeticae* and *artes rhythmicae* emerges in the treatises of Deschamps and the authors of its *seconde rhétorique* on French vernacular poetry. Fulgentian allegorizing continues unabated in the *Ovidius Moralizatus* of Petrus Bercorius, the *Fulgentius Metaforalis* of John de Ridevall; and the *Epître d'Othéa* of Christine de Pisan. It is complemented by the vogue of allegorical poetry illustrated by the *Roman de la Rose,* Chaucer's *Book of the Duchess,* and Gower's *Confessio Amantis.* Such works are of great literary interest, but they are not central to the history of criticism. We can also pass over the tradition of the *ars dictaminis* and *ars praedicandi.* These traditions were continuous from the twelfth century through the Renaissance, but they properly belong to the history of rhetoric.

It is in Italy, then, that the important critical developments occur. The reason for their occurrence—if we rely on the documents themselves—is that the humanists had begun to make claims for poetry that conservatives found unacceptable. When they stated their objections, the battle was joined. Petrarch's major statement on poetry is his *Invective Against a Physician.* Other statements are scattered widely through his letters, often as replies to specific questions or criticisms. Mussato's critical theory was formulated as a reply to a specific adversary, Fra Giovannino of Mantua. Boccaccio's most important essay, Book XIV of the *Genealogy of the Gentile Gods,* is an answer to charges made by unnamed "cavillers" who were obviously conservative clerics.

If we draw back from the debate a little way, we can see that the major point at issue was the placement of poetry among the sciences. The idea that poetry is (or can be) a kind of theology is explicit in Mussato and Boccaccio. The corollary of this position is that poets, like religious prophets, are divinely inspired. If so, poetic fables can be regarded as veils covering esoteric truths or as symbolic statements necessitated by the impossibility of directly expressing transcendent experiences in language. Obscurity may be inevitable in great poetry as in scripture. Moreover, since the *prisci poetae* were inspired theologians, such pagan poetry, especially mythological poetry, may anticipate the truths of Christian revelation.

St. Thomas himself had been willing to consider poetry an instrument of moral instruction. However, in the heat of debate the opponents of poetry reverted to a more radical position: poetry is simply a "faculty." It has no content and the claim that it teaches morality is exaggerated if not a lie. Petrarch's response was to reassert the traditional didactic theory of poetry. He flirted with the idea of the divinity of poetry and the theory of allegory, but typically he considers poetry a means of instruction and a storehouse of examples of eloquence. To the traditional belief that poetry offers *doctrina* he adds the idea, anticipated by Cicero's *Pro Archia Poeta,* that poetry arouses patriotism. He thus anticipates the association between poetry and nationalism which is a typical feature of sixteenth-century criticism.

The belief that poetry is inspired and that poets express esoteric wisdom in their fables is associated during the Middle Ages with Platonism. That a Platonic critical frame could accept didacticism without strain we know from Plato himself and Proclus. During the high Middle Ages and the early humanistic period, Platonic theory blended easily with Ciceronian and Horatian criticism. Petrarch and Boccaccio argue at length that poetry is morally uplifting and in no sense a threat to Christian orthodoxy. They differ somewhat in emphasis. In the Genealogy, instruction is a secondary rather than a primary function of poetry. The major emphasis, which Boccaccio shares with Mussato, is on poetry as theology. In this Boccaccio both echoes the theories of Proclus and anticipates those of the Florentine Platonists of the fifteenth century. Petrarch, conversely, anticipates the more sober strain in Renaissance humanism which runs through the work of the educators, the rhetorical theorists, and the philologists; and which emerges finally in the seventeenth century as an important component of neoclassic criticism.

The selections below are intended to illustrate, as fully as possible within the limited space, the scope and historical development of medieval criticism as outlined above. Where possible, I have used standard translations, as noted at the end of the introduction to each selection. In three cases—the selections from Evanthius, Fulgentius, and Averroes—I have made my own translations.

The problem of providing bibliography for a body of material as broad and as varied as that represented by the following selections is formidable. In the end it seemed best to include all bibliographies in a single section categorized according to period and, to a certain extent, according to topic. The alternative —providing a general bibliography after the General Introduction, and more specialized bibliographies after each specific introduction—would have involved much repetition of entries for general works and would have required frequent cross-checking by the reader with the attendant possibility of overlooking important items. Footnotes have been avoided in the introductions. The studies and editions used may be readily ascertained, however, by reference to the bibliography. In general, the bibliography emphasizes works in English and translations where these are available. It is selective. For Dante in particular, the body of relevant material is so large that no attempt has been made to cover it, and the interested reader is referred to the standard editions and bibliographies.

EVANTHIUS AND DONATUS

(4th century A.D.)

INTRODUCTION

Classical stage drama disappeared completely during the Middle Ages. Knowledge of classical drama, however, persisted. It is clear from the plays of Hroswitha of Gandersheim that Terence was read, at least sporadically, in the schools. During most of the Middle Ages the major source of information concerning classical drama was the body of definitions and descriptions preserved in encyclopedias, floralegia, and the like, and transmitted lovingly from generation to generation. Isidore of Seville's *Encyclopedia* (seventh century) and Vincent of Beauvais' *Speculum Morale* (thirteenth century) are particularly important in this regard.

A. P. MacMahon has documented the continuity of definitions of comedy and tragedy from the late classical period to the early Renaissance. Beginning in the fourteenth century classical drama began to be read and imitated. Knowledge of its history developed rapidly, as did understanding of the ways it was produced, its typical forms, and the classical terminology associated with it. The new knowledge did not replace the old but supplemented it. Humanists did not so much reject Isidore of Seville and Vincent of Beauvais, for example, as go behind them to the documents that were the ultimate sources of their information.

The three most important late classical sources of information about classical drama are the essays *On Drama* (*De Fabula*) of Evanthius and *On Comedy* (*De Comedia*) of Aelius Donatus, and the section on drama in Diomedes' *Ars Grammatica*. These essays directly or indirectly provided most of the historical information and the definitions incorporated into medieval tradition. During the Renaissance the essays of Evanthius and Donatus were widely reprinted in editions of Terence. They continued to be used extensively in critical treatises, commentaries, prefaces, and the like, through the seventeenth century.

Of Evanthius we know only that he was a fourth century grammarian. Throughout the Middle Ages it was assumed that his essay was by Donatus. Donatus, on the other hand, was so widely known during the Middle Ages that the term "donet," meaning a Latin grammar, became a common noun in Middle English. The two grammars of Donatus, referred to as the *Ars Major* and the

39

Ars Minor, were used widely through the sixteenth century. They are reprinted in Heinrich Keil's *Grammatici Latini.* Donatus' commentary on Terence, which is a sixth-century redaction of the original text, was widely reprinted during the Renaissance and is available in the edition of the commentary of Donatus on Terence by Paul Wessner, together with an excellent introduction summarizing available information on Donatus and the history of the text. *On Drama* and *On Comedy* are evidently based on standard handbook information that was the stock-in-trade of the Roman grammar schools. No specific source has been discovered for either essay. The occasional citation of conflicting opinions in both essays suggests that they are compilations from several works. Ultimately, they go back through the Roman schools and Alexandrian criticism to Theophrastus and Aristotle, especially Aristotle's essay *On the Poets.* Mac-Mahon summarizes the evidence that they contain echoes of the *Poetics,* but the echoes, if they are there at all, are very faint.

    On Drama begins with a brief history of tragedy and comedy. The standard etymologies of both forms are given. It is of some interest that Evanthius traces both forms to religious ceremonies. Tragedy arose from Bacchic festivals and comedy from festivals to Apollo. Evanthius agrees with Aristotle that tragedy was the earlier form. His reasoning involves a bit of elementary *ex post facto* anthropology: tragedy deals with somber events. It is therefore associated with the early stages of civilization—with "barbarism and brutality"—while comedy, which is lighter in tone, is associated with the time when "towns were founded and life became more mild and easier." Thespis and Eupolis "along with Cratinus and Aristophanes" are cited as the founders of tragedy and comedy. We then turn to a more detailed history of comedy, which moves, following Horace in the *Ars Poetica,* from old comedy to satyr play (branching off into Lucilian satire) to new comedy, "especially Menander and Terence." The section ends with observations on the decline of the chorus, on differences between Greek and Roman drama, and on meter. Like Aristotle, Evanthius considers Homer a teacher of dramatic poets. He adds the point, made also, for example, by "Longinus," that the *Iliad* anticipates tragedy, the *Odyssey,* comedy.

    The essay continues with a discussion of Roman comedy. Terence emerges as the foremost Latin comic poet. He is praised for his relaxed meter, which is close to prose, for his characterization, including his willingness to defy convention, for his observance of comic decorum, and for his double plots. In the conclusion Evanthius lists the standard types and parts of Roman drama.

    Probably the most important part of this section is the contrast between tragedy and comedy:

> In comedy the fortunes of men are middle-class, the dangers are slight, and the ends of the action are happy; but in tragedy everything is the opposite—the characters are great men, the, fears are intense, and the ends disastrous. In comedy the beginning is

troubled, the end tranquil; in tragedy events follow the reverse order. And in tragedy the kind of life is shown that is to be shunned; while in comedy the kind is shown that is to be sought after. Finally, in comedy the story is always fictitious; while tragedy is often based on historical truth.

This definition omits any reference to staging. It points the way toward the later medieval conception of tragedy and comedy as poems to be recited rather than plays to be acted. This conception is illustrated by the "tragedies" narrated by Chaucer's Monk and by Dante's defense of the "comic" nature of *The Divine Comedy* in the *Epistle to Can Grande della Scala*. The Evanthius definition is structural, and its differentiation between tragedy and comedy is entirely different from that found in the *Poetics*. Aristotle was willing to approve a tragedy like *Iphigenia in Tauris*, which ends happily, and he cited the *Antheus* of Agathon to show that an entirely fictitious plot can be as satisfactory as an historical one. By contrast, Evanthius insists that the end of tragedy must be sad, and that the tragic action must be based on history. Again, Aristotle is indifferent to moral lessons. By contrast, Evanthius asserts that tragedy shows what is "to be shunned" and comedy, what is "to be sought after." In sum, this passage contains the seeds of the most widespread clichés of medieval dramatic criticism and of Renaissance theory and practice.

On Comedy repeats much that is found in Evanthius. Cicero's definition of comedy as "an imitation of life, a mirror of character, and an image of truth" was quoted widely during the Renaissance. It comes from Donatus, since it is not found in any of Cicero's extant works. The quotation from Horace's *Ars Poetica* confirms the outlines of the history given by Evanthius and Donatus. The remainder of the essay consists of technical terms, most of them already introduced by Evanthius. The summary of the parts of a classical drama—prologue, protasis, epitasis, and catastrophe—is of interest because of the influence of these terms, demonstrated by T. W. Baldwin in *Shakespeare's Five-Act Structure*, on Renaissance dramatic practice.

The translation here used is my own. For bibliography, see especially pp. 481–84.

Evanthius: ON DRAMA

Tragedy and comedy began in religious ceremonies which the ancients held to give thanks for a good harvest.

The sort of song which the sacred chorus offered to Father Bacchus when the altars had been kindled and the sacrificial goat brought in was called tragedy.

This is from *apo tou tragou kai tes oides*—that is, from "goat," an enemy of vineyards, and from "song." There is a full reference to this in Vergil's *Georgics* [II.380 ff.], either because the poet of this sort of song was given a goat, or because a goatskin full of new wine was the usual reward to the singers; or else because the players used to smear their faces with wine-lees prior to the introduction of masks by Aeschylus. "Wine-lees" in Greek is *truges*. And the word "tragedy" was invented for these reasons.

But while the Athenians were not yet confined to the city and Apollo was called "Nomius" [shepherd] and "Aguieus" [guardian]—that is, guardian of shepherds and villages—they erected altars for divine worship around the hamlets, farms, villages, and crossroads of Attica and solemnly chanted a festival song to him. It was called comedy *apo ton komon kai tes oides*—the name composed, as I think, from "villages" [*komai*] and "song" [*oide*]. Or else it was composed *apo tou komazein kai aidein*—going to a revel singing. This is not unlikely since the comic chorus was drunk or engaged in love making on the sacred day.

And once the historical sequence has been established, it is clear that tragedy appeared first. For man moved little by little from barbarism and brutality to a civilized condition. Later towns were founded and life became more mild and easier. Thus the matter of tragedy was discovered long before the matter of comedy.

Thespis is thought to be the inventor of tragedy by those who study ancient history. And Eupolis, along with Cratinus and Aristophanes, is thought to be the father of old comedy. But Homer, who is, as it were, the copious fountainhead of all poetry, provided exemplars for these sorts of poetry and established almost a law for their composition. We know that he wrote the *Iliad* in the form of a tragedy and that the *Odyssey* has the form of a comedy. In the beginning such poems were crude and not all polished and graceful as they later became. And after Homer's excellent and copious work they were regularized in their structure and parts by clever imitators.

Now that we have discussed the early history of the two forms in order to determine their origin, let us proceed to necessary matters. But, keeping within the limits of the title of this work, we will defer those subjects that are proper to tragedy for a later time, and will talk of the sorts of drama that Terence imitated.

Old comedy, like tragedy, was once simply a song, as we previously observed. The chorus sang it to a flute accompaniment while grouped around the smoking altar. At times the chorus walked, at times stood still, and at times it danced in circles. Then one character was taken from the group who spoke to the group, each taking alternate turns—that is, . . . [lacuna; perhaps the Greek word *amoibaios*, "alternately"]—and with a different melody. Then there appeared a second and a third character; and at length, as the number of characters was increased by various authors, masks and *pallia* [robes] began to be used, and boots and the comic sock and the other adornments and costumes used by the actors. Eventually, each type of character came to have his own costume. Finally, as there were actors who played in the first part, the second, the third, the fourth, and the fifth, the whole drama was divided into five acts.

While comedy was still, as it were, in its cradle and had hardly begun, it was called *archaia komoidia* and *ep'onomatos,* because it was "old" [*archaia*] in comparison to what has been discovered more recently. And *ep'onomatos* [by name] because the fable has, as it were, the historical validity of a true story, and real citizens are named and freely described.

The early poets, unlike the moderns, did not write fictional plots but wrote openly about things which citizens had done, often using real names. This was very beneficial to the morals of the society since every citizen avoided immorality in order not to become a public spectacle and a disgrace to his family. But as the poets came to use their pens with greater license and began to pillory good men right and left just for the fun of it, they were silenced by a law forbidding anyone from writing a poem slandering another person.

From this situation a new type of drama, satyr play, originated. "Satyr play" derived its name from satyrs, who are, as we know, supernatural beings always involved in games and wanton sports, although some wrongly think the word has a different derivation. Satyr play took the form of a poem which, through the device of crude and, as it were, rustic jesting, attacked the vices of citizens without mentioning specific names. This species of comedy was damaging to many poets since they were suspected by powerful citizens of making their deeds worse than they really were, and of disgracing the upper class by their manner of writing. Lucilius began composing this kind of poem in a new way, and he wrote "poesy"—that is, a single poem in several books.

Forced by the abuses already mentioned to give up satyr play, poets invented another kind of poem—*nea komoidia*—that is, "new comedy." This kind of poem was concerned with more typical situations and in general terms with men who live a middle-class life. It gave the spectator less bitterness and more pleasure, being close-knit in plot, true to life in characterization, useful in its sentiments, delightful for its wit, and apt in its prosody. Just as those earlier works were celebrated for their authors, so new comedy is the work of many earlier and later writers, and especially Menander and Terence.

Although a great deal can be said about these matters, it will be enough to instruct the reader, to summarize what the writings of the ancients say about the comic art. Old comedy consisted in the beginning of the chorus. Little by little it expanded, by increasing the number of characters, into five acts. Eventually, as the chorus was reduced and thinned out, it came about that in new comedy the chorus is not only not brought onstage, but there is not even a place left for it. As times became more leisurely, the audience grew more sophisticated and as the play changed from the acted part to the singing the spectators began to grow restless and leave. The poets learned from this and reduced the choral part, leaving almost no place for it. Menander left out the chorus for this reason and not for another, as some other writers think. Eventually the poets did not leave any place at all for the chorus. The Latin comic poets wrote in this way, and this is why it is difficult to decide where the divisions of the five acts occur in their plays.

Moreover the Greeks do not have prologues, which we Latins customarily include. Like the Greeks, all the Latin writers but Terence have *theoi apo mechanes*—that is, "gods from a machine"—to narrate stories. Besides, the other comic writers do not readily admit *protatika prosopa*—that is, characters drawn from outside the plot—while Terence often uses them since the plot becomes clearer through introducing them.

The ancient poets were rather careless in meter, demanding only an iamb in the second and fourth place. But they are outdone by Terence, who, by relaxing the meter, reduced it as far as possible to the nature of prose.

As for the laws of characterization in respect to moral habits, age, station in life, and type roles, no one was more diligent than Terence. He alone dared— since verisimilitude is required in fiction—to defy the comic prescriptions, and at times to introduce prostitutes who were not evil. There is both a reason given for their goodness and the fact itself gives a certain pleasure.

Terence did these things most artistically, and it is especially admirable that he kept within the bounds of comedy and tempered the emotional element so that he did not slide over into tragedy. This effect, along with others, was seldom achieved, we observe, by Plautus and Afranius and Appius and the many other comic poets. Among the other virtues, it is also admirable that Terence's plays are so well controlled in style that they neither swell up to tragic elevation nor degenerate into the baseness of mime.

Add that Terence never brings in abstruse material or things that have to be glossed by antiquaries, as Plautus often does, and that Plautus is more obscure than Terence in many places. Add that Terence is careful about plot and style; that he always avoided or was very circumspect about topics that could give offense; and that he joined the beginning, middle, and end so carefully that nothing seems extraneous and everything appears to be composed from the same material and to have a single body.

It is also admirable that he never brings four characters together in such a way that their differences are unclear. And further, that he never has a character address the audience directly, as though outside the comedy, which is a frequent vice of Plautus. It also seems laudable, among other things, that he chose to make his story more full by means of double plots. Except for *Hecyra*, which deals with the love of Pamphilus alone, the other five comedies have two young couples.

It is clear that after new comedy the Latins developed many kinds of drama. For example, the *togata*, based on Roman events and stories; the *prae-*

textata, from the dignity of its noble characters taken from Roman history; the *Atellana*, from the town of Campania where this kind of drama was first acted; the *Rinthonica*, from the name of the author; the *tabernaria* from the lowness of the plot and style, and the *mime* from constant imitation of base subject matter and wanton characters.

Of the many differences between tragedy and comedy, the foremost are these: In comedy the fortunes of men are middle-class, the dangers are slight, and the ends of the actions are happy; but in tragedy everything is the opposite— the characters are great men, the fears are intense, and the ends disastrous. In comedy the beginning is troubled, the end tranquil; in tragedy events follow the reverse order. And in tragedy the kind of life is shown that is to be shunned; while in comedy the kind is shown that is to be sought after. Finally, in comedy the story is always fictitious; while tragedy often has a basis in historical truth.

Latin dramas were first written by Livius Andronicus. The form was so new that he was both the author of his dramas and acted in them.

Comedies are either "active" or "quiet" or "mixed." The "active" are more turbulent, the "quiet" are more tranquil, and the "mixed" have elements of both.

Comedy is divided into four parts: prologue, protasis, epitasis, and catastrophe. The prologue is a kind of preface to the drama. In this part and this part only it is permissible to say something extrinsic to the argument, addressed to the audience and for the benefit of the poet or the drama or an actor. The protasis is the first act and the beginning of the drama. The epitasis is the development and enlargement of the conflict and, as it were, the knot of all the error. The catastrophe is the resolution of the course of events so that there is a happy ending which is made evident to all by the recognition of past events.

Donatus: ON COMEDY

Comedy is a form of drama dealing with the various qualities and conditions of civil and private persons. Through it one learns what is useful in life and what, on the contrary, is to be avoided. The Greeks define it as follows: "Comedy deals with the acts of private persons in a story that lacks serious danger." Comedy, says Cicero, is "an imitation of life, a mirror of character, and an image of truth."

Comedy received its name from an ancient custom. In early times this kind of song was sung "in the villages" [*apo tes komes*]—as is the case with the "crossroads festivals" [*compitalia*] in Italy. A term was added for the spoken part with which the audience was entertained during the changing of the events. That is, they were held by the acting out of the lives of men who live "in the villages" because of the middle state of their fortunes, not in royal palaces like the characters of tragedy. And comedy, because it is written to imitate life and character with verisimilitude, employs gesture and speech.

No-one knows who invented comedy among the Greeks. The Roman inventor is known. Livius Andronicus was the first Roman to write comedy, tragedy, and *fabula togata*. He said comedy is "a mirror of daily life" and the observation is just. When we gaze into a mirror we readily see the features of truth by means of the reflection. Likewise, by reading comedy we readily discover the image of life and custom.

The original concept came in from foreign cities and with foreign customs. When the Athenians, the guardians of Attic propriety, wanted to rebuke anyone for an immoral life, they used to gather together from all sides, happily and eagerly, at the villages and crossroads. There they used to describe the vices of individuals publicly and with proper names. Comedy was named from this custom.

At first they sang their songs in grassy meadows. And there was no lack of prizes to incite the wits of the more learned to writing. And gifts were offered to the actors to encourage them freely to use pleasing modulations of voice to gain sweet commendation. A goat [*tragos*] was given to them as a reward, because the animal was considered an enemy of vineyards. From this custom the name "tragedy" arose. Many authorities, however, prefer the idea that "tragedy" was derived from *amurca*—that is, oil-lees—which has a watery quality, the word being suggested by "trygodia" [from Greek *truges*, "lees"].

Since these revels were performed at ceremonies in honor of Father Bacchus, the writers of tragedy and comedy began to worship and venerate the spirit of this god as though he were present. This is the probable explanation of the matter: these primitive songs were written for the purpose of setting forth and celebrating the fame and glorious deeds of Bacchus.

Little by little the reputation of this art form grew. Thespis first brought it to the attention of all. Aeschylus wrote next, following the example of his predecessor. On these matters, Horace writes in the *Ars Poetica*:

> Thespis is said to have invented tragedy, a type unknown previously, and to have carried his plays around in carts, to be performed by actors whose faces were smeared with wine-lees. After him came Aeschylus, who introduced the tragic mask and robe. He designed a stage built of small planks and taught the players to speak in a grand manner and wear the tragic buskin. Then came

old comedy, which won popular praise, but the freedom it employed degenerated into excess and violence that had to be restrained by law. Prevented from attacking people's characters, the chorus lapsed into shamed silence. The Latin poets have left no style untried. Nor do those poets deserve the least honor who dared to forsake the track laid out by the Greeks and celebrate the deeds of their own country, whether in the tragedy *praetexta* or the *togata* form of comedy. [*Ars Poetica*, 274–88]

Drama is a general term. Its two chief parts are tragedy and comedy. Tragedy, if it concerns Roman subjects, is called *praetexta*. Comedy has many species. It is *palliata* or *togata* or *tabernaria* or *Atellana* or *mime* or *Rinthonica* or *planipedia*.

Planipedia is named from the baseness of the subject matter and the lowness of the actors, who do not act on a stage or platform in the boot or sock, but act "in bare feet"—or else because the subject matter does not include things appropriate for people living in houses with towers and large halls, but only things appropriate for those in low and humble places.

They say that Cincius Faliscus was the first to use masks in comedy, and in tragedy, Minucius Prothymus.

The titles of all comedies are taken from four areas: name, place, deed, and result. Names as exemplified in the *Phormio, Hecyra, Cruculio,* and *Epidicus.* Places in the *Andria, Leucadia,* and *Brundisina.* Deeds in the *Eunuchus, Asinaria,* and *Captivi.* Result in the *Commorientes, Crimen,* and *Heautontimorumenos.*

There are three forms of comedy. *Palliata* uses Greek dress; *togata* exhibits the sort of people who wear a Roman toga—many people call this form *tabernaria*—; and the *Atellana* which is based on wit and jests that have no value except their antiquity.

Comedies are divided into four parts: prologue, protasis, epitasis, and catastrophe. Prologue is the first speech, so called from Greek *protos logos* ["first word" or "first speech"] preceding the complication of the plot proper [*ho pro tou dramatos logos*]. There are four types. There is the *sustatikos*—the "commendatory"—where the poet or the story is praised. Then the *epitimetikos*—the "relative" prologue—where the poet either curses some rival or praises the audience. Then the *dramatikos*—"relating to the story"—which explains the argument of the drama. And there is the *miktos*—"mixed"—which includes all these things.

There is this difference according to some between a *prologue* and a *prologium*: a *prologue* is where the poet is vindicated or the story praised. A *prologium*, however, says something about the story.

Protasis is the first action of the drama, where part of the story is explained, part held back to arouse suspense among the audience. *Epitasis* is the complication of the story, by excellence of which its elements are intertwined. *Catastrophe* is the unravelling of the story, through which the outcome is demonstrated.

In most dramas the title came before the name of the author; in several the authors were named before the dramas. In ancient times there was a diversity of practice. For when men first presented dramas to the public, the titles were announced before the poet to prevent his being discouraged because of hostility. But when the poets had gained reputations as a result of presenting many dramas, then their names came first so that the name might draw attention to the drama.

It is clear that plays were presented at various kinds of games. There are four kinds of games which the officials provide for the public: the Megalenses, dedicated to the major gods, whom the Greeks call *megaloi* ["great"]; the *Funebres*, devised to draw the attention of the people while funeral ceremonies in honor of some noble person were performed; the *Plebei*, held for the benefit of the people; and the *Apollinares*, in honor of Apollo.

Usually, two altars were placed on the stage. The right one was sacred to Bacchus. The left was sacred to the god whose games are being celebrated. Thus Terence says in the *Andria*: "Take some consecrated boughs from the altar" [IV.iii.724].

They always have Ulysses wear a *pilleus* [cap] either because he once feigned madness so that he would not be recognized and forced to go to war, or because of his singular wisdom which often made him a protection and aid to his companions. He had a special talent for deception. Many commentators note that the inhabitants of Ithaca wore the *pilleus*, as do the Locrians. The costumes of Achilles and Neoptolemus include diadems although neither hero ever possessed the royal sceptre. Proof of this is the fact that they never joined the other Greek youths in the sacred oath to wage war on the Trojans, nor were they ever under the command of Agamemnon.

Old men in comedy wear a white costume, because white is associated with old age. Youths wear a varicolored costume. Slaves in comedy are clothed in a short garment in token of their age-old poverty, or so that their actions will be unencumbered. Parasites come on with a *pallium* [cloak] wrapped around them. The successful man has a white garment; the unlucky man wears an old one; the rich man a purple one; the poor man a Phoenician [reddish-purple] robe. A soldier wears a short purple cloak. A girl wears a foreign costume. A pimp wears a cloak of various colors; a prostitute wears a yellow one symbolizing greed.

Syrmata [robes with a long train] are named from the fact that they are dragged along the ground—this garment was invented by the luxurious Ionians. When worn by characters in mourning they symbolize carelessness resulting from self-neglect. Embroidered *aulaea* [curtains] are also spread out in front of the stage. This ornate decoration was taken from Attalus' palace in Pergamum all the way to Rome. Later, a *siparium* [comic drop-curtain] was used instead of *aulaea.* There was also a mimer's curtain used to block off the audience's view while the scene was being changed.

The actors spoke their lines in iambic dialogue, but the songs had melodies invented not by the poet but by a skillful musician. And a single song did not have a single melody. Rather, the melodies were often varied, and this is indicated by three numbers used to mark the comedies. These different numbers indicate the varying melodies of the song. The name of the musician who composed the melodies was placed at the beginning of the drama following the names of the author and principal actor.

Songs of this kind were played on flutes. When they were heard many of the spectators could tell what drama the players were going to present, even before the title was announced. The songs were played by matched flutes for the right and left hand, and by unmatched flutes. The flutes for the right hand played grave music and foreshadowed the serious kind of comedy. Those for the left hand foreshadowed the sportive kind of comedy by their high pitch. And when the drama called for flute playing for both right and left hands, both seriousness and sport were foreshadowed.

PROCLUS

(ca. 410–485)

INTRODUCTION

In Book X of the *Republic* Plato develops his famous theory of imitation. There is the idea of a bed, says Socrates, which is the true bed, eternal and changeless. Then there is a primary imitation of the bed by a carpenter. The material bed is necessarily imperfect and mutable, but since it is made by a craftsman it is relatively close to the idea. Finally there is a picture of a bed. The artist who paints it knows nothing of the craft of bed-making and studies only appearances. His bed is farthest from the true bed. If man's highest good is to know truth, art leads us away from truth. At best it is trivial; at worst it is positively harmful, as when Homer depicts the gods not as they are but as the myths reveal them— erratic, often cruel, and subject to the lowest human passions.

Elsewhere, in Plato's *Ion* and *Phaedrus* especially, there are suggestions of a different approach. In the *Ion* Socrates flirts with the idea that poets are inspired —that they see more, rather than less, than the average mortal.

The history of Neoplatonism as it impinges on art is the history of the substitution and elaboration of ideas in the *Ion* at the expense of those in the *Republic*. In this process the most important figure is Plotinus (205–269/70). The foundation of Neoplatonic aesthetics is *Enneads* I.6, "On the Beautiful." There we learn that beauty is more than a matter of symmetry; it is a joy felt by the soul in the perception of that which is akin to the soul—a delight in higher spiritual experience rather than appearances. God, the first principle, is both the Good and the Beautiful. The perception of true beauty does not involve gazing at material things but closing the eyes of sense and seeking transcendent vision. In *Enneads* V.8, this line of thought is carried further. True beauty is intelligible beauty. It is found in the work of artists—Plotinus cites statuary rather than poetry or music—as the form, or spiritual element, conferred on the material. Art is thus a higher, almost visionary activity. It imitates nature only in the sense that it imitates the source from which nature derives. Phidias did not use a model for Zeus but made him as he might be if he should decide to manifest himself to human eyes. This sort of creation takes place in the soul. The artist, by implication, is a visionary using faculties that transcend reason. His work communicates this vision and leads others along the path taken by the artist himself.

As important as these ideas are, it remained for Proclus, a late disciple of Plotinus, to relate them directly to literature. Neoplatonic critics had previously dealt with literature. Maximus Tyrius had devoted several essays in his *Dissertations* to poetic questions, especially the probity of Homer. Philo Judaeus, Clement, and Origen had used Neoplatonic concepts in biblical exegesis, and Porphyry had discovered allegory, in a manner analogous to that of Macrobius in his commentary on *Scipio's Dream,* in the cave of the nymphs passage in Homer. But Maximus Tyrius is pedestrian and Philo, Origen, and Porphyry are tied to specific texts and an allegorical method that limits their discussion of general critical issues. It is Proclus who first applies Neoplatonic theory to the outstanding problems of literary criticism. Although it is impossible to trace the influence of the essay here reprinted, the ideas which the essay brings into remarkably sharp focus form a leitmotif in medieval and Renaissance critical thought. They are paralleled in the fourth-century cult of the poet-seer as reflected in Servius and Macrobius, they recur in conjunction with the rediscovery of Dionysius the pseudo-Areopagite following the translation of his work into Latin in the tenth century by Scotus Erigena, they are found in the Platonizing authors of the twelfth-century Renaissance, especially Bernard Silvestris, and they impinge deeply upon humanistic defenses of poetry from Boccaccio to Sir Philip Sidney. Their hallmark is the idea that poetry is a more profound philosophy, a form of theology, a kind of vision. Their corollaries include: (1) the idea that poetry is necessarily allegorical (its vision is untranslatable; or it begins with images but ascends to truth; or its profound revelations must be concealed by the veil of fable from the profane rabble); (2) the notion of the poet as seer; (3) the positing of a faculty (imagination) higher than reason; (4) the idea that this faculty seems irrational to the uninspired, so that poets often are compared by the uninitiated to madmen and drunkards; (5) rejection of the classical theory of imitation (that poetry is an image of nature, a mirror of life); (6) qualification of the nearly universal idea that the chief benefit of poetry is that it teaches good morals (that poets must profit as well as delight); and (7) the idea that the experience of art is not an entertaining diversion but something akin to religious experience. In sum, Neoplatonic theories of literature leavened the rather dry and matter-of-fact critical tradition transmitted to the Middle Ages by writers like Horace, Cicero, and Donatus. They implemented the strong mystical tendency inherent in biblical exegesis and are involved, if only at third or fourth hand, in the conception of art evident in Bernard Silvestris, Alanus de Insulis, and Dante. After Marsilio Ficino had resurrected Plato in a Neoplatonic guise in the late fifteenth century, they provided a vital stimulus to the critical theory and literary practice of humanists during the sixteenth and seventeenth centuries. It is significant that rationalists like Castelvetro and Bacon attacked poetry for precisely the qualities emphasized in Neoplatonism—its claim to higher vision, its allegory, and its resistance to logical paraphrase. And it is significant that one of the most common Neoplatonic terms for inspiration (*enthusiasm*) became a term of ridicule in the eighteenth century.

Proclus wrote extensively on poetic questions in his voluminous commentaries on Plato. The essay reprinted here has been chosen because it is self-contained and because its general observations on literature are supplemented by specific comments intended to answer the objections which led Socrates in *Republic* X to banish Homer from his ideal state.

Proclus begins with psychology. He observes that there are three faculties in the soul. The first, which would later be called the intuition, intellect, or *mens,* is allied to the divine. The second is allied to human life and the world revealed to the senses. It is the rational soul which makes "intellect and science . . . the principle of its energy." Reason is a discursive faculty. It abstracts general principles from what is known, according to the rules of logical inference. The third faculty does not abstract but is captive of images as they enter the mind (and are combined by chance associations) from the senses. This faculty is *phantasia* or fancy.

Corresponding to the three lives of the soul, there are three kinds of poetry. The first exhibits what may literally be called "a rage for beauty." It is produced by "divine inspiration" and is related to a madness (*mania*) that is better than the "temperance" advocated by reason. Being concerned with beauty, it is also concerned with "adornment"—which is objectified in poetry as "measures and rhythms." The impulse evident here emerges during the Renaissance (in Tasso, for example) as a striving toward poetic "magnificence"—toward maximum use of the imagery, word effects, stanza forms, sheer variety, and the like—which is the concomitant of truly inspired poetry.

The kind of poetry produced by the reason is essentially didactic. It presents the lore of science in attractive forms and teaches "prudence and every other virtue to those of a naturally good disposition." Interestingly, the lowest type of poetry—that of the fancy—is equated with imitation. The Platonic distaste for artistic imitation is retained here, but in a context which completely overturns Plato's low estimate of artists. Being limited to "the world as it seems to be," "phantastic poetry" depends on appearances. It is less artistic than the poetry of reason which abstracts impressions into general systems. In a single paragraph, Proclus has repudiated the hallowed classical tradition that imitation, in the sense of mirroring life and custom, is the highest function of art.

For support, Proclus brings in the *Phaedrus* and the *Ion.* His citations reveal the profound ambiguity in Plato's view of art. They are valid, but they ignore the *Republic,* and, like most Neoplatonists including Ficino, Proclus reads the *Ion* as an exposition of "*furor poeticus*," ignoring the fact that Socrates may be (probably is) speaking ironically when he couples enthusiasm and divine inspiration with madness. When Plato's reservations in the *Republic* finally are introduced, Proclus stresses that the tales of the gods are "concealed in these symbols, as under veils." The passing remark in *Republic* III that certain fables have a higher allegorical sense is taken as a *carte blanche* for mythology considered as allegory, while the later very strong attack on poets for falsifying the true nature of divinity is ignored. Likewise, in the discussion of imitative poetry, subdivided into the assimilative and phantastic categories, Proclus implies that Plato's discussion in the *Republic* is consciously limited to a single category of art rather than to art as a whole. Again, the approach is—if not a conscious distortion—an egregious case of special pleading.

The essay ends with a eulogy of Homer. Homer is a master of all three kinds of poetry "but especially the enthusiastic, according to which, as we have said, he is principally characterized." Likewise, Homer represented a model for tragic poets, particularly as these, being committed to pleasing the masses, draw on the phantastic elements in his work.

The essay ends with a brief explanation of why Plato criticizes Homer so severely. Plato wrote at a time when philosophy was "despised" and the worst sort of poetry was admired. Plato did not condemn Homer because of deficiencies in his moral outlook, but because the poets of Plato's day appealed to the lowest common denominator in society. Instead of instructing the masses they devoted their energies to entertainment by means of the lowest (imitative) form of poetry, concentrating on the least edifying emotions. The tragedians, who most appeal to a popular audience, are the worst offenders in this respect. In spite of this abuse, however, Homer remains pre-eminent among poets: "so far as he is possessed of the Muses, he is divine; but as far as he is an imitator, he is the third from the truth."

Thomas Taylor's translation, which was published in the preface to his edition of Aristotle's *Poetics, Rhetoric, and Nicomachean Ethics* (London, 1818), has been revised for this volume by Kevin Kerrane. For bibliography, see especially pp. 482–84.

PROCLUS ON THE MORE DIFFICULT QUESTIONS IN THE *REPUBLIC*: THE NATURE OF POETIC ART

There are three lives in the soul. The best and most perfect is through the faculty which allies and conjoins it with the gods, so that the soul lives a life united to them through the highest similitude. The soul, no longer existing in itself, but deriving life from a divine source infusing the mind, is filled with ineffable impressions of the divine, and connects like with like—its own light with that of the gods, and that which is most uniform in its own essence and life with that which is above all essence and life. The second life of the soul is through a faculty of middle dignity and power: the soul, not divinely inspired, realizes its own individuality by ordaining intellect and science as the principle of its energy, evolving the multitude of its reasons. It surveys the various mutations of forms, unites through abstraction the intellect and its object, and expresses in images an intellectual and intelligible essence. The third life of the soul is that which accords with its inferior faculties: the soul, expressing itself through them, employs phantasies and irrational senses, and is filled entirely with things of a subordinate nature.

Just as there are these three forms of life in souls, so poetry, as it proceeds from the various faculties, is diversified into the first, middle, and last modes of being. The first kind of poetry has the highest existence: it is full of divine goods, and it establishes the soul in the causes themselves of things, according to a certain ineffable union, leading that which is filled into sameness with its replenishing source. The soul subjects itself to spiritual illumination, and the divine is impelled to a communication of light—thus, according to the Oracle, "perfecting works, by mingling the rivers of incorruptible fire." This kind of poetry produces one divine bond, a union of participation, in which that which is subordinate partakes of that which is more excellent, so that the divine energy infuses all. The inferior nature withdraws, and conceals itself in that which is superior. This, then, in short, is an apparent madness better than temperance, and is distinguished by a divine quality. And as every different kind of poetry subsists according to a different hyparxis, or summit of divine essence, so this first kind of poetry, proceeding from divine inspiration, fills the soul with symmetry, and hence adorns even its least energies with measures and rhythms. And just as we define prophetic fury as according with truth, and the amatory inclinations as according with beauty, so in like manner we define the poetic mania as according with divine symmetry.

The second kind of poetry, which is subordinate to this first and divinely inspired species, and which has a middle existence in the soul, derives its being from a scientific and intellectual faculty. Hence this kind of poetry embodies the essence of things, strives to contemplate beautiful works and reasonings, and leads everything toward a measured and rhythmical interpretation. For you will find many works of good poets to be of this kind, rivaling the wisdom of great men—full of admonitions, the best counsels, and intellectual harmony. This kind of poetry teaches prudence and every other virtue to those of a naturally good disposition, and it explores and reflects on the periods of the soul, its eternal reasons, and various powers.

The third species of poetry, subordinate to these, is mingled with opinions and phantasies. It is composed by means of imitation; it is said to be

—and is nothing other than—imitative poetry. Sometimes it uses likeness-making alone, and sometimes it relies on a likeness that is only apparent, not real. It strongly intensifies very moderate passions, astonishing the hearers; using appropriate names and words, mutations of harmonies and varieties of rhythms, it changes the dispositions of souls. It indicates the nature of things not as they are, but as they appear to the many, being a certain adumbration, and not an accurate knowledge of things. It also establishes as its goal the delight of the hearers, and looks particularly to the passive part of the soul, which is naturally adapted to rejoice or be afflicted. But of this species of poetry, as we have said elsewhere, one division is *assimilative,* in which the imitation is accurate, while the other is *phantastic,* affording only apparent imitation.

Such, then, in short are the species of poetry. It now remains to show that these are also mentioned by Plato, and to treat other matters compatible with his teachings about each. First we shall discuss those wonderful conceptions of divine poetry which may be collected by anyone who reads Plato attentively. And once these are clear, I think it will be easy to understand the other two species of poetry.

In the *Phaedrus* Plato calls divine poetry "a possession from the Muses, and a mania" [244–45], and says that it is imparted from above to a tender and solitary soul. Its employment excites and inspires with Bacchic fury, in odes and other poetic forms, and its purpose is to instruct posterity in celebrating the infinite deeds of the ancients.

From these words it is perfectly evident that Plato identifies the original and first-operating cause of poetry as the gift of the Muses. For just as the Muses fill with harmony and rhythmical motion all the other divine creations, both the apparent and the unapparent, so in like manner they produce a vestige of divinity in those souls they take possession of, and this illuminates inspired poetry. I think that Plato calls such an illumination a *possession* and a *mania* because the whole energy of the illuminating power is divine, and because that which is illuminated gives itself up to this energy and, abandoning its own habits, yields to the force of that which is divine and uniform. He calls it a possession because the whole illuminated soul surrenders itself to the present effect of the illuminating deity. Plato calls it a mania because such a soul abandons its own proper energies for those of the illuminating powers.

In the second place, Plato describes the characteristics of the soul possessed by the Muses, and says that it ought to be tender and solitary. A soul hard and resisting, and disobedient to divine illumination, would oppose the energy of divinely inspired possession, because it would exist in itself rather than through the illuminating power, and it would be incapable of appreciating the gifts of this power. And a soul given over to various opinions, and filled with thoughts alien to a divine nature, would obscure the process of inspiration by mingling itself and its energies with those derived from the Muses. The soul which is to be possessed by the Muses must therefore be tender and solitary—so that it may be properly receptive to divinity and harmonize with it, and it should be unreceptive to and unmingled with other things.

In the third place, Plato mentions the common occurrence of such an aptitude in combination with possession and mania from the Muses. For to excite and inspire with Bacchic fury is the province both of that which illuminates and that which is illuminated, and the two processes become one: the divine force moving from above, and the soul surrendering itself to this motion. Excitation is a purified energy of the soul, lifting it from the world of matter and time and into divinity. Bacchic fury is a divinely inspired motion and, as it were, an unwearied dance upward toward the divine, giving perfection to the possessed. But again, a correct disposition of the soul is as necessary as the divine power, so that the possessed will not incline to that which is worse, but will easily be moved to a more excellent nature.

In the fourth place, Plato adds that the purpose of this divine poetry is to instruct posterity in celebrating the infinite deeds of the ancients. This implies that human affairs become more perfect and splendid when they are presented by a divinely inspired poet, and that such poetry produces true learning in its hearers. It does not aim primarily at the training of the young, but is directed more toward those already schooled in civic virtue, who still need a greater spiritual understanding of divine matters. More than any other kind of poetry, this species instructs the hearers, once its divine nature becomes manifest to them. Hence Plato very properly prefers this poetry, which subsists from the Muses in tender and solitary souls, to every other human art: "For the poet who approaches the poetic gates without such a mania will be imperfect, and his poetry, so far as it is dictated by prudence, will vanish before that which is the outcome of fury" [*Phaedrus* 245]. Thus does Socrates in the *Phaedrus* instruct us in the peculiarities of divine poetry—which differs both from divine prophecy and from prudent, calculated art—and he attributes to the gods its first unfolding into light.

Socrates' comments in the *Ion,* when he is discoursing with the rhapsodist about this species of poetry, confirm these views. Here Socrates states clearly that the poetry of Homer is divine, and that it is a source of enthusiastic energy to those conversant with it. For when the rhapsodist says that he can speak copiously on the poems of Homer, but not at all on the writings of other poets, Socrates explains this by saying: "It is not from technical skill that you speak well concerning Homer, but because you are moved by a divine power" [533D]. And the truth of this is indeed perfectly evident. For those who do something by means of art are able to produce the same effect in all similar situations. But those who work by means of divine inspiration on something truly harmonious cannot regularly produce the same effect when working with other, similar things. The rhapsodist receives divine inspiration when reciting Homer, but not when reciting other poets. Socrates then instructs us by using the stone commonly called Herculean as a clear analogy to perfect possession by the Muses: "This stone, then, not only draws to itself iron rings, but imparts to them a power to attract similar things, so as to enable them to draw other rings, and form a chain of rings, or pieces of iron, each hanging from the other" [533D-E].

Let us now consider Socrates' continued remarks on divine poetry. "Thus then," he says, "the Muse makes men divine; and, from these men thus inspired, others catch the sacred power to form a chain of divine enthusiasts" [533E]. Here, in the first place, he speaks of the divine cause in the singular number, calling it the Muse and not, as in the *Phaedrus,* a possession from the Muses. Socrates refers to the divine cause as a single mania affecting a whole multitude, in order to attribute all enthusiastic power to one spiritual substance, the primary principle of poetry. For poetry subsists uniformly and mysteriously in the first mover, but secondarily and indirectly in poets moved by that spiritual power, and still more indirectly in the rhapsodists, who are led back to the first cause through the agency of the poets. By thus extending the principle of divine inspiration as far as the rhapsodists, Socrates celebrates the fecundity of the first moving power. At the same time he clearly states that poets themselves participate in inspiration: the poets' ability through their poems to excite others to a divinely inspired state indicates that a divine nature is conspicuously present in their souls. Consequently, Socrates adds this comment: "The best epic poets, and all who similarly excel in composing any kind of verse to be recited, do not frame their admirable poems from the rules of art; but, possessed by the Muse, they write from divine inspiration. Nor is it otherwise with the best lyric poets, and all other fine writers of verse to be sung"[533E]. And again, afterwards, he says: "For a poet is a thing light and volatile, and sacred, nor is he able to write poetry till he becomes divine, and has no longer the command of his intellect" [534B]. And lastly, Socrates adds: "Hence it is that the poets indeed say many fine things, whatever their subject, just as you do concerning Homer; but not doing it through any rules of art, each of them succeeds through a divine calling in that species of poetry to which he is uniquely impelled by the Muse" [534C].

In all these citations, it is evident that Plato traces divine poetry to a divine cause, which he calls a Muse. In this he emulates Homer, who at one time refers to a multitude of Muses and at another to the union of the Muses in a single principle—as when he says "O Muses, sing" and "Sing me the man, O Muse." Midway between this divine cause of enthusiasm and the last echoes of inspiration in the responses of the rhapsodists, Plato locates poetic mania. Moving and being moved, filled from on high and transferring to others the illumination thus derived, the poetic mania joins together even the last participants in a communion with the divine substance.

With these things we may also bring into accord what the Athenian Guest says about poetry in the third book of the *Laws,* and what Timaeus says about poets. The Athenian Guest says that "poetry is divinely inspired," and that "it composes sacred hymns, and, with certain Graces and Muses, relates many things that have been truly transacted" [682]. Timaeus exhorts us to follow poets inspired by Apollo, in that they are "the sons of gods, knowing their fathers' concerns, even though their assertions are not probable and are unaccompanied by demonstrations." From all this it is easy to understand what Plato thought about divine poetry, and how he characterized inspired poets as special messengers of divine powers, eminently acquainted with the affairs of their fathers. When, therefore, Plato takes notice of mythical fictions, and corrects the more serious part of the writings of the poets—such as those dealing with bonds, castrations, loves, sexual connections, tears, and laughter among the gods—we must say that he also especially testifies that these things are properly presented as allegorical, concealing the idea as under veils. For whoever thinks that poets are particularly worthy of belief in affairs respecting the gods, even though they speak through inspiration rather than logical demonstration, must certainly admire the divine fables through which they deliver the truth concerning the nature of the gods. Whoever calls poetry divine cannot also ascribe to it an impious and exaggerated treatment of the divine. And whoever shows that the assertions of poets are attended with certain Graces and Muses must certainly judge an inelegant, unharmonious, and ungraceful phantasy to be very remote from the theory of poetic inspiration. Thus, when Plato in his *Republic* establishes by law that poetry and allegorical fables are not adapted to the ears of the young, he is very far from despising poetry itself; he merely protects the juvenile mind, which is inexperienced in hearing such things, from fiction of this sort. For, as he says in the *Second Alcibiades,* "The whole of poetry is naturally enigmatical, and is not obvious to the understanding of everyone" [147]. And hence in the *Republic* he clearly says that "youth is not able to distinguish what is allegory and what is not" [II.377]. We must say, therefore, that Plato entirely approves of inspired poetry, which he calls divine, and thinks it proper that those who compose it should be venerated in silence. This concludes our examination of the first kind of poetry, which subsists, from a divine origin, in tender and solitary souls.

Now let us contemplate that species of poetry which has a scientific knowledge of things, and which proceeds according to intellect and prudence. It reveals to men many spiritual essences, and brings to light many probable tenets in practical philosophy. It investigates the most beautiful symmetry in human behavior, and examines the disposition to vice. And it adorns all of these things with proper measures and rhythms.

The Athenian Guest in the *Laws* says that the poetry of Theognis is of this kind, which he praises beyond that of Tyrtaeus, because Theognis is a teacher of the whole of virtue, including the whole of political life. Theognis teaches a fidelity which receives its completion from all the virtues, expelling from politics that most pernicious vice sedition, and changing the lives of those who are persuaded. On the other hand, Tyrtaeus merely praises the habit of fortitude by itself, preaching it to those who neglect other virtues. But it will be better to listen to Plato's own words: "We also have the poet Theognis as a witness in our favor, who was a citizen of Megara in Sicily. For he says, 'Who keeps his faith amid seditious cries/Is worth his weight in silver and in gold.' We say therefore that such a person will conduct himself better in the most difficult kind of war, much in the same degree as justice, temperance, and prudence, when united with fortitude, are better than fortitude alone. For no one can be both faithful and effective in civil strife without the whole of virtue" [*Laws* I.630]. Here, therefore, Plato recognizes Theognis as partaking of political science, and all the virtues.

In the *Second Alcibiades* Plato, defining the most right and healthy mode of prayer, attributes it to a certain wise poet: "To me, Alcibiades, it seems probable that some wise man or other, happening to be connected with certain persons void of understanding, and observing them to pursue and pray for things for which it were better for them to be without, but which appeared to them good, composed for their use a common prayer in words like these—'King Jupiter, grant us what is good, whether or not it is the subject of our prayers, and avert from us what is evil, even if we should pray for it' " [142–43]. For only the scientific man, in whom a divine nature is adapted to the middle faculties of man, knows how to distinguish between good and evil in daily life. And on this account Socrates calls the poet who composed the prayer a wise man: through science alone, rather than through divine inspiration or right opinion, the poet formed a judgment on the natures and habits of those who prayed, and he reserved to the gods that which falls under their beneficent power. For it was the work of wisdom and science, and not of anything casual, to have converted those people through prayer to the one kingly providence of Jupiter, to have attributed the existence of good to the power of divinity, to have prevented the generation of true evils by calling upon the benevolence of a more excellent nature, and in short to have asserted that these things were unknown to those who prayed and were instead within the province of the divinity. Very properly, therefore, we say that such poetry is wise and scientific. For the poetry which is able to adapt truths to the middle faculties of man must itself exist by means of perfect science.

In the third place, let us now speak about imitative poetry, which, as we have already said, sometimes makes accurate likenesses of things, and at other times expresses things according to mere appearance. In the *Laws* the Athenian Guest clearly explains to us the assimilative part of this poetry, but in the *Republic* Socrates describes its phantastic part. And in the *Sophist* the

Eleatean Guest apprises us of how the assimilative and phantastic species of imitation differ from each other:

> GUEST: For I seem to perceive two species of imitation —one being the art of making likenesses, which is executed when someone produces an imitation by copying an original model in all proportions (length, breadth, and depth) and colors.
> THEAETETUS: Do not all imitators try to do this?
> GUEST: Not those who perform or paint any great work. For if sculptors, for example, were to follow the exact proportions of their models, then the upper parts, which we see from farther off, would appear smaller than they should be, and the lower parts would seem too large.
> THEAETETUS: Entirely so. And thus artists forego accuracy in their imitations; they do not produce in images truly beautiful proportions, but only those which appear to be so. [235].

Very properly, I think, does the Eleatean Guest at the end of the dialogue, wishing to bind the sophist by the definitive method, distinguish between assimilative imitation (in which the image is a true likeness of the model) and phantastic imitation (in which the likeness is only apparent).

In the second book of the *Laws* the Athenian Guest speaks only of assimilative poetry, and he discusses music which, rather than making pleasure its end, aims at a true imitation of its model. On the other hand, Socrates in the *Republic* deals with phantastic poetry. And having shown that a poet of this kind is third from the truth and merely derivative, Socrates compares such poetry to a picture which represents not the works of nature but of artificers— and these not as they truly are, but only as they appear to be. Thus Socrates clearly shows that the phantastic species of poetry aims only at delighting the audience. Of the two kinds of imitative poetry, the phantastic is inferior to the assimilative for this very reason: whereas assimilative poetry is concerned with accuracy of imitation, phantastic poetry is concerned merely with how the power of the phantasy can produce pleasure in the audience.

Such, then, are the species of poetry which Plato thought worthwhile to distinguish—one as better than science, another as scientific, a third as conversant with, and a fourth as falling off from, right opinion.

Having clarified these matters, let us now return to the poetry of Homer and contemplate every poetic habit that shines in it, especially those concerned with truth and beauty. When Homer is filled with enthusiastic energy, is possessed by the Muses, and communicates mystical ideas about the gods themselves, then he operates according to the first and divinely inspired principle of poetry. When he speaks of the life of the soul, the diversities in its nature, and its relation to civic virtue, then he especially speaks scientifically. When he presents forms of imitation truly similar to specific things and persons, then he employs assimilative imitation. And, finally, when Homer directs his attention not to the truth of things, but only as they appear to the multitude, and thus seduces the souls of his hearers, then he produces phantastic poetry.

I wish now to illustrate these poetic habits in Homer, beginning with phantastic imitation. He sometimes describes the rising and setting of the sun, not by accurately recounting in his verses each of these as it actually happens, but merely as it appears to us from a distance. These and all similar examples may be called the phantastic part of his poetry. But when Homer imitates heroes as warring or consulting or speaking according to the forms of real life—some as prudent, others as brave, and others as ambitious—then I would call this assimilative poetry. The scientific habit of poetry is manifested, I believe, when Homer unfolds and teaches the workings of the soul, based on his knowledge of the various faculties within it or of the relation between an image and the soul's use of it, or when he deals with the order of the elements within the universe (earth, water, fire, air), or other similar matters. And I would say that Homer is filled with enthusiastic energy, and is possessed by the Muses, when he devises fables that teach us about such mysteries as the demiurge, the triadic emanation of the one, the bonds of Vulcan, or the relation between the paternal ideas of Jupiter and the fertile divinity of Juno.

In addition, Homer's portrayal of Demodocus the bard [*Odyssey*, Book VIII] attributes to him an energy originating from the gods. Ulysses says that Demodocus was impelled by a god when he began his song, that he was divinely inspired, that the Muse loved him, and that God is the leader of the Muses: "The Muse, Jove's daughter, or Apollo, taught/Thee aptly thus the fate of Greece to sing,/And all the Grecians, hardy deeds and toils" [488–90]. It is a standard interpretation that Homer intended to represent himself in the character of Demodocus, and their personal calamities are indeed similar. There seems to be a direct reference to the fabled blindness of Homer in the statement that the gods "With clouds of darkness quenched his visual ray,/But gave him power to raise the lofty lay" [62–64]. Homer thus clearly contends that Demodocus says what he says by means of divine inspiration.

It is well that we have mentioned Demodocus and his inspired song, for it seems to me that the musicians Homer thought worthy of mentioning illustrate the various poetic habits discussed above. Demodocus, as we have said, was inspired, both in narrating divine and human concerns, and is said to have received his songs from the gods. On the other hand, the Ithacan bard Phemius is characterized merely according to a scientific knowledge of divine and human affairs. In Book I of the *Odyssey* Penelope addresses him: "Alluring arts thou knowest, and what of old/Of gods and heroes sacred bards have told" [337–39]. A third bard is the lyrist of Clytemnestra, who seems to have been an imitative poet, employing right opinion. He performed melodies of temperance for

Clytemnestra's benefit, and as long as he remained with her she perpetrated no unholy deed: the disciplining effect of his song converted her irrational tendencies into temperate behavior. A fourth musician, Thamyris, may be taken to represent the phantastic species of poetry. It is said that his song made the Muses indignant, so that they caused it to cease, for he practiced a music much more diversified and sensuous, and calculated to please the vulgar. By preferring a more varied music than the simpler mode adapted to the Muses, Thamyris is said to have fallen into contention with them, and to have lost the benevolence of the goddesses. The anger of the Muses does not refer to any passion in them, but indicates that Thamyris was unsuited to participate with them: his kind of song is phantastic and most remote from truth, calling forth the passions of the soul, and possessing no value with respect to imitation, right opinion, or science.

We may therefore behold all the kinds of poetry in Homer, but particularly the enthusiastic which, as we have said, principally characterizes him. Nor are we alone in this opinion: as we observed earlier, Plato himself in many places calls Homer a divine poet, the most divine of poets, and a proper imitator in the best sense. But imitative and phantastic poetry has a very obscure place in Homer's work, since he uses it merely in order to gain the credibility of the vulgar multitude, and only when it is totally unavoidable. If a man entered a well regulated city and beheld intoxication employed there for a certain useful purpose, he might decide to imitate not the prudence or whole order in the city, but intoxication itself alone. In such a case the city is hardly to be blamed for his conduct, which is due rather to the peculiar imbecility of his judgment. And in like manner, I think, the tragic poets, who emulate the phantastic species of Homer's poetry, should refer the principle of their error not to Homer, but to their own weakness. Homer may therefore be called the leader of tragedy, insofar as tragic poets emulate him in other respects and distribute the different parts of his poetry—imitating phantastically what he asserts assimilatively, and adapting to the ears of the vulgar what he composes scientifically. But Homer is not only the teacher of tragedy (for he is this merely by means of the phantastic element of his poetry), but he is also the teacher of all that is imitative in Plato, and of the whole theory of that philosopher.

It seems to me that the reason Plato wrote so severely against Homer, and against the whole species of imitative poetry, was the corruption of the times in which he lived. Philosophy was then despised, some calling it useless and others condemning it entirely. By contrast, poetry was then held in immoderate admiration. Its imitative power was the subject of emulation, and it was considered as adequate by itself for purposes of discipline. And poets, because they imitated everything, persuaded themselves that they knew all things, as is evident from what Socrates says in the *Republic*. Hence Plato, indignant at the prevalence of such an opinion, shows that poetry and imitation wander far from the truth imparted by philosophy, the savior of souls. In the same benevolent spirit in which he criticizes the sophists and popular orators for their inability to contribute anything to virtue, Plato also criticizes the poets—particularly the composers of tragedy, and those imitators who devise works to charm the audience without promoting virtue, enchanting the multitude without instructing them. And Plato considers that Homer deserves a similar criticism, insofar as he is the leader of this species of poetry and the model for the tragedians' emulation. It was necessary for Plato to do this in order to recall the men of his age from their total admiration of poetry, because their immoderate attachment to it led to a neglect of true discipline. And so with a view to the instruction of the multitude, to correct an absurd phantasy, and to exhort men to a philosophic life, Plato reproves the tragedians (who were then thought of as public teachers) for directing their attention to nothing rational. At the same time, Plato gives up his reverence for Homer and, ranking him in the same class with tragic poets, blames him as an imitator.

It should not seem strange for Plato to call the same poet both divine and third from the truth. For insofar as Homer is possessed by the Muses, he is divine; but insofar as he is an imitator, he is third from the truth.

FABIUS PLANCIADES
FULGENTIUS

(ca. 500–600)

INTRODUCTION

The *Exposition of Vergil* was written probably in the sixth century A.D. by Fabius Planciades Fulgentius. Next to nothing is known of its author. He was obviously a Christian, probably a cleric, and he was deeply interested in pagan literature, especially its esoteric meanings. This interest is illustrated by two other works, the *Three Books of Mythology*, containing allegorical interpretation of the most important pagan myths, and a brief allegorical exegesis of the *Thebiad* of Statius.

Today it is easy to regard the *Exposition* as an absurd jumble of ideas totally foreign to the *Aeneid* as we now read it. However, as Domenico Comparetti has shown in his *Vergil in the Middle Ages,* Fulgentius was an influence on the interpretation of Vergil throughout the Middle Ages and on into the Renaissance. Among the authors who drew on his work are Bernard Silvestris, Francis Petrarch, Giovanni Boccaccio, and Christoforo Landino. Fulgentian concepts of epic poetry—if not Fulgentius himself—are evident in Tasso's essay on the allegory of *Gerusalemme Liberata* and in both Spenser's *Letter to Raleigh* explaining *The Faerie Queene* and in the poem itself. In other words, the *Exposition* was a living document, influencing both the theory of epic poetry and the way epic poets went about their task from the sixth to the sixteenth century. George Saintsbury sums up the liabilities and assets of the work:

> If it were not written in a most detestable style, combining the
> presence of more than the affectation and barbarism of Martianus
> [Capella] with a complete absence of his quaintness and full-
> blooded charm, it would be rather agreeable to read. Even as it
> is, it is full of interest.

The *Exposition* comes last in the series of Vergil commentaries that includes the work of Servius, of Macrobius, and of Tiberius Claudius Donatus.

These late classical commentaries are by-products of the "reading of the poets" which formed a regular part of the ancient grammar curriculum. Like the grammatical commentaries of Aelius Donatus on Terence and of Arcon and Porphyrion on Horace, the commentary of Servius on Vergil is essentially a series of footnotes to the text. In a sample analysis of Servius on *Aeneid* II, Bolgar finds that about 60 percent of the notes are on points of language, especially the meanings of unfamiliar words. Of the remaining 40 percent, many are brief allegorical explanations of myths and mythological details. For example, the golden bough given to Aeneas is the Pythagorean "Y," symbol of virtuous choice; Tartarus is equated with "earth," the river Styx symbolizes the anger and lust suffusing the temporal world, and its nine circuits represent the nine spheres. Julian Ward Jones has found 183 instances of allegorical interpretation in Servius. This is a tiny percentage of the whole commentary, and the Servian allegories are unrelated to each other—they do not add up to an allegorical reading of Vergil. What they illustrate is that by the fourth century allegorical readings of Vergil were accepted by learned pagans. As allegory gained prestige, especially in Christian circles where allegorical reading of the Bible was the rule rather than the exception, more ambitious allegorical readings of the *Aeneid* became inevitable.

The Vergil commentary of Tiberius Claudius Donatus takes quite a different approach. In an introductory letter to his son, Donatus complains of the superficiality of the grammarians. He will approach the *Aeneid* as an orator rather than a writer of linguistic footnotes. In fact, his commentary is a continuous essay rather than a gloss. Like a good Ciceronian, Donatus emphasizes Vergil's wisdom. The *Aeneid* contains a pattern of human life as well as many useful and pithy maxims. It is also a masterful exercise in rhetoric. Rather surprisingly, Donatus avoids the jargon and the mindless listing associated with treatises on "figures of diction and of thought" and the *colores rhetoricae*. His emphasis is on larger, less technical points—the order of the narration, the use of digressions, *doctrina,* transitions, set speeches, and the like.

Donatus begins by "placing" the *Aeneid* in a specific department of rhetoric. Its form is *certe laudativum;* that is, it is a poem of praise following the formulas of demonstrative (or epideictic) rhetoric. Other materials are brought in, but "they are used to add to the praise of Aeneas." The result is a long essay—rather tedious to the modern reader, but generally informed and balanced—unified by the theme of praise.

If Donatus retains a balanced perspective, we begin to encounter in Macrobius' *Saturnalia* the kind of bardolatry to which Vergil was subjected in the later Middle Ages. The *Saturnalia* is a rambling dialogue treating the Roman calendar, history, mythology, philosophy, and various scientific and literary topics. Books III to VI treat Vergil. Vergil is praised for his deep knowledge of Roman religious rites, his mastery of every rhetorical device and emotion;

his imitation of the major Greek and Roman authors; and above all for his prowess as an orator. In fact, he is superior to Cicero, for Cicero excelled in only one style, while Vergil excels in all three. If Quintilian compared Homer to an ocean, Macrobius compares Vergil to Nature herself.

Between these commentaries and Fulgentius' *Exposition* there is a gap of about two hundred years. The *Exposition* employs a labored, involuted Latin which looks barbarous today but was probably the result of conscious effort to write according to the formulas of Asiatic (as against Attic) style. In terms of content, we can detect echoes of earlier traditions, but—rather surprisingly—no direct borrowings.

The full title of Fulgentius' essay is *The Exposition of the Content of Vergil According to Moral Philosophy*. This accurately defines its purpose. Fulgentius is not interested in footnotes or glossing hard lines, nor is he particularly concerned to demonstrate Vergil's rhetorical skill. His main objects are, first, to show that Vergil concealed a consistent system of ethics under the veil of fable; and second, to outline this system. The *Exposition* is thus different in fundamental conception from earlier Latin commentaries. Servius produced a treatise for the grammar curriculum, and Donatus and Macrobius wrote rhetorical criticism. The *Exposition*, on the other hand, turns from the trivium to a formal category of advanced learning, ethics. At the same time, Fulgentius has obviously learned at first or second hand from his predecessors. The fashion of allegory *via* etymology had already been applied to the *Aeneid* by Servius. More interesting, because more influential on the shape of the essay as a whole, Fulgentius agrees with Donatus that the *Aeneid* is a poem of praise following the prescriptions of demonstrative rhetoric. Commenting on the word order of *arma virumque cano* (and assuming that *arma* symbolizes valor), he remarks, "According to logic one should mention the person first and then the things relating to the person, so that substance precedes accidents—for example, 'man' would come first and then 'arms,' since the virtue is in the person. But I wrote according to the formulas of praise, and therefore I mentioned the merit of the man before the man himself." The plot of the *Aeneid* is also based on praise. An oration in praise of someone is an encomium, and the rhetorical prescriptions for the encomium are precise. An encomium should begin at or before birth and should summarize the life of the subject in a series of representative episodes. The rationale of the encomium is not flattery but teaching by example. The episodes should therefore be idealized in the interests of moral instruction. The standard virtues both in oratory and epic poetry are fortitude and wisdom, but temperance, magnanimity, justice, chastity, piety, and the like are also appropriate.

Clearly, if an encomium is written to embody a moral system, a critic can reduce it back to this system. This is the approach taken by Fulgentius. Having established that the *Aeneid* is written according to the formulas of praise, he attempts to penetrate the fable in order to abstract its basic content.

The extent to which Fulgentius is willing to go in this direction is evident in his treatment of the first episode in the *Aeneid,* the shipwreck of the Trojans on the shore of Carthage. Normally, this is considered a prime example of the epic convention of *in medias res* (in the midst of things). But Fulgentius is committed to the position that the *Aeneid* is an encomium, and an encomium should begin *ab ovo*—at the beginning. His solution is to assert that the shipwreck episode is an allegory of the birth of the soul into a tempestuous and painful life. Thus, what appears superficially to be *in medias res* is in reality the first episode in the life of the encomium hero.

As we move forward, Fulgentius remains relentlessly chronological and relentlessly exemplary. Aeneas becomes a kind of everyman engaged in the struggles and trials that beset us all at various stages in life. The tale of his wanderings is an allegory of childhood. His love for Dido symbolizes the awakening of passion in the adolescent, and Mercury, who commands him to leave Carthage, symbolizes the reason that must control passion. The death of Anchises represents the freeing of youth from parental authority. The descent into the underworld represents the formal study of philosophy. Finally, books VII–XII, which recount the wars of the Trojans in Italy, are an allegory of the active man following the path of labor (Lavinia) and resisting the temptations of drunkenness (Metiscus) and rage (Turnus). Throughout this extraordinary reading, Fulgentius emphasizes the virtues suggested by the opening words *arma* and *virum*— that is, valor and wisdom. The order in which the good life is attained is, first, natural talent, the inborn ability to learn the ways of virtue; second, education; and third, what Fulgentius calls adornment, which is the embodiment of virtue in action and the benefits that come from such action.

To describe the mechanism whereby Fulgentius extracts moral philosophy from the *Aeneid* is useful, for the *Exposition* is the first sustained allegorical reading of a Latin poetic classic that has survived. Equally, if not more, significant are several themes that run through the *Exposition*: poetry as esoteric wisdom, the poet as inspired prophet, and poetic truth as revelation.

The first of these themes is plain enough in the assumption that Vergil concealed his teaching under the veil of fable. The veil is so heavy, in fact, that in the essay Fulgentius has to summon the ghost of Vergil to lift it. Before Vergil appears, Fulgentius explains that the *Eclogues* and *Georgics* contain "the secrets of almost every art." He will not explain them, however, because they are very dangerous—evidently, they might corrupt Christian readers. The "secrets" which interest Fulgentius are ethical, for in ethics pagan wisdom based on natural law supplements (and at times anticipates) Christian revelation. The motif of hidden wisdom is further objectified in the imagery of darkness and light which runs through the *Exposition*. As Vergil is about to appear, Fulgentius exclaims, "Send me now the Mantuan Bard, so that I can lead his fugitive meanings into the light." Later Vergil remarks that although he did not know the truths of revelation, "still, truth sprinkled its sparks in my darkened mind." Discussing the burial of Anchises, Vergil states that he wants the meaning of the episode "to shine out with perfect clarity." The magical bough is "golden" says Vergil, "because I wanted to symbolize the splendor of eloquence." The scenes which Aeneas witnesses in Hades show that "unless learning has been mastered and darkness dispelled by profound knowledge, one sees the empty shapes of dreams."

The second motif, the notion of the inspired bard, is evident throughout the *Exposition.* Fulgentius is taking the same position adopted by Macrobius in the *Saturnalia*, but his viewpoint is more mystical, less rationalistic. Vergil is more than a genius. He emerges as a *vates*, a prophet, who sees to the heart of every mystery. His wisdom is so profound, in fact, that a mere mortal cannot hope to understand it. Supernatural assistance is required, and this is provided by none other than the ghost of Vergil himself. "Behold," says Fulgentius, "he comes toward me well-filled with a draught of the spring of Mount Helicon. He is a proper image of a Bard with his tablets raised in order to treat his topic, and with a fixed frown murmurs some mysterious truth that wells up within him." This is more than a clever invention. It parallels the appearance of the elder Africanus to expound the secrets of the afterlife in *The Dream of Scipio,* and it foreshadows the appearance of Vergil as a guide to the underworld in *The Divine Comedy.* It is another way of affirming what the concept of the poet as *vates* directly asserts—that certain works contain supra-rational truths; that they are texts having the authority of direct revelation.

The third theme, poetic truths as revelation, complements the second. Although Fulgentius emphasizes that he is interested only in ethical lore, he occasionally rises to more challenging topics. He cites Vergil's Messianic *Eclogue,* which was the standard example throughout the Middle Ages of Vergil's mysterious prophetic ability. In five instances, he remarks that Vergil's insights parallel those in Scripture. When Vergil states that the *Aeneid* begins by celebrating virtue and wisdom, Fulgentius exclaims, "If I understand you, most excellent Bard, Holy Writ sang Christ, the Redeemer of our world, as virtue and wisdom, because Divinity assumed the shape of a perfect Man." When Vergil comments on the symbolism of the first line of the *Iliad*, Fulgentius adds, "You did not speak poorly in this. Divine Wisdom, far surpassing your understanding, began in like manner, saying 'Blessed is the man who walks not in the counsel of the ungodly'." It is here that Vergil admits that "truth sprinkled its sparks in my darkened mind." Again, when Vergil comments on the excellence of contrition, Fulgentius adds, "I approve your sentiment. Our divine and lifegiving teaching tells us that God does not despise a humble and contrite heart."

In these and similar passages there is an echo, however dim, of the view of pagan literature taken by Philo Judaeus, Clement of Alexandria, and Origen. For these Alexandrians, the divine *logos* manifested itself in all cultures although it revealed itself most fully in Scripture. Consequently, one could expect to find anticipations of scriptural truths throughout pagan literature, although only those who have been properly prepared by study and meditation should be encouraged to undertake the search.

The translation here used is my own. For bibliography, see especially pp. 482–85.

THE EXPOSITION OF THE CONTENT OF VERGIL ACCORDING TO MORAL PHILOSOPHY

[TO CALCIDIUS THE GRAMMARIAN]

O most holy of Deacons, because of my age I thought complete silence proper. Not only did my mind cease to recall what it had learned, but it was becoming forgetful that it lived at all. But because I am subject to the New Law of charity, and the rule of love makes refusal impossible, I have touched on the hidden natural lore of Vergil, avoiding those things which are more dangerous than praiseworthy. Woe to me, I say, should I know and possess anything improper.

Therefore I have omitted the *Eclogues* and *Georgics* in which are interwoven concepts so profound that in those books Vergil has included the inner secrets of almost every art. In the first, second, and third eclogue he has given in philosophic terms the characteristics of the three kinds of life [contemplative, active, voluptuary]. In the fourth he treated the art of prophecy. In the fifth, priestly matters. In the sixth, with his exquisite meters, the art of music, and in part of this eclogue he explained physiology according to the Stoic view. In the seventh he touched on botany. In the eighth he described the art of music and also magic, and at the end, omens, which he continued to discuss in the ninth. In the eighth he says:

Lo, while I hesitate to carry it away,
The ash itself has spontaneously
Enveloped the altar with flickering flames,
May the omen be good!
Something has been determined; and the dog Hylax barks at the gate.
[II. 105–7]

In the ninth he says: "I remember this was forecast by the oaks struck by heaven" [not *Eclogue* IX but I.17]; and again, "Wolves beheld Moeris first" [1. 54].

The first *Georgic* is astrological throughout and toward the end deals with omens. The second deals with physiognomy and medicine. The third deals entirely with augury. And he also touches on this subject in the sixth book of the *Aeneid,* where he says: "Plucking the topmost hairs between the horns,/[The priestess] lays them on the fire as first offerings" [245–46]. The fourth is wholly concerned with music, and has interpretative comments on the art of music at the end.

I have, then, omitted teachings exceeding the limits of the times so that he who seeks reputation will not end by fracturing his skull. Be content, my Lord, with the modest posy that I have picked for you from the flowery gardens of the Hesperides. For, if you seek golden apples, you must play Eurystheus[1] to some other stronger man, who, like Hercules, is willing to risk his life. You will be able peacefully to take many ideas from this posy which will gratify your wishes. Now, laying aside the rancid bitterness of the Hellebore of Chrysippus, I will say something pleasing to the Muses:

> O Maids of Helicon—and I do not call
> On Calliope alone—assist me.
> Give your blessing to my mind.
> I undertake a more difficult task.
> A single Muse will not suffice.
> Run, Pierian Maidens, you are my greatest care.
> Strike the Arcadian lyre with an ivory plectrum.

I think this little invocation will satisfy the Vergilian Muses.

Send me now the Mantuan Bard in person, so that I can lead his fugitive meanings into the light. And behold—he comes toward me well filled with a draught of the spring of Mt. Helicon. He is a proper image of a Bard with his tablets raised in order to treat his topic, and with a fixed frown murmurs some mysterious truth that wells up from within him.

I said: "If you please, put aside your frowning expressions, o most famous of Italian poets. Sweeten the bitter sauce of your difficult ideas with the condiment of sweet honey. For I do not search your words for what Pythagoras says about harmonic numbers, or Heraclitus fire, or Plato ideas, or Hermes the stars, or Chrysippus numbers,[2] or Aristotle entelechies.[3] Nor am I interested in what Dardanus says about powers, or Battiades about daemons, or Campester about spirits of the underworld and ghosts. I seek only the easy things taught by grammarians to their childish pupils for monthly fees."

Then, wrinkling his brow, Vergil said: "I thought, little man, that you were too foolish for me to load my heavier burdens on your heart. You are more dense than a dirt clod and will sleep through anything weighty."

I said: "Save that sort of knowledge, I pray, for your Romans for whom it is honorable and harmless. It will be enough for me to touch the lowest hem of your robe."

He said: "As far as your coarse intelligence and the timidity of your age permit you to learn, I will dip out just a few drops from the fountain of my swelling genius and explain these matters to you. This small measure will prevent you from becoming so drunk that you get sick. Now make the seats of your ears vacant so that my words can enter."

And then, settling into the posture of an orator, with two fingers erect in the form of an "I" and the third pressing the thumb, he began: "In all my works I treated subjects relating to natural philosophy. And in the twelve books of the *Aeneid* I revealed fully the condition of man's life. And I began the exordium with 'Arms and the man I sing'—referring to virtue[4] by 'arms' and wisdom by 'man.' For perfection consists of virtue of body and wisdom of mind."

I said: "If I am not mistaken about your meaning, most excellent bard, Holy Scripture sang Christ the Redeemer of our world as virtue and wisdom because God assumed the condition of a perfect man."[5]

"He said: "You know what true Majesty has taught you. Meanwhile, I can only relate what I think. Now it is proper according to logic to speak of the person first and then the things relating to the person so that substance comes first and then the accidents—as it were, to mention 'man' first and then 'arms,' since virtue is inherent in the man. But because I wrote according to the forms of praise,[6] I mentioned the merit of the man before the man himself. Thus we come to the person with his merit already recognized. This, in fact, is how things are commonly done in letter-writing, where we first write 'Most excellent' and then the name of the man addressed."

"But to understand more readily that I have written in the form of praise, notice the wording of the lines that follow. I say 'an outcast through fate' and 'by the power of the gods' to show that Fortune was to blame for the flight of Aeneas, not lack of virtue. He exposed himself to danger because of the gods, not through lack of wisdom. This accords with the ancient maxim of Plato, 'The spirit of man is his god.'[7] If it is worthy, God will be kindly. And Carneades in the *Telesias* says, 'All Fortune resides in the intelligence of the wise man.' "[8]

"Moreover, I wanted to mention 'virtue' first then 'wisdom' because, although wisdom rules virtue, wisdom flourishes in a virtuous soul. A lack of virtue is a weakness in wisdom because when wisdom intends to do something, if the virtue to accomplish it is inadequate, wisdom is cut off in its effects and languishes."

"Now about beginning with 'arms'—I knew that the word 'man,' if placed first, would indicate the sex of the individual, not his honor. There are many men, but not all of them are praiseworthy. Therefore, I placed first the word suggesting the 'virtue' for which the man is praiseworthy. In this I followed Homer, who says, 'The wrath, O goddess, sing of Achilles' [*Iliad* I.1]—mentioning the wrath of the man before the man himself. Moreover, Homer symbolizes virtue in the figure of Minerva, and he writes: 'She caught the hair of Achilles' [*Iliad* I.197]."

I said: "You did not speak badly in this. Divine Wisdom, far surpassing your understanding, began in like manner, saying, 'Blessed is the man who walks not in the counsel of the ungodly' [Psalms 1:1]. Note that the most perfect teacher of the righteous life, the Prophet David, placed the reward for virtuous living—'blessedness'—before the sweat of the struggle."

He said: "I rejoice, little fellow, at these added sentiments, because, although I did not know the full truth concerning the nature of the righteous life, still, truth sprinkled its sparks in my darkened mind with a kind of blind favor."

"Now, as I began to say, 'virtue' is related to substance, and 'wisdom' is what controls substance. As Sallust said, 'All our strength is in our soul and body' [*On Cataline's Conspiracy*, I.2]."

"To satisfy your mind more fully, there are three phases in human life: first possession, second control of what you possess, and third graceful adorning of what you control. Note that these three phases are included in my first line; that is, 'arms,' 'man,' and 'first.' 'Arms'—that is, virtue—refers to a natural characteristic. 'Man'—that is, wisdom—to a mental characteristic. And 'first'— that is, foremost—to judgment. Thus the order is: to possess, to control, and to adorn."

"Thus through an historical allegory I have shown the whole condition of human life, which involves first nature, second learning, and third success. Be careful to understand these phases. As I said before, first comes inner capacity which is a gift of nature and permits man to improve—for you cannot educate a creature that is not born with the ability to be educated. Second comes learning which enhances nature as it improves. This is like gold, for gold is malleable and beautiful by nature, but it is brought to perfection by the hammer of the workman. Like gold, the mind is born capable of expansion. It improves because it was born, and success comes along to adorn what improves."

"These phases of life should be followed by the young children to whom my poem is taught. Every worthy person is born capable of education. The person is educated so that his natural capacity will not be wasted. He is adorned with success so that the gift of learning will not be useless. Plato, explaining the triple order of human life, said: 'Each good is either inborn, or learned, or imposed.'[9] It is born through nature, learned through study, and imposed through experience."

"Now, having completed the preliminaries, I proceed to the beginning of the story. But to make sure that I am not explaining my story to untutored ears, tell me the content of the first book. Then, if all is well, I will explain the book to you."

I said: "If the memory of past studies does not fail me, first Juno asks Aeolus to cause shipwreck of the Trojans. Aeneas escapes with seven ships. He reaches the shore of Libya. He sees his mother but does not recognize her. He and Achates are enveloped in a cloud. Then his soul is stirred by pictures. After dinner he is soothed by the music of a lyre. You now have a brief summary of the contents of the first book. Now I wish to know what you meant by them."

He said: "The shipwreck symbolizes the perils of birth in which the mother suffers birth-pangs, and the infant endures the danger of being born. All human beings necessarily share in this. And to make this meaning very plain, the shipwreck is caused by Juno, the goddess of childbirth. And she sends Aeolus: Aeolus in Greek is *eonolus* [aion + oloos]—that is, 'the destructiveness of time.'[10] As Homer says, 'The destructive wrath that brought woes innumerable on the Achaeans' [*Iliad* I.2]. And note what is promised to Aeolus: Deiopea, Juno's nymph, as his bride. *Demos* in Greek means 'public'; *iopa* is 'eyes' or 'vision.' To those being born the temporal world is dangerous. But an unclouded vision of perfection is promised by the goddess of birth to Aeolus. Next Aeneas escapes with seven ships. This is symbolic, for seven is the harmonic number of birth. I will briefly explain the reason for this if you like."

I said: "I discuss this sufficiently in the book that I recently wrote about medicine. There I commented on the whole arithmetic significance of seven and nine, and I would be wordy if I put in one book what I included in another. Anyone who wants to learn about such matters can read my book on physiology. Now I await what remains."

He said: "As I began to say, as soon as Aeneas reaches land, he sees his mother Venus but does not recognize her. This symbolizes infancy because those recently born can see their mothers from the moment of birth but do not immediately recognize and respond to them. Next Aeneas is enveloped in a cloud and recognizes his companions but cannot speak to them. Note how plainly I have depicted the characteristics of the very young children. They have the ability to recognize people but not to speak. And I placed Achates with Aeneas at the beginning. Achates is his arms bearer after the shipwreck, and he is also enveloped in the cloud. Achates is Greek *aconetos* [achos + ethos]; that is, 'the habit of sorrow.' Humanity is doomed to hardship from infancy, as Euripides says in the tragedy of *Iphigenia*:

> Nothing can be described that is so terrible—
> Be it physical pain or heaven-sent affliction—
> That man's nature could not bear it.[11]

That is: there is nothing so terrible and no experience so dire that human nature has not endured it. There is no armor against sorrow except tears. Infants console and call attention to themselves by crying. Although we are scarcely able to laugh by the fifth month, tears flow freely on the very threshold of life."

"That Aeneas vainly feasts his soul on a picture clearly symbolizes childish thought. An infant can see but he cannot understand what he sees—just as pictures can be looked at but lack rational meaning."

"Then Aeneas is taken to dinner and soothed by the sound of the lyre. Little children characteristically seek nothing more than to be pleased by sweet music and filled with food. And note the name of the lyre-player. Iopas in Greek is *siopas* [siope]—that is, the silence of a child. Infants are always soothed by the sweet words and songs of nurses; and to symbolize this I described Iopas with long hair like that of a woman [cf. *Aeneid* I.740]. And also, Aeneas sees Cupid [I.715–17]. Youth is always wanting or desiring something. And therefore I wrote the verse that comes in the second book after the lyre playing is over: 'Who could refrain from tears' [II.8]."

In the second and third books Aeneas is diverted by tales of the sort that usually amuse talkative young children. At the end of the third book [613ff.] Aeneas sees the Cyclops after Achaemenides describes them. *Achos* [achos] means sorrow in Greek; *ciclos* [kuklos] means 'circle.' Also, *pes* [pais] means 'boy.' The sense is that the child, when released from fear of his guardians, does not yet have rational knowledge of grief and gives himself over to the wandering of wild youth. The Cyclops is described as having a single eye in his forehead because the wandering of wild youth is not directed by a full or a rational vision, and the whole of youth rests on Cyclopean vanity. The single eye in the head of the Cyclops symbolizes that he cannot see and understand anything but vanity. The wise Ulysses put out the eye: that is, vainglory is blinded by the flame of reason. And I called him Polyphemus—that is, *apolunta femen* [apoleipo + pheme], which means 'loss of reputation' in Latin. For a blind later life follows youth's pride and indifference to reputation."

"To make the sequence perfectly obvious, Aeneas next buries his father. As the child grows up he rejects the force of paternal authority. He buries his father at the port of Drepanum [III.707]. *Drepanos* is *drimpedos,* and *drimos* [drimos] means 'keen' and *pes* [pais] 'boy.' This symbolizes the fact that immaturity rejects parental discipline."

"And now that the soul of Aeneas is free of his father's authority, in the fourth book he goes hunting and is aroused by the fire of love. Driven on by a storm and mist—symbolizing a disturbed mind—he commits adultery. And when he has dallied for a long time, he gives up his immoral love at the urging of Mercury. Mercury is the god of reason. This symbolizes that at the prompting of reason the more mature person breaks the bonds of lust. And indeed, the object of passion [i.e. Dido] dies when it has been rejected. Totally consumed, it wastes away to ashes. When lust is expelled from the youthful heart by reason, it flickers out and is buried in the ashes of oblivion."

"In the fifth book Aeneas is aroused by the memory of his father and engages in the sports of young men. This symbolizes that when one reaches the age of prudence, he follows examples provided by his father's memory and exercises his body in manly activities."

"Note that they engage in boxing. That is, Entellus and Dares [V.362ff] practice a manly sport. *Entellin* [entello] in Greek means 'command' and *derin* [dero] 'cudgel'—which masters often do when teaching."

"Then the ships are burned [V.641]. They are the dangerous instruments that lure a youth onto the stormy seas of vanity where he is constantly buffeted by tempests, as it were, of dangerous impulses. By the excellent fire of reason all these are destroyed, and, as knowledge is added to intelligence, they all vanish like dreams in the ashes of oblivion. And Beroë—that is, 'the order of truth'— makes the fire."

"In the sixth book Aeneas comes to the temple of Apollo and descends into the underworld. Apollo is the god of learning and he is a friend of the Muses. Now the shipwreck and dangers of youth are over, and Palinurus has been lost. Palinurus is *planonorus* [plane + horao]—that is, 'wandering vision.' Therefore in Book IV [363] I wrote concerning amorous glances, 'her silent glances *wander* over the whole man'; and also in the *Eclogues*, 'the *wandering* footsteps of a bull' [VI.58]."

"Having put these things behind him, Aeneas now comes to the temple of Apollo—that is, learning from studies. And there he ponders the course of his future life and seeks out the path to the underworld. This symbolizes that whenever anyone considers the future he must penetrate the hidden and secret mysteries of knowledge. And Aeneas must bury Misenus first [VI.227]. *Misio* [misos] in Greek means 'spite' and *enos* [ainos] 'praise.' Unless you reject ostentatious and vain praise you will never reach the secrets of wisdom. The appetite for vain praise never seeks truth but thinks that false things flatteringly attributed to the self are truly possessed. Also there is the contest between Misenus and Triton with his horn and shell [VI.171–76]. Note how precise the symbolism. The bubble of vain praise is puffed up by a windy voice and Triton destroys it. Triton is *tetrimemenon* [?tetinmenos] in Greek, which we Latins call 'contrition.' Contrition always deflates vain praise. And for this reason Tritonia is called the goddess of wisdom: contrition always makes a man wise."

I said: "Having better knowledge on this subject, I approve your sentiment. Our divine and life-giving teaching tells us that God does not despise a humble and contrite heart [Psalms 50:19]. And this is true and manifest wisdom."

He said: "To make my story fully and explicitly clear, I wrote that

Carineus [Corynaeus; VI.227] cremated the body of Misenus in a fire. *Carin* [charis] in Greek means 'favor'; and we call *eon* [aion] 'time.' This symbolizes that through the favor of time the ashes of vainglory are inevitably buried.''

"But no one learns about hidden knowledge until he has plucked the golden bough; that is, the study of philosophy and letters. I intended the golden bough to symbolize knowledge, recalling that my mother dreamed she gave birth to a branch,[12] and because Apollo is painted holding a branch. Moreover, the bough is said to be *'apo tes rapsodias,'* that is, 'from writings' by Dionysius [?Thrax] in his book on Greek expressions. And I called the bough 'golden' because I wanted to symbolize the splendor of eloquence, recalling the saying of Plato that when Diogenes the Cynic attempted to steal Plato's estate, he found nothing there except a golden tongue. Tiberianus recounts this in his book *On the God of Socrates.*[13]

"I referred to ten golden apples in the *Eclogues*: that is, the polished eloquence of the ten eclogues. Hercules took golden apples from the Hesperides. And the Hesperian maidens are said to be Aegle, Hespera, Medusa, and Arethusa, which in Latin are study, understanding, memory, and eloquence. First comes study, second understanding, third memorization of what you understand, and then adorning in eloquent language what you retain. In a similar way virtue seeks to grasp the golden prize of learning."

I said: "Most learned man, you are surely speaking the truth. Just now I recalled a passage in Scripture which speaks of a golden tongue and virtuous skills stolen from iniquity,[14] just as eloquence may be recovered from the gentiles. But pray go on to what remains."

He said: "As I previously remarked, having taken up the golden bough, that is, learning, Aeneas enters the lower regions and investigates the secrets of knowledge. In the outer chamber of Hades he sees sorrow, disease, wars, discord, old age, and poverty. This symbolizes that when all things in the mind and heart of man are considered, when learning has been mastered and the darkness dispelled by higher knowledge, one sees that old age and its cousin death are empty dreams, and war the child of greed, and disease the offspring of disorder and intemperance, and quarrels the consequence of drunkenness, and hunger the handmaid of laziness and sloth."

"So Aeneas descends into Hades and there he witnesses the punishments meted out to evil men and the rewards of good ones and sees the sad confusion of lovers."

"Charon the ferryman carries him and he crosses Acheron. This river symbolizes the boiling emotions of youthful activity. It is called 'muddy' because youths do not have mature and clear ideas. *Acheron* [akairos] is Greek for 'without time.' Charon is *ceron* [kairos] which means 'time.' Therefore he is said to be the son of Polidegmon. *Polidegmon* [polus + deigma] is Greek for 'much knowledge.' This symbolizes that when one has reached the age of much knowledge he moves past time—muddied waters and the dregs of his own bad habits."

"He drugs three-headed Cerberus with a morsel dipped in honey [VI.420]. I [that is, here, Fulgentius] have already explained in my *Mythologies* that the Tricerberus story is an allegory of quarreling and legal wrangles. Petronius says of Euscios, 'Cerberus was a trial lawyer.'[15] For men learn quarreling slander and use eloquence in other people's affairs simply for money, when true learning should be used for improvement—as is seen even today among lawyers. The bitterness of altercation, treated with the honey of wisdom, regains its sweet taste."

"Now that Aeneas has been admitted to the secrets of wisdom, he looks on the shades of heroic men. That is, he considers the achievements and monuments of virtue. And he sees the punishment of Deiphobus. Deiphobus is Greek for either *Dimofobus* [deima + phobos] or *demofobus* [demios + phobos]— that is 'fear of terror' or 'fear of the people.' Whatever kind of fear is intended, it is properly depicted with hands cut off and blinded and without ears [VI.495–97]. The reason is that fear never perceives what it sees or knows what it hears or, lacking hands to feel, recognizes what it does. And Deiphobus was killed by Menelaus when sleeping. Menelaus is *menelau* [mene + laos] that is 'valor of the people,' for this valor always overcomes slothful fear."

"Then Aeneas sees Dido, now an empty shadow of love and lust. But to the wise man the memory of lust, even though it has been deadened by indifference, brings penitent tears."

"We have now reached the place where I say:

In front stands the huge gate and pillars
Of solid adamant, so that no human power
Not even the sons of heaven, can uproot them in war.
There stands the iron tower soaring high.
[VI.552–55]

Note how obvious I have made this image of pride and vanity. I put adamantine columns on the tower because this kind of rock is indestructible. The Greek [*adoneo*] means, in fact, 'untouched'—for neither fear of the gods nor human virtue nor fear of a bad reputation can control pride. 'An iron tower soaring high' signifies high and unbending arrogance. And who sustains this arrogance but Tisiphone, meaning 'raging voice' [?*tisis* + *phone*]. When I said 'The Hydra still more cruel with fifty black and gaping throats' [VI.576], I symbolized nothing less than that the swelling vanity in the heart of proud men is worse than the hot air of boasting coming from their mouths. When I said 'Tartarus itself yawns open twice as far' [VI.577–78], this symbolizes the final punishment of pride. The punishment for pride is to be thrown down. The more arrogant a proud man is, the more anguish he will endure when his arrogance collapses. Whoever is raised up by pride will therefore be doubly struck down. On this subject, recall the epigram of Porphyrius:

> Fortune aids you Quintus (by my soul)
> And takes your sneering face all over town.
> By heaven it's true: You are some stinking hole:
> The bigger you get, the more men stare you down.[16]

"Next Aeneas sees the giants [VI.580] and Ixion [VI.601] and Salmoneus [VI.585] all damned to punishment for pride, and Tantalus also [VI.602]. Tantalus is Greek *teantelon* [?te + anta + ethelo]; that is, 'greedy to see,' for avarice is reluctant to use a thing and is fed merely by looking at it."

"But here the judge Rhadamanthus of Cnossos appears [VI.566–77]. Rhadamanthus is Greek *tarematadamonta* [ta rema + ta damonta]—that is, 'ruling the word'—and *gnoso* [gnosis] means 'understand.' That is, he who knows how to control the force of words punishes and denounces pride. Next, Aeneas is frightened by loud noise. That is, the honest man flees the call of pride and fears the punishment meted out to evil men. Then, fixing the golden bough on the sacred doorposts, he enters Elysium. This symbolizes that when the labor of learning is over, one celebrates a perfected memory. Learning is fixed in the memory forever, like the golden bough on the sacred doorposts.

"Aeneas enters the Elysian Fields. *Elisis* [eleusis] is Greek for 'freeing' —that is, after the fear of teachers, life becomes like a holiday. And Proserpine is queen of the Underworld. That is, memory is the queen of knowledge. Extending [*proserpens*] itself, it reigns forever in the liberated mind. The golden bough of learning is dedicated to memory. Concerning memory, Cicero used to say that it was the store-house of knowledge [*de Oratore* I.v.18]."

"In the Elysian Fields Aeneas first sees Musaeus [VI.66]—as it were, 'the gift of the Muses'—exalted above all the rest. Musaeus introduces him to his father Anchises and shows him the river Lethe. He is shown his father to emphasize the need to retain a grave character. He is shown Lethe to bring out the need to forget the levity of youth. And note the name Anchises. Anchises is Greek *ano scenon*—that is, 'living in one's homeland.' There is one God, Father and King of all, dwelling alone on high, who is discovered whenever knowledge points the way. Note what Anchises teaches his son:

> In the beginning an indwelling spirit
> Infused the heavens and the earth
> And the watery plains and the shining orb
> Of the moon and the stars of Titan
> [VI.724–25]

You can see that the creator must be God and that Anchises teaches about the hidden mysteries of nature, and describes the souls returning again and again from life, and reveals the future."

I said: "O truest of Italian bards, how could you have obscured your brilliant genius in the darkness of such a stupid line of defense? When you were writing allegorically in the *Eclogues,* you once said: 'Now a virgin returns and the reign of Saturn returns. / Now a new race is promised by high heaven.' [IV.6] But here, snoring out some sort of Academic tripe while your wit is drowsing, you say: 'Heavenly souls go up to heaven / And then return again to sluggish bodies.' [VI.720] Why did you put blackberries among so many sweet apples and obscure the torch of your brilliant genius?"

Smiling he said: "If I had not mixed something Epicurean in with so many Stoic truths, I would not have been a pagan. No people except you Christians on whom the sun of truth has shone can know all of the truth. But I did not come here to explain your Scripture and argue about what I should have known, but to explain those things that I did know. Now listen to what remains."

"In the seventh book Caieta the nurse is buried [VII.2]—that is, the heavy burden of fear of one's teachers. Caieta means 'forcer of youth.' Among the ancients *caiatio* meant 'the yielding of children.' Thus Plautus in his comedy *Cistolaria* wrote, 'Are you afraid your doxy will not *yield* herself to your arms?' And I made it very plain that Caieta symbolizes discipline when I said, 'Dying you gave eternal fame, O Caieta' [VII.2]. Although the discipline of learning is eventually removed, it passes on the eternal seed of memory."

"Therefore, having buried school matters, Aeneas arrives at his much-desired Ausonia—that is, 'increase of good' toward which the desire of wise men eagerly hastens. *Ausonia* is from *apo tu ausenin* [apo toi auxanein]—that is, 'of increase.' Another explanation is that even at this age the body continues to grow."

"Next he seeks Lavinia as his wife—that is, 'the path of hard work.' About this time of life, everyone chooses labors which increase his worldly advantages. And Lavinia is called the daughter of Latinus, a descendent of Caunus [i.e., Faunus; VII.47]. *Latinus* is from *latitando* [lying in wait] because hard work lies in wait in many different places. *Latona* is from *luna* [moon] because at one time she conceals her upper parts, at another her lower parts and then, at another, is entirely concealed. *Caunus* is *camnonus* [kamno + nous]—that is, mental labor. And Caunus is married to the nymph Marica—that is, *merica* [merimna] or 'counsel.' As Homer says, 'His heart within his shaggy breast was divided in *counsel*' [*Iliad* I.189]."

"In Book VIII Aeneas seeks Evander as an ally. *Evandros* [eo + andros] in Greek is 'good man.' This symbolizes that the perfected individual seeks the companionship of good men. From Evander he hears of the excellence of goodness—that is, the glory of Hercules [VIII.193ff.] and how he slew Cacus, a name [i.e., *kakos*] that means 'evil' among the Latins. Then he puts on the armor of Vulcan [VIII.612ff.]; that is, the protection of the alert intelligence against all the temptations of evil. *Vulcan* is *bulencauton* [boule + kautes], or, as we say, 'ardent wisdom.' All the virtues of the Romans are displayed on this armor because all happiness is either provided by or foreseen through the careful protection of wisdom. To act well is the harbinger of future good, and he who acts well insures good for himself. Thus wisdom both produces good things and can look forward to them."

"In Book IX, assisted by the arms of Vulcan, Aeneas fights Turnus. *Turnus* is *turosnus* [thouros + nous] in Greek—that is, 'raging mind.' The arms of wisdom and intelligence always oppose rage. As Homer says, '[Athena] spoke and led the raging Ares from battle' [*Iliad* V.35]."

"Next Aeneas kills Mezentius, the belittler of the gods [X.907–8]. God ordains all things and commands them to be good. But when the spirit which inhabits the body despises the good it fails in its proper duty and neglects goodness to its own harm. The wise man sallies out to slay wrongdoers and slays Mezentius and his son Lausus [X.815–16]."

"This symbolizes the wise man's conquest of his own soul. And who is said to be the friend of Turnus? Messapus—that is, *misonepos* [misos + epos], which is 'threatening speech' in Latin. As Euripides says in his tragedy of *Iphigenia*, 'Nothing can be described that is so terrible . . .' [*Orestes* 1]."

"After overcoming Messapus, victorious Aeneas gravely balances out the armor of Messapus on the scales and displays his effigy."

"Then Juturna is forced to desist from war [XII.875]. She was driving the chariot of her brother. Juturna symbolizes calamity because calamity always [*diuturne*] threatens. Calamity is the sister of rage. And the chariot of Turnus which she uses to drive him away and save him from death is also calamity because it can cause rage to go on without end."

"First Turnus had Metiscus as his driver. *Metiscos* [methusko] is Greek for 'intoxicated.' Intoxication first produces rage. Then calamity arrives to prolong rage. But while Juturna is said to be eternal, Turnus is mortal. Rage can cease in a short time, but calamity continues forever. And Juturna drives the chariot everywhere—that is, she continues for a long time. The wheels symbolize time. Fortune is said to have a wheel, symbolizing the mutability of time."

The end.

Farewell, my Lord. Read cautiously these thorny outgrowths of my heart.

Here ends the exposition of the content of Vergil according to moral philosophy by the distinguished Fabius Planciadis Fulgentius.

AVERROES

(1126–1198)

INTRODUCTION

Aristotle's *Poetics* was written between 347 and 322 B.C. In view of the prestige which the treatise now enjoys, it often comes as a surprise to the contemporary student of criticism to learn that after Aristotle's death the *Poetics* disappeared almost without trace from the ancient literary scene. Obviously the text must have been copied during the classical and Byzantine periods; otherwise we would have no manuscripts at all. The influence on all later manuscripts of a single source, the eleventh-century manuscript designated Paris 1741, indicates, however, that the manuscript tradition of the Greek *Poetics* is relatively uncomplicated. Evidently there was little demand for the work in antiquity. Efforts to reconstruct the history of the text before the eleventh century have produced tenuous, often contradictory results. The same may be said for efforts to trace the influence of the *Poetics* on post-Aristotelian criticism, such as those made by McMahon, Rostagni, and (most recently) C. O. Brink. If Aristotle's *Poetics* had any influence, it was via two or three intermediaries, which, by warping its thought to fit the prevailing assumptions of rhetorical criticism, obliterated just those qualities that are today considered characteristically Aristotelian. The fragmentary essay *On the Poets* appears to have been far more widely known than the *Poetics,* and Theophrastus, Aristotle's pupil and popularizer, had far more influence on later critical thought than his master.

The version of the *Poetics* that influenced the Middle Ages was not Greek but Arabic. According to the best guesses of Margoliouth and Tkatsch, the source of the Arabic tradition is a Greek manuscript dating before the year 700 and independent of the archetype that is the source of Paris 1741 and its descendents. As translated into Arabic (through Syriac) in the tenth century, this version of the *Poetics* departed widely in vocabulary from the original, and thus initiated the process of assimilating Aristotle by misinterpretation that continued throughout the later Middle Ages.

The next phase in the history of the medieval *Poetics* is the result of the adoption by Arab philosophers of a scheme originally formulated by Alexander of Aphrodisias and other late Greek commentators on Aristotle. According to this scheme, Aristotle divided human knowledge (*scientia,* often translated as "science") into four main branches. First come the instrumental sciences of the *Organon.* These are sciences of technique or "faculties," and they have no "content" in the Aristotelian sense of that term. The other three branches, which *do* have content, are the theoretic (including metaphysics, mathematics, astronomy, and physics), the practical (including politics, economics, and ethics), and the productive (including most professions and crafts). It is the *Organon* that is important for present purposes. Today, scholars agree that the *Organon* is made up of six works; namely, *Categories, On Interpretation, Prior* and *Posterior Analytics, Topics,* and *Sophistic Refutations.* To these six books the late Greek commentators and their Arab disciples added the *Rhetoric* and the *Poetics.* The most influential Arab expression of this theory is the *Catalogue of the Sciences* written by al-Farabi in the tenth century. This work was twice translated into Latin during the twelfth century, first by Gerard of Cremona and second by John of Seville. The theory which it proposes may be called the "context theory" of the *Poetics,* since it arises from the context within which Aristotle was thought to have placed his treatise. To include the *Poetics* in the *Organon* is to assert that it is an essay on method, and that the method itself is a "faculty" without "content." Furthermore, since each of the logical faculties was supposed to be distinguished from the others by its use of a unique logical device, the inclusion of *Poetics* in the *Organon* shifted emphasis from "imitation," the key term in the Greek *Poetics,* to the "device" which differentiates poetry from its sister faculties.

This interpretation ignores imitation, plot, characterization, catharsis, and most of the other subjects stressed by Aristotle in favor of an element—the imaginative syllogism—for which the reader of the Greek text will search in vain. It also ignores the moral "purpose" usually attributed to poetry in the Middle Ages, because to bring in moral questions would be to assign a "content" to poetry—in Aristotelian terms, to treat it as a sub-division of "practical science" rather than of the *Organon.*

The most important Arab student of the *Poetics* was Averroes (Ibn Rushd). Averroes is considered the greatest of the Arab philosophers of the Middle Ages, and he is also the Arab philosopher who most deeply influenced the Latin West. During his long and active career he wrote commentaries on all of Aristotle's major works, and all but two of these were translated into Latin during the scholastic renaissance of the thirteenth century. Medieval interest in the *Poetics* must therefore be understood as a by-product of scholasticism, and in particular, that phase of scholasticism which was a self-conscious revolt against the earlier, Platonizing tradition of medieval thought.

Two key ideas, both of them foreign to Aristotle, run through Averroes'
commentary. The first is the notion derived from al-Farabi and Avicenna that
poetry is a branch of logic. The second also owes something to earlier Arab
commentaries, but its basic source would seem to be the vocabulary of the Arab
translation. This is the idea that poetry can be defined as the art of praise and
blame. Praise and blame are rhetorical techniques, explained at length in Books
I and III of Aristotle's *Rhetoric*. They are brought into the *Poetics* in Chapter 4,
where Aristotle asserts the first two forms of poetry were "lampooning verses"
and "praises of famous men." Averroes could understand this theory much
better than the complex theory of imitation developed in the first three chapters
of the *Poetics*. Better still, it seemed consistent with what he knew of the history
of Arab poetry, whose early forms tend heavily to invective and encomiastic
verse. From this apparent point of contact between the *Poetics* and Arab literary
tradition, Averroes moved outward to the genres and function of poetry. Not
only did poetry originate in praise and blame, its major forms fall into one or
the other category. Epic and tragedy are poems of praise; comedy (by which
Averroes means satire) is a form of blame; and ode is a mixed form that employs
both techniques. Good poets praise good men in order to lead their readers to
virtue, while base poets satirize and vituperate evil men and thus war against
vice. This approach, it should be noted, assigns poetry an ethical function and
is incompatible (or, at least, hard to reconcile) with the theory that poetry is a
branch of logic. Averroes either failed to perceive the conflict or was indifferent
to it, for the two theories exist side-by-side in his commentary, and no effort is
made to harmonize them.

The Arabic *Poetics* was translated in 1256 by Hermannus Alemannus, a
monk living in Toledo. Twenty-three manuscripts of the Hermannus translation
survive, and it was printed in 1481, thus becoming the first version of Aristotle's
literary theory published during the Renaissance. Its compatibility with medieval
critical ideas is attested by the fact that in 1278 William of Moerbeke, Bishop of
Corinth, made a remarkably accurate translation from the Greek, which was, however, ignored; William's translation exists in only two manuscripts, both dating
from the thirteenth century, and it was not printed until 1953. The obvious moral
of this tale is that the late Middle Ages was not prepared to assimilate the *Poetics*.
On the other hand, Averroes' commentary was easy to assimilate. The distortions
which disconcert the modern reader are the very features which made the work
intelligible and attractive to the medieval audience. In effect, it enlisted Aristotle
in support of the most characteristic (and most un-Aristotelian) features of medieval poetic theory.

In a preface referring to both the *Rhetoric* and the *Poetics*, Hermannus discusses the placing of these works in Aristotle's system of the sciences and quite
explicitly locates the *Poetics* in the *Organon*. To avoid possible confusion, Hermannus cites the two common rival theories of poetry—first, the theory that

considered rhetoric and poetry a part of "civil" philosophy, by which he means "practical" or "moral" philosophy; and second, the theory associating poetry with grammar. The first theory, attributed justifiably to Cicero, is the didactic theory, which considers poetry a device of ethical instruction. It is commonplace in medieval criticism, and both Averroes and Hermannus subscribed to it in practice. In his preface, however, Hermannus takes pains to call attention to the *difference* between it and the allegedly Aristotelian theory, which emphasizes technique rather content. The second theory, which Hermannus attributes to Horace, leads to emphasis on the prosodic element of poetry. Classical grammar included the study of syllables and quantity, and hence the study of the various poetic meters. According to the grammarians, the difference between poetry and nonpoetry is the use of meter; and the differences between the various poetic genres are the meters themselves. This inverts the normal relation between form and content. Poetry becomes "heroic," for example, by using dactylic hexameter, and only secondarily by narrating the deeds of noble heroes. In the same way, the essence of elegy is the elegaic distich, of satire and comedy, iambic meter, of the ode, lyric strophes, and so forth. Again, Hermannus explicitly rejects the *ars metrica* in favor of the logical theory attributed to Aristotle and justified by "al-Farabi, Avicenna, Averroes, and various others."

Hermannus' emphasis on the logical "placement" of poetry is apparent from the first section of the commentary where, with the help of hints taken from Chapter 20 of the *Poetics*, poetry is defined in terms of its use of the technical device of *comparison*. The Aristotelian concept of poetry as an imitation of action, human character, and/or nature is replaced by the concept of poetry as the skillful manipulation of similes, metaphors, and analogies.

The relation of poetry to logic continued to be debated until late in the sixteenth century. On the other hand, the theory destined to have the greatest influence on later critics is the one which is dominant in the Averroes commentary. This is the theory of praise and blame. Returning to Averroes' discussion of Chapter 1 of the *Poetics*, we find that the initial definition of poetry, offered as a quotation from Aristotle himself, is as follows: "Aristotle says: Every poem and all poetic speech are either blame or praise (*aut vituperatio aut laudatio*). And this is evident from examination of poems themselves, especially the poems which are concerned with matters of choice, either honest or base." The passage is, of course, not in the *Poetics*. Like the definition of imitation, it is an interpolation required to reconcile the text with the presuppositions of the commentator. Unlike that definition, however, it has some Aristotelian precedent. Averroes has transposed the notion that the original poetic forms were encomia and lampooning verses from Chapter 4 to Chapter 1 and converted it from an observation about primitive poems to a categorical assertion about poetry in general.

The praise-blame theory was attractive to Averroes for two reasons. First of all, it furnished a point of contact between Arab and Greek poetry. Second, it justified poetry by making it an instrument of moral instruction. These ideas are combined in a comment on Chapter 2 of the *Poetics*, where, after remarking that the Greeks had many excellent poems of praise, Averroes adds, "Children should be brought up to read those poems which incite and incline one to acts of fortitude and magnificence. In their poems the Arabs treat only these two virtues, although they do not incite to these virtues because they are good in themselves but because they are a means of attaining honor and glory." The didactic motive is also reflected in an interpretation of Aristotle's "objects of imitation" as virtue and vice.

The exotic combination of additions, transposed passages, and warped interpretations continues in the later sections of the commentary. According to Aristotle, the *Iliad* anticipates tragedy in its seriousness, its sustained plot, and its emphasis on dialogue, while the *Margites* antcipates comedy by dramatizing "the ludicrous" rather than continuing the earlier Greek tradition of personal satire. Because he knew neither Homer nor Greek drama, Averroes failed completely to understand these distinctions. (His problems are portrayed amusingly but sympathetically in Jorge Luis Borges' short story "Averroes' Search.") Homer, he says, "established the first principles of these arts, and there was no one before him whose achievement either in praise or blame had anything worth mentioning." Tragedy is defined simply as the *"ars laudandi"*—the art of praising, while comedy is *"ars vituperandi"*—the art of rebuking "not only everything that is bad, but what is despicable and almost beyond cure; that is, what is base and almost worthless." If this not only misses but inverts Aristotle's thoughts about the geniality that Homer introduced into comic tradition, it also wholly ignores the distinction between dramatic and narrative form. We are reminded here of the medieval habit, illustrated in the work of Dante, Lydgate, and Chaucer among others, of referring to narrative poems as "comedies" or "tragedies." Averroes' commentary did not create this misconception but may well have encouraged it. Benvenuto da Imola, for example, found that the Averroes commentary provided just the theory needed to explain the organization of Dante's *Comedy*.

Needless to say, the confusion of the commentary concerning poetic form produces a distorted interpretation of the six "parts" of tragedy listed by Aristotle in *Poetics* 6. Plot becomes *sermo fabularis;* character *consuetudines,* a category that includes both actions and morals; thought becomes *credulitas;* diction *metrum;* song *tonus;* and spectacle something called *consideratio,* by which Averroes seems to mean the gestures and facial expressions used by orators to emphasize their arguments. Equally characteristic, the concepts of probability and necessity are interpreted morally, with the surprising result that the poet is denied the right to create fictions: "And it is evident from what has been said about poetic speeches that representations that are based on lies are not proper to the poet's work." Again, reversal is treated not as a sudden change in the action of a work but as a shift in poetic technique from praise to blame or vice versa.

As a final example of Averroes' misinterpretation of Aristotle, we can turn to his comments on *Poetics* 12, which deals with the Greek terms used to designate the structure of tragedy—parode, episode, stasimon, and the like. Averroes solves the problem by substituting terms from rhetoric:

> [Aristotle] mentions in this discussion the parts that are proper to Greek poems. Of these, the parts that are found in Arab poems are three. First comes the part that resembles the exordium of rhetoric. It is the part where the Arabs speak of houses and noble buildings and of ruins and remains. . . . And the second is the praise proper; and the third is the part that is like the rhetorical conclusion. And this third part is usually either an invocation or petition to the man being praised, or a commendatory section praising the value of the poem itself.

This is an outline of the contents of the classic Arabic ode form, the *quasīda*. Its chief significance, however, is its suggestion that the formulas of rhetoric for organizing speeches are equally applicable to literature. This would doubtless have seemed a gratifying confirmation of what many Latin readers of the commentary already believed. The original passage in the *Poetics,* conversely, would have been as unintelligible to them as to Averroes.

References to the Averroes commentary begin almost immediately after its translation into Latin. Roger Bacon referred to the translation of "master Hermannus" with qualified approval, and a fourteenth-century manuscript of what appear to be lecture notes on the commentary has recently been discovered by Professor William Boggess of the University of Georgia. The first critic to make extensive use of the commentary may have been Benvenuto da Imola, one of the fourteenth-century commentators on Dante. Benvenuto knew the Hermannus translation well. Confidently claiming "Aristotle's authority" for his definition, he asserts that "it is manifest to whoever contemplates the forces of poetry . . . that all poetic discourse is either praise or blame." Later he cites Averroes rather than Aristotle to support the idea that poetry is morally edifying. Evidently, he considered both writers equally authoritative and did not differentiate between them.

Benvenuto's general acknowledgment is complemented by his analysis of the structure of the *Divine Comedy*. It is, he believes, a poem fully in accord with Aristotle's rules. The *Inferno* is a work based on "blame." It consists of a series of vignettes showing the ugliness of vice and its terrible consequences. It thus warns the reader to reform. After the *Inferno* comes the first of two "reversals" of the sort advocated by Averroes. The *Inferno* stresses unhappiness, the despair of the damned. In the *Purgatory* the tone abruptly changes to hope. The *Purgatory* contains some "blame"; but however wicked, the characters in this section have redeeming qualities which are "praised" by Dante. The second reversal comes

at the beginning of the *Paradiso*. Here the tone changes from hope to joyful fulfillment, and the technique from a mixture of blame and praise to unqualified
praise of men of preeminent virtue whom the reader is encouraged to emulate.
As Benvenuto remarks, "no other poet ever knew how to praise or blame with
more excellence. . . . [Dante] honored virtue with encomia and lacerated vice
and vicious men."

Although Benvenuto's commentary was known in the sixteenth century,
he remains primarily a medieval figure. It is significant that the next critic to be
influenced by the Averroes commentary is Coluccio Salutati. Salutati is the most
famous of Petrarch's disciples and was regarded during the sixteenth century as
a full-fledged humanist. Among his many works, his allegorical interpretation of
the life of Hercules, *De Laboribus Herculis*, is especially significant. It stands midway between Boccaccio's *Genealogy of the Gentile Gods* and the allegorized
mythologies of such sixteenth-century writers as Comes (or Conti) and Cartari.
The first book of the *De Laboribus* is a little "art of poetry," in which Salutati offers a theory that in parts may be accurately described as Averroes expanded and
ornamented by examples from the Latin classics. In Chapter 2 Salutati attempts to
differentiate between rhetoric and poetic. This is difficult because, following
Averroes, he believes that the two disciplines share the same "matter"—that is,
praise and blame. They are eventually distinguished by the assertion that poetry
is (1) in meter (an echo of the *ars metrica*) and (2) employs "imaginative and
figurative discourse," an idea derived from Averroes' definition of imitation.
Later, the tired classical definition of the orator as *vir bonus dicendi peritus*—the
good man skilled in speaking—is reworked to apply to the poet, who is called
a *vir optimus laudandi vituperandique peritus*—a perfect man skilled in praise
and blame. Even Horace is assimilated into the system. The "delight and instruct"
formula from the *Ars Poetica* is explained in the following way: "The reprehension of vice may profit right away, but does not immediately please; praise pleases
but does not immediately profit. Therefore blame is primarily for utility, praise
for pleasure; although in a secondary way the former may please and the latter
profit." As is appropriate for a forward-looking humanist, Salutati compliments
modern poets on their ability to "celebrate virtue and criticize vice" in the way
prescribed in "[Aristotle's] little book."

Averroistic ideas remained attractive during the sixteenth century, although
they were occasionally attacked and more frequently disguised by an increasingly
heavy overlay of erudition. Savonarola, Robortello, Segni, Maggi and Lombardi,
and Mazzoni all debate the "placing" of poetry among the sciences and all decide
that poetic is at least in part a branch of logic. Pietro Vettori was not only aware
of Averroes, he edited the commentary for the Giunta "Aristotle" of 1552, eight
years before composing his own analysis of the *Poetics*. Almost every one of these
writers cites the Averroes commentary directly and with respect, often to buttress
his own position. As late as 1575, in fact, Alessandro Piccolomini appealed to

"the authority of Averroes which has always had great force with me" to refute Robortello's theory of the origin of poetry. Throughout the sixteenth century, it may be added, the didactic theory of poetry existed side-by-side in rather uncomfortable proximity with more precisely Aristotelian doctrines. The fact is that the *Poetics* was difficult to accommodate to the moralistic attitudes of the humanists, whereas Aristotle as interpreted by Averroes is not only moral but oppressively so. In the early part of the century, before the publication of the great commentaries on the *Poetics*, the problem was not fully understood. Aulo Parrasio, for example, was responsible for the first of many efforts to harmonize Horace with Aristotle. His "Commentary on the *Ars Poetica*" appeared posthumously in 1531. Although one reference in the commentary seems to be to the Greek *Poetics*, the remainder of his allegedly Aristotelian principles are evidently quotations or paraphrases from Hermannus Alemannus. Obviously, such an approach became increasingly difficult as time went by. The tension between didacticism and Aristotelian criticism finally became an open break in Lodovico Castelvetro's *Poetica d'Aristotele vulgarizzata et sposta*, published in 1570. Although Castelvetro himself radically distorted the *Poetics*, his interpretation is free of the influence of Averroes. For this reason, he was viewed with suspicion by his great humanistic contemporary Torquato Tasso. In the *Discorsi del poema eroico*, published in 1594, Tasso attacked Castelvetro's rather hardheaded view that praise is irrelevant to heroic poetry. "Without doubt," Tasso wrote, "Castelvetro erred when he said that praise is not appropriate to the heroic poem, because if the heroic poet were to celebrate virtue, he would have to exalt it clear up to the heavens with his praises. On the other side, St. Basil says that Homer's *Iliad* is nothing but a praise of virtue, and Averroes has the same opinion in his commentary on poetry, and Plutarch too. . . . Therefore, leaving aside the followers of Castelvetro in their ignorance, let us follow the opinions of . . . St. Basil, of Averroes, of Plutarch, and of Aristotle himself."

In the last decade of the sixteenth century, in other words, the most eloquent spokesman of Italian humanism found Averroes not only worthy of citing, but in some respects more truly Aristotelian than the most informed student of the *Poetics* that the age produced.

The translation which follows is my own. The Roman numerals inserted in the translation are my suggestion (sometimes my guess) as to what chapter in the *Poetics* Averroes may be referring. For bibliography, see especially pp. 488–89.

(It is worth noting that Averroes uses several terms which are roughly equivalent to Greek *mimesis* and English "imitation." Among these are *assimilatio, representatio,* and *imitatio.* Although these terms are frequently used in doublets and even triplets, they are presumably not exact synonyms. In general I have translated *imitatio* as "imitation," *representatio* as "representation," and *assimilatio* as "likening." In spite of obvious drawbacks, this strategy recognizes (a) the difference between *imitatio* and *assimilatio,* and (b) the tendency of Averroes to view poetic imitation as the making of poetic images, as well as the process of representing characters and actions in poetry.)

THE MIDDLE COMMENTARY OF AVERROES OF CORDOVA ON THE *POETICS* OF ARISTOTLE

Hermannus Alemannus says: After finishing my translation of the *Rhetoric* of Aristotle with no small labor, wishing to set my hand to his *Poetics*, I encountered such great diffculty because of the diversity of the system of writing poetry in Greek and Arabic and because of the difficulty of the vocabulary and for many other reasons that I did not trust myself to be able to make a full translation of this work for Latin-speaking readers. Therefore I chose the commentary of Averroes on this work by Aristotle. The commentary explains what Averroes could understand of the *Poetics*. And I translated the commentary as well as I could into Latin.

Considerable aid in understanding the *Poetics* is provided by the *Ars Poetica* of Horace, just as Cicero's writings on rhetoric aid in understanding Aristotle's theory of rhetoric. Let the studious receive this translation if they will and rejoice that in it they have the completion of Aristotle's thought about logic.

Here begins the commentary of Averroes on the *Poetics* of Aristotle.

Averroes says: My intention in this work is to determine what is contained in Aristotle's *Poetics* concerning the universal rules of poetry common to all nations or most. Much of what is said in this book either deals with rules proper to Greek poems and Greek conventions or is not found in Arabic or is found in different forms.

[Chapter I] Aristotle says: My purpose is to discuss the art of poetry and the kinds of poem. Properly, one who wishes the rules of this art to proceed in an orderly sequence, should discuss first what each kind of poetry does, and the elements from which poetic compositions are formed, and how many subjects poetry has. Aristotle rightly concentrates on this material in his treatise and begins with those first principles that are natural to us in this subject.

Aristotle says: Every poem and all poetry are either blame or praise. This is apparent from examination of poems and the subjects that are proper to them which deal with matters of choice, both good and bad. This holds true for the arts of representation that follow the lead of poetry, like lyre or harp music or flute or pipe music and dancing, for these arts are adapted by nature to these two subjects. Poetry is based on image-making. There are three kinds of image-making or "likening"—two simple and one composite. The first of the simple forms is "likening" of one thing to another and the comparison of the first to the second. This is done in all languages by words proper to them, like the Latin words *quasi* [like] and *sicut* [as] and similar expressions called "particles of comparison"—

or else through the use of the thing which is "like" together with the thing to which it has "likeness" or in place of it. And in the art of poetry this is called a trope. For example, a certain poet[1] wrote concerning a man who was extremely generous, *He is a sea everywhere flooding the emptiness of those who approach him, and filling it in a copious tide.*

You should know that this category includes forms which the moderns call analogy and metaphor. For example, *the meadow smiles* or *he plows the sand* [i.e. "he labors in vain"]; and, as a poet[2] writes, *There are mares that in their youth reject the saddle and bridle, and female camels that cannot bear saddle bags.* And metaphors can very properly be called tropes on attributes or characteristics of a thing.

An analogy is a trope based on proportion. For example, when *a* is related to *b* as *c* is to *d*, then the word for *c* can be used for *a* and vice versa. The varieties of these tropes have already been treated in the *Rhetoric.*

The second of the two simple types is when the "likening" is reversed, as when you say, *the sun is like a woman* or *the sun is a woman*—not *this woman is like the sun* or *this woman is the sun.* The third kind is a composite of these two simple types.

Aristotle says: Certain men naturally imagine humans and represent them in actions—for example some men make representations using colors and shapes and sounds, and this either through art or habit on the part of the imitators themselves or through long-established artistic conventions. By the same token, some men are naturally drawn to representation by speech.

Image-making and representation in poetry involves three elements: harmony and rhythm, and likening. Each of these elements is sometimes found by itself and without another—as sound in pipe or flute music, and rhythm in dance. And representation or imitation occurs in language alone—that is, in representational or imaginative speeches composed without meter or rhythm. And sometimes all three elements are combined.

This occurs among the Arabs in the so-called "song" [i.e. the Mozarabic folkforms, *muwashshahah* and *ghazal*] recently discovered or invented by the inhabitants of this region [Spain] in their own language, that is, Arabic. This form of poem developed naturally and uses two elements [words and music] together. Natural forms are only discovered by peoples living close to nature. Indeed, *symphonia*, or rhyme, used not to exist in Arab poems—only meter by itself or meter with representation.

And since this was the case, there were three imaginative arts which created the imaginative effect: the art of rhyme, the art of meter, and the art of making representational speeches. This is the part of the art of logic with which this book [the *Poetics*] deals.

Aristotle says: Often we find compositions which are called poetry but which have no poetic invention except meter, like the compositions of

Socrates and the works of Empedocles on natural philosophy, in contrast to what is contained in the poems of Homer. In Homer's poems one finds both elements [representation and meter] together.

Aristotle says: Therefore no work can be properly called a poem unless it contains these two elements. The others are better called "this or that composition" than poems. Likewise the author of metrical works on natural philosophy should be called a "discursive author" rather than a poet. Also, imaginative speeches which include mixed meters are not poems. Aristotle observes that poems are found among the Greeks using rhythm or mixed meters. This, however, is not found among the Arabs.

It is now clear from what has been said how many manners of representation there are and from what arts representational works in language are composed so that the effect is achieved.

[Ch. II] Aristotle says: Since imitators and makers of likenesses wished through their art to impel people toward certain choices and discourage them from others, they had to treat subjects that, being represented, would suggest either virtues or vices. All action and character are concerned with one of these two—that is, virtue or vice. It necessarily follows that good and virtuous men represented only virtues and virtuous men; while bad men represented evil and evil men. Since all "likening" and representation occurs through showing the proper or the improper or base, it is evident that representation aims at nothing but the encouragement of what is proper and the rejection of what is base. Necessarily, then, there are imitators of virtue—that is, men who naturally incline to representing the more virtuous and better sorts of men—and imitators of evil, who are less perfect and nearer to evil men. From these two kinds of men, praise and blame arose—that is, praise of good men and blame of bad ones.

And because of this certain poets are especially adept at praise but not at blame. And conversely certain poets are adept at blame but not at praise. Moreover these two different approaches—that is, commendation of good and criticism of what is base—run through all imitative poetry. But these two differences are only found in the arts of "likening" and representation that use language—not in representation using meter or rhyme alone. And there are three types of poetry of "likening." First, there is "likening" which compares one thing to another, which is comparable, without showing virtue or vice, and aiming only at accuracy. This kind of "likening" is capable, as it were, of being modified and varied toward either of the two extremes. That is, it is sometimes used to show goodness through strong emphasis in this direction, and sometimes modified to show badness by a similar use of emphasis.

Aristotle says: This was the practice of Homer, whose "accurate likening" is used to express goodness and badness. The excellence of certain writers consists in accuracy alone, and of others in showing goodness and badness, and of others in the combination of both, as is the case for Homer. Aristotle gives examples of each kind of poetry, citing poets who were famous or notable among the Greeks and are in their histories and used each of the three manners of "likening" [i.e., accuracy, emphasis on good, emphasis on evil.]

It will not be hard for you to find examples of these in Arab poems, although as al-Farabi says, most Arab poems are simply intended to give pleasure. The sort of poem they call "elegy" is nothing but an incitement to sexual intercourse, which they hide and disguise under the name of love. Therefore children should be kept from reading such poems and instructed and exercised in poems that incite and encourage acts of fortitude and generosity. Indeed, in their songs the Arabs incite readers to these two virtues alone out of all the virtues. They do not do this simply for the sake of virtue but because through fortitude and generosity one achieves supreme honor and glory.

The kind of poetry which seeks only accuracy is common in Arab songs. Often they describe the properties and characteristics of metals and other minerals and even of things that grow in the earth and of animals. The Greeks do not often include such things in their poems except insofar as they contribute to the object of teaching readers to seek virtues or avoid vices or of instructing them in various other kinds of good that can be done or known.

From this passage in the *Poetics* it is clear that there are three kinds of "likening" and three differences. It is also clear what the three differences and three kinds are. And when one considers various poems it seems clear that there is no fourth kind of "likening" and no fourth difference among the kind.

[Ch. IV] Aristotle says: There seem to be two causes in human nature for the origin of poetry. First, the tendency to liken one thing to another and to represent one thing by another exists naturally in man from birth. Indeed, this tendency to liken and represent is found even in infants. This tendency is proper to man in contrast to the other animals. And the reason is that only man, among all the other animals is delighted by "likening" things that he has perceived in his mind, and by their representation and imitation. A sign of this—that is, that man naturally enjoys and rejoices in "likening"—is that we are delighted and rejoice in representations of certain things that did not delight us when we perceived them directly. We are especially delighted when the representation very artfully expresses the thing represented, as happens with the images of many animals, represented by skilled sculptors and painters. This is why we use examples in teaching—so that what we say can be more easily understood through use of the power of images. For the mind will grasp a subject more perfectly when it experiences the delight arising from examples. And learning is not only for philosophers but is for all men, who share in this to some degree with philosophers.

Learning proceeds naturally from one man to another in the way that a teacher is related to a pupil. Since examples are nothing but likenesses of things which have already been perceived in the mind, it is clear that they are used simply

to make understanding what is said more rapid and more easy. They make understanding more rapid because of the pleasure of the image of the thing that they
represent. And this is the first cause for the origin of poetry.

The second is the pleasure that man naturally takes in meter and melody.
Concerning melody, it appears to be adapted to the meter by those who have a
natural talent for hearing and judging melody and meter. Thus the natural
pleasure of the soul in representation and meter and melody was the cause of the
invention of the art of poetry—and specifically, by men who had a special natural
talent for it.

As soon as people began to gather together and formed a social group, the
art of poetry began to develop among them. The development was gradual, however. At first they discovered a small part of it, and then another part, until at
length the art attained perfection. Also the kinds of poetry reached perfection according to the capacity of various types of men for greater or lesser delight in this
or that kind of poetic song.

In addition, virtuous and noble souls naturally first discovered the art
of songs praising and reciting beautiful and excellent deeds. Less noble souls discovered songs blaming and denigrating base and immoral deeds. However, the
poet who intends to denigrate evil men and deeds must approve and praise good
men and good and virtuous deeds so that by this means evil and ignoble deeds
can be more fully revealed—i.e., so that when the poet has narrated bad deeds
he has placed the opposite sort next to them.

This, then, is what is contained in the chapter [Poetics IV] concerning
things that are common to all nations or most. The rest of what Aristotle says in
it is all or mostly about matters that are proper to the poems of the Greeks and
their poetic conventions. He defines the kinds of poetry that were written by
the Greeks, and what natural origin and beginning each one had, and which of the
parts preceded the other in its appearance, and especially the art of praise and
blame, which was very highly regarded among the Greeks. He also tells who first
began each of the standard kinds of poetry and who added to them and who
perfected them. And in this chapter he especially praises Homer, noting that he
provided the first principles of these kinds and that there was no one before him
who achieved anything worth mentioning in the art of praise or the art of blame
or any of the other poetic kinds known to the Greeks.

Aristotle says: The more defective and briefer kinds of verse came first in
time because in the beginning human nature understood them more easily.
"Briefer" refers to the kind of verse that is made up of few syllables. And "defective" refers to poetry that has few melodies or sections.

Aristotle says: A sign that these kinds of verse came first and first revealed
themselves to men's souls is that, in arguments, the speakers often use half a verse
of a poem for the sake of rapidity and leave off the other half, wishing to make
their arguments brief. In my opinion, he is referring to what lawyers frequently do

when they argue, as when they say, "No, no, no," raising their voice during this. And when they say, "This is not so," also raising and increasing the volume of their voice. Negative responses of this sort are close to being half-verses having melody and meter. But fuller and more complete verses did not appear until later, as happens also in other arts.

[Ch. V] Aristotle says: The art of blame seeks to represent not all that is evil, but what is debased and almost diseased; that is, what is so abject that it is almost beyond cure.

Aristotle says: The sign that these three elements should be present in evil that is almost beyond cure or despicable is that in the face of the despicable man these three elements appear. That is, a wrinkled and ugly expression, a contemptible disposition, and a lack of desire to improve. And the same is true, given the different emotion, of the face of an angry man. That is, the expression is twisted, there is certain narrow-mindedness, and there is a vehemence like fire against the man who offered the provocation.

Aristotle says: Excellent poems of praise [i.e., the epic] use a lengthy, not a short meter. Therefore later writers rejected the brief meter used formerly in this art and in other kinds of poetry. The most proper kind of meter is uniform, not mixed. But it is most important that this not lead to tedious lengthiness. And the end in respect to content—that is, what makes the content of the art of praise meaningful—is that it should be the likeness and representation of a complete virtuous act of choice which has universal application to virtuous activities and not a particular application to an individual instance of virtue. I add, a representation which arouses in the soul certain passions which move it to pity or fear or to other like passions which the representation arouses and stimulates by what it makes virtuous men imagine about virtue and corruption. Representation does not deal with dispositions that follow virtue because of wise habits and the like [i.e., when will is not involved], for one cannot represent these things in images.

Representation in language is completed when melody and meter are joined to it. Reciters of songs have other abilities, in addition to those which are found in meter and language, which make the language more representational —that is, movements of the head and changes of expression, as has already been explained in the *Rhetoric*.

The first of the parts of the art of praise is to express [in words] noble concepts through which imaginative stimulation occurs. Then those concepts are enhanced by melody and meter appropriate to what is being expressed. The melody of the poem prepares the soul to receive images of the thing represented. The melody makes the soul receptive and thus sensitive to the likeness and representation of the thing whose likeness is intended. Indeed, the melody proper to each kind of poem shapes the soul in a way appropriate to each kind through its harmony and composition. Thus we find that a sharp or acute tone fits a kind of speech for which a "heavy" tone is inappropriate. This is the opinion we should have about harmony and meter and their composition.

The impressions created by those who recite and represent and enhance the imaginative content of the poetic speeches themselves (which contain three elements—that is, likeness and rhythm and melody) are two in number. The first is the impression of character and habit—as when one recites the speech of an intelligent man or the speech of a wrathful man. The second is the impression of human belief or opinion. For the impression made by a man who speaks from factual certainty is different from the impression made by a man who is uncertain when he speaks. The impression made in reciting and representing speech in tragedy should be the impression and image of one who is certain, not doubtful, and saying serious, not playful things. Such speech resembles the speech of men of the finest character, thought, and actions. It is the impression of the deeds and fortunes of men like this that those who give [tragic] recitations must create.

And fables which involve likening and representation or imitation are imitative works conveying the two impressions just mentioned. I refer to a fable composed of material whose representation is based on either what the material truly is in itself, or on the material as it is conventionally feigned in poetry, even though it is a fiction. This is why poetic speeches are called "fables."

Reciters and enunciators, to sum up the matter, are men who have the ability to represent human character and belief [i.e., thought].

[Ch. VI] Aristotle says: In tragedy, that is, the art of praise, there should be six parts. These are: representational speeches in the form of fables [i.e., plot]; character; meter or accent; belief [i.e., thought]; deliberation; and melody. A sign of this is that all poetic speech is divided into the "likening" and the means by which the "likening" is expressed. And there are three parts through which "likening" is expressed—representation, meter, and melody. And there are three parts which are "likened" in the poetry of praise, character, belief, and deliberation. Deliberation is proof of the truth of a belief.

Thus there are six parts of tragedy. The most important parts of this song of praise are character and belief. Tragedy is not an imitation of men in themselves as they are perceived individually, but is a representation of their honest characters and praiseworthy actions and praiseworthy beliefs. And character includes actions and moral attitudes. Therefore character is one of the six parts, and therefore action and morals are included in this part.

"Deliberation" is the demonstration of the rightness of the belief which makes a man praiseworthy. It is not found at all in the poems of the Arabs, but it is found in legal speeches. And three things—that is, character and belief and signification—are represented by the three means by which representation occurs—that is, imaginative speech and meter and melody.

Aristotle says: The parts of spoken fable [i.e., plot] which make it representational are two in number. All representation either defines itself through representation of its contrary and is then changed to its proper intention—this is the technique that the Greeks call "indirection" [i.e., reversal]—or else it presents the thing itself making no mention of its contrary—and they called this "signification" [i.e., discovery]. The part which is, as it were, the principal and fundamental one of the six is representational speech used in fable [i.e., plot]. The second part is character. In early times representation concentrated on character—that is, it concentrated on the thing represented. And representation or imitation is indeed the main prop and foundation in the art because there is no delight in mentioning a subject without representing it. But there is delight and stimulus when it has been represented. Therefore we are usually not delighted by seeing the form of something existing in nature, but we are delighted by its representation and image in drawings and colors. This is why men practice the arts of painting and description.

The third part of tragedy is belief. This is the power to represent a thing as it is or is not. This resembles what we seek in rhetoric when we assert that a thing exists or does not exist, except that rhetoric does this through persuasive speech and poetry through representational speech—and this sort of representation is also found in legal speeches.

Aristotle says: The makers of the laws of Sparta were content to strengthen belief in the minds of the citizens by poetic speech; while later men began to travel the road of rhetoric.

The difference between poetic speech which depicts and influences belief and poetic speech which depicts and influences character is that the speech that influences character impels us to perform and do something or to reject and withdraw from it. But speech which influences belief only influences us to believe that something exists or does not exist, not to seek it or reject it.

The fourth part is the meter or rhythm. The perfection of this part is to be appropriate to the purpose or intention. At times a certain rhythm is appropriate to one purpose and not to another. The fifth part, in order, is melody. It is the most important part for impressing and moving the soul.

The sixth part is deliberation—that is, argument or proof, not using persuasive speech, of the correctness of belief or action. Persuasive speech is not involved in the poetic art nor is it appropriate. The poetic art uses representational speech. Indeed, the poetic art—and especially tragedy—does not consist of logical arguments or philosophical speculation. Therefore the poem of praise does not use the techniques of gesture or of facial expression as they are employed in rhetoric.

Aristotle says: The philosophic art which shows or teaches from what and how poems are composed is more important and more perfect than the making of poems themselves. Every theoretical art which includes under itself the techniques for performing its tasks is more worthy than the techniques which are included in it.

[Ch. VII] Since we have said what tragedy is and from what it is composed and how many parts it has and what they are, let us now speak of the matters which lend excellence and goodness to those elements from which poetry arises. We must speak of these things in respect to tragedy and the other forms of poetry, for they are, as it were, the first causes and basis of existence of these forms.

The principles from which arts arise are of two kinds. Some are necessary and others provide completion or adornment.

We may say, then, that tragedy should achieve the end appropriate to its purpose—that is, it should attain through 'likening' and representation the end which its nature permits it to attain. Several factors make this happen. First, what is intended should have a certain definite magnitude so that it is whole and complete. Now that is whole and complete which has a beginning, middle, and end. The beginning precedes the main subject and must not be mixed with the things to which it is a beginning. The end follows those things to which it is an ending and must not precede them. The middle follows and precedes. The middle is better than the two extremes, since it occupies a position between what precedes and what follows. In war the bravest men occupy the same position—that is, the middle position between the cowards and bold and rash men. This is the middle place, and for this reason excellence in composition is in the middle and the middle is derived from the extremes and the extremes are not derived from it. Nor should the middle be merely the middle in respect to composition and location, but also in magnitude and excellence. When this happens the poetic subject will have a beginning, middle, and end, and each one of the parts will have an appropriate size. Likewise, the whole composed of these parts will have a definite size and will not be indeterminate.

Excellence in composition arises from two factors. One is arrangement and the other is magnitude—for we do not say, when discussing the general characteristics of things, that a very small animal is excellent or beautiful.

Arrangement in poetic speech is like arrangement in lecturing. That is, if the lecture is shorter than it should be, it hinders understanding; and if it is too long, it is difficult to retain and encourages the learner to be forgetful. In this respect arrangement is like one's stance when observing the appearance of something visible. The view is good when there is a proper distance between the observer and the object—neither too close nor too far.

What happens in teaching also happens in poetic speeches. That is, if the poem of praise is briefer and more compressed than the subject demands, it will not include all the praise that the subject warrants; and if it is too long, its parts will not be retained in the memory of the audience, and as they hear the last parts they will forget the first ones.

Rhetorical speeches used in controversy as confirmation or refutation do not have a size naturally determined. This is why men needed to measure the time of an argument between adversaries by water clocks, as was the custom among the Greeks, who chiefly used enthymemes; or by sundials as is our custom, since in our legal wrangles we employ much material extrinsic to the argument in order to bolster our credibility. If tragedy consisted of argumentative speech, men would need to measure the time of the dispute either by water clocks or some other device; but since this is not the case, the poetic art should have a natural limit as do the magnitudes of things existing in nature. All living things, if they are not impeded in their growth by some unfortunate accident, reach a magnitude defined by nature, and this should be true of poetic speeches and especially the two kinds of representation that employ either change from representing the contrary of a thing to the thing itself, or direct representation of the thing without reference to its contrary.

[Ch. VIII] Aristotle says: If the composition of a poem is to be excellent and attractive it should not be drawn out by mention of all the things that happened to the single subject that the poem depicts. Many things happened to a single subject, and likewise, many actions are found in the same subject.

Aristotle says: And it seems that not all poets concentrated on a single subject. Rather, they skipped from subject to subject and did not concentrate on the same material—all, that is, except Homer.

You find this frequently in the poems of the Arabs, both in the new or modern poems [*muwashshahah, ghazal*]; and especially in their songs of praise [*quaṣīda*], when they have any subject to praise, like an energetic horse or a precious sword, they digress from the subject at hand and waste much time in praising whatever subject presents itself.

And to sum things up, art in this should imitate nature; that is, whatever is done should be done according to a single subject and a single end. This being so, it follows that "likening" and representation should have unity; and the subject treated through them should be one; and the parts should have a definite magnitude. And there should be a beginning, middle, and end, and the middle should be best, since matters which depend on arrangement for their unity—and also the excellence derived from proper arrangement—will not achieve their potential effect if they are not properly organized.

[Ch. IX] Aristotle says: It is clear from what has been said about the object of poetic speeches that representations which are false and made up are not part of the poet's work. These compositions are called proverbial tales and exemplary tales, as, for example, the stories in Aesop's book and similar fabulous writings. It is the poet's task to speak only of things that exist or may exist. Such things are presented as desirable or to be avoided or as accurate likenesses, as was observed in the chapter on representation. The composition of proverbs and fables is not the work of poets, although men compose proverbial tales and fables and such things in meter. Although they use meter, the effect of both proverbial tales and fables is achieved through the stories themselves as they would be even if meter were not used. They convey a kind of instruction in prudence. The poet does not contribute to the achievement of this effect by stimulating the imagination, only by meter. The maker of made-up proverbial tales and fables invents or feigns individual things which obviously do not really exist and gives them names. But the poet only gives names to things that exist. And at times poets speak in universal terms. Therefore the art of poetry is closer to philosophy than is the art of making up proverbial tales. And this is what Aristotle says about Greek poetry that imitates nature and about the poetry of societies living close to nature.

Aristotle says: In the art of praise or tragedy one should be sure that most of the things on which the imitative representation is based are things that exist in nature, not things that are made up or imaginary, with made-up names. For the poems are intended to influence voluntary choices. When their actions are possible and like real actions, their persuasive power stimulates the soul more deeply—that is, it arouses the poetic belief that moves the soul to seek something or reject it. In tragedy names are never given or made up for things that do not exist in nature—or only rarely—as, for example, when poets treat generosity as though it were a person and then attribute to this person actions proper to a generous man and represent him and write poem after poem in his praise. And if this is at times effective and no small help because of the similarity of the actions and passions of such a made-up subject to things existing in nature, it is not therefore proper to rely on such devices in tragedy. For this kind of imaginative stimulation is not what appeals to most people. Rather, most people deride it and attack or revile it. And among the Arabs the poetic excellence discussed in this chapter can be seen in the lines of al-Asa, although they do not incite to virtue:

> Because of my life many eyes have gazed
> At the light of a fire
> Burning on the mountain-tops.
> So that two cold eyes passing the night in its brilliance
> Grew warm from its radiance.

Given these facts, it is clear that the poet is not a poet except through the making of fables [i.e., plots] and meters or rhythms with a magnitude sufficient to produce likenesses and imitative representations. And the poet only uses "likening" for matters relating to choice that exist in nature. And it is his task to imitate and represent not only what exists, but also what people think can possibly exist. He is a poet in this latter function no less than when he treats things that exist. Nothing prevents him from treating those things as he treats things that exist today. This sort of invented fable is not lacking in poetic stimulation of the imaginaton.

The skilled or perfect poet does not need to enhance his representation through extrinsic aids like dramatic gestures and facial expressions. Only those who parade as poets (although they are really not poets) use these devices. True poets only use such devices when they wish, through this, to show up the practice of false poets. They do not use these devices against skillful poets.

At times perfect poets are forced by place and time to aid themselves by using devices that are extrinsic or outside of the basic elements of poetry. This is because imitation is not always of complete things whose imitation can be definite and complete, but also of incomplete things whose imitation in language is difficult. Aid in imitating these subjects is therefore provided by extrinsic devices—especially when the imitation involves belief. It is difficult to make the reader imagine things that are neither actions nor substances.

Sometimes extrinsic devices are mixed with poetic images. If this happens by chance and without being planned it is a marvel, since that which occurs because of chance is marvelous by its very nature.

[Ch. X] Aristotle says: The excellence of many poetic speeches consists in simple imitation not having much variation. And there are many whose excellence consists in variation of the "likening" and imitation. The same thing holds true in other activities, for certain activities are performed in a simple, single action, and some require complex actions. This is true in imitation or representation. Simple imitation is a form that uses one of the two ways of presenting the material —that is, either the one called "indirection" [i.e., reversal] or the one called "directness" or "direct presentation" [i.e., discovery].

A mixed imitation is one that uses both kinds—that is, it can begin with "indirection" and proceeds to "directness" or it can begin with "directness" and proceed to "indirectness." The form to be used is the one beginning with "indirection" and proceeding to "direction." There is a great difference between beginning with "indirection" and moving to "direction," and beginning with "direction" and moving to "indirection."

Aristotle says: I mean by indirection imitation of the opposite of what is to be praised, so that the soul first rejects and despises the one, and then there is a change from the negative to the imitation proper of what is to be praised. For example, if one should want to imitate or represent success and things related to it, he would begin first by imitation of failure and things related to it and then change to imitation of success and things pertaining to it. And he will do this by presenting the opposite of what he used to represent failure.

Direct imitation treats the thing itself.

Aristotle says: Directness is more excellent when mixed with indirectness.

Aristotle says: At times directness and indirectness are used for animate and inanimate things not to move people to seek or reject them but merely to arouse the imagination. I call this "accurate imitation." The method of "directness"—really, "directness" and "indirectness"—is most often applied to inanimate things in Arab poems. For example, there is the passage of the poet al-Mutanabbi,[3] who writes:

> As often as you visited hidden doorways—
> Visits more sly than those made by the wolf when all are asleep—
> So often did I visit them;
> And the blackness of the night protected me.
> And I returned and the white dawn met me.

The first part of this poem is "direct" and the second part "indirect." Since the two parts include the two methods of imitation, they are excellent or beautiful in effect.

Aristotle says: Among men, "directness" and "indirectness" are used for inquiry and rebuttal.

The method of "directness" and "indirectness" can move the soul at times to pity and at times to fear. This is what is needed in the art of praising laudable and moral human actions and in blaming base and immoral ones.

Aristotle says: These two parts which we have described are parts of tragedy. There is a third part—that is, a part that generates animal passions, like pity and fear and sorrow. He includes in this category all pitiable events like dangers experienced by friends and deaths of parents and other similar things that often happen to men. These, indeed, are what arouse pity and fear. And this element forms a large proportion of the parts of Greek poems that incite to praiseworthy actions which the poem is written to praise.

[Ch. XII] Aristotle says: The qualitative parts of tragedy have been described. Now we must speak of the quantitative parts. He mentions in this section parts which are proper to Greek poems. Three of these parts are found among the Arabs. First, there is the part that appears in poems in the manner of a rhetorical exordium. This is the part where the Arabs mention mansions or noble buildings and ruins and remains. After this, they include preludes and consolations in it. The second part is praise itself. The third part is what resembles a rhetorical conclusion. Most of this part among the Arabs is either an address or prayer to the man they have praised or a commendation of the value of the poem itself.

The first part is more noteworthy and better known than the last. Therefore they call the change from the first part to the second a "following." And at times they go directly to praise, leaving out the exordium, as in the passage by Abu Tammam: "Certainly, I should hesitate both to speak and act." And there is the passage by al-Mutanabbi: "One enjoys what he has been accustomed to all his life, and the lance of Saifu ad-Daulati has been accustomed to pierce his enemies."

[Ch. XIII] After Aristotle completes his list of the parts of Greek poems, he says: We have now listed the parts of tragedy according to quality and quantity. Let us next discuss the matters from which the effect of the art of praise, that is tragedy, is derived, adding this to what has preceded.

[Ch. XIV] Aristotle says: As has been said, the composition of songs of praise should not be by simple imitation but should mix elements of all three methods together—that is, the methods of "directness," of "indirectness," and of imitations arousing or inducing the passions of pity and fear and thus moving the soul. The ode, that is the poem of praise, which intends to impel the reader to virtue should be composed of representations of virtues and of matters inducing fear and pity, from which perturbation arises, like misfortunes happening to good men without cause. Indeed, this constitutes a powerful stimulation of the soul to receive virtue.

A change by the poet from representation of virtue to representation of vice or from representation of virtuous men to representation of vicious men accomplishes nothing toward impelling a man or forcing him, as though terrified, toward virtuous actions, if the change creates neither intense love nor fear. Both of these emotions should be found in songs of praise. This happens when the change is from representation of virtues to representation of misfortune and the evil accidents happening to good and worthy men; or when there is a change from this to representing those who are extremely virtuous. Truly, these representations arouse the soul and make it eager to receive virtue. And you will find many representations included in legal speeches which are like those that Aristotle discusses, since these are speeches of praise inciting to praiseworthy actions. For example there is the story of Joseph and his brothers and other similar stories from past history, which are called "hortatory examples."

Aristotle says: Pity and compassion are aroused when we tell of misery and misfortune befalling one who did not merit it, and without cause. Terror and fear arise from telling such things because of the thought of deserved harm that could befall those who are less worthy than the characters in the poem— that is, the audience, who know that they are less worthy than the characters. Sadness and pity arise from telling such things because they happened to a man who did not deserve it. When one simply mentions virtues by themselves, this does not involve fear of loss, nor pity, nor love. A poet who wishes to move to virtue must therefore devote part of his representation to things that arouse sadness and terror and pity.

Aristotle says: Songs of praise which are beautiful and excellent in terms of the art of poetry are poems based on this sort of composition—that is, narration of virtue, and of sad events, and of things that arouse fear and move to pity and compassion.

Aristotle says: Those men err who criticize a poet who devotes part of his poem to fictional or historical tales and includes indications of how these parts are useful to the praise. And in poems of praise dealing with war, things are added that arouse and signify wrath. Wrath is a kind of sorrow and perturbation accompanied by a powerful desire for revenge. This being the case, recalling the murder of parents and similar events that have befallen active and virtuous men, can move and arouse in the hearers a zealous love of virtue and a fear they may someday be deprived of the benefits of virtue.

Some poets include representation of vices or defects in songs of praise because they give rise to a certain measure of "indirection." But the reprehension and ridicule of defects is more proper to satire than to tragedy. Therefore their presence in tragedy should not be related to its principal intention and should only be included for the sake of "indirection." And when there is mention of defects in a poem of praise, then there is no excuse for not immediately mentioning enemies of the man praised and those who hate him.

A poem of praise is written only to recall the deeds of friends and loved ones. Enemies of enemies and friends of friends are not commemorated in praise or blame, since they are neither friends nor enemies of the man praised.

Aristotle says: Fictional invention should be so fearful and sorrowful that it occurs "before your eyes" and has almost the reality of something seen. For when a fictional story is ambiguous and is based on doubtful material, it does not produce the action that it seeks to produce. For what a person does not believe cannot move him either to fear or pity. What Aristotle says here explains why many people who do not believe the stories in the Bible are vile and depraved. Men are naturally moved by two kinds of speech—logical and non-logical. The kind of man just mentioned is prevented from being moved by either of these two types of speech that one finds in the Bible.

Aristotle says: Certain poets include in tragedy representation of things that arouse admiration alone without fear or sorrow. You find many passages of this kind in the Bible, though songs praising virtue are not found in Arab poetry and are not found in our own day except in the Bible.

Aristotle says: There is absolutely no efficacy in this form of tragedy [i.e., of admiration]. The art of poetry does not seek any sort of pleasure but seeks the level of pleasure which moves to virtue through imagination. This is the pleasure proper to tragedy.

Aristotle says: We know the things whose representation produces pleasure without suffering of fear. Things whose representation produces suffering and fear along with pleasure can be determined by asking what the difficult and harsh experiences are among those which tend to befall mankind, and what things are small and unimportant so that great sorrow and fear do not arise from them. The ideal kinds are things that happen intentionally between friends like the slaying of parents and dangers and misfortunes and other similar injuries, and not what happens between enemies. One is not saddened nor is he pained or terrified by an evil act performed by enemies in the same way that he is saddened and offended by an evil act caused by friends. And if a certain degree of suffering results from the first sort of deed, it is not comparable to the suffering that comes from an evil act performed by loved ones—like the slaying of a brother by a brother or a father by a son or a son by a father. The story of Abraham is a case in point. He was commanded to sacrifice his most beloved son. This is truly pitiable and produces an extreme impulse toward suffering and pity and fear.

Aristotle says: Praise should only be of excellent actions proceeding from free choice and knowledge. Some actions are based on free choice and knowledge. Some are based on neither choice or knowledge. Some are based on knowledge but not on choice, and some on choice but not on knowledge. Likewise some things are done by agents who are recognized, and some by agents who are not recognized. A deed that is done in ignorance and without free choice is not worthy to be called "praise." The same is true of a deed done by agents who are not recognized. This is far more appropriate to fabulous tales than poems. Therefore it should not be represented. Deeds which clearly proceed from free choice and knowledge and agents who are recognized are most worthy to be called "praise" and true commendation.

[Ch. XV] Aristotle says: We have now sufficiently discussed the proper treatment of the things from which poems are made and how they are to be composed. We will now discuss character—that is, what qualities are to be represented in praise.

We say, then, that there are four aspects of character or qualities worthy and excellent to represent in praise—that is, qualities that seem excellent to the audience.

Certain ones are characteristics which are good and virtuous qualities innate to the man who is praised. The soul is receptive to the representation of qualities truly existing in the man praised. And there is some good in any kind of man, although some things not good may be found in the man.

Second are attributes pertaining to the subject of praise and appropriate to it. Some attributes pertain and are convenient to a woman and do not pertain to a man and are not appropriate to a man.

Third are characteristics existing or invented in terms of the completion of the whole, when it is possible to discover characteristics that are verisimilar and appropriate.

Fourth are characteristics which are moderate and means between extremes.

And the case in respect to these matters is such that no-one is praised on account of bad and perverse customs and character. Likewise, no-one is praised for qualities that are not appropriate to him, even if they are good qualities. Likewise no-one is praised for appropriate qualities if they are not highly probable on the basis of verisimilitude and appropriateness, or are not adequate to the purpose.

Qualities which are good and express good and praiseworthy character are such according to truth or the opinion of many; or are similar to these. All of these are proper to praise—that is, qualities that are good according to truth or are similar to those which are truthful or thought by many to be true or are similar to these.

Aristotle says: The epilogues or conclusions of poems or metrical compositions should state in summary form the subject commemorated and the qualities of character which gave rise to the praise, just as happens in rhetorical conclusions. Also the poet should exclude from his poem representations extraneous to the speech except what those to whom the speech is directed can tolerate. Thus he will not be criticized for too much or too little or wandering from the path of poetry.

Aristotle says: Likeness and representation relate to praise of things which are at the summit of virtue and goodness. Just as the skilled artist depicts an object as it is in reality, so that he can represent anger and humor and sloth by his paintings—though the characteristics of these are primarily of the soul—in the same way in his representation the poet should depict and form the object as it is in itself and as he is able to do it, so that he imitates and expresses the character and habits of the soul. Here Aristotle mentions the poet Homer and his poem in which he depicted the character of a certain man [Achilles—*Poetics* XV.1454B]. Poetry of this type—I mean a poem that causes a quality of the soul to be imagined and represents it—is illustrated by the passage in al-Mutanabbi describing a certain messenger of the Romans coming to the presence of a certain Arab king named Saifu ad-Daulati and written with the intention of celebrating the king. He wrote:

When he came to you,
For fear, the head almost denied the neck on which it was placed.
All his joints almost dissolved for terror.
As though between battle lines drawn up on either side
He advanced toward you,
While he forced his trembling legs forward
Though his shaky will wanted to turn them back.

Aristotle says: In arousing the imagination and in imitative representation the poet should employ materials that are customary, and in making metaphors he should not stray from the paths of poetry.

[Ch. XVI] Aristotle says: The kinds of indicative signs which function in this way are many. One is that the representation of visible things be by means of sensible images which, by their nature, leave the spectator in doubt, making him believe the things themselves that are represented are present because of

the ability of the images to communicate the forms of the things being represented. For example, they call certain constellations "crab" and "spear-bearer"
because on hearing these terms, one can imagine from their shape and organization the things which they symbolize, as though the images were the things
themselves. Much metaphoric resemblance among the Arabs is of this sort.
They call words of comparison "doubtfuls," and the more apt the images—
that is, the expressions arousing the imagination so that it "doubts" whether or
not the thing represented is truly present—the more perfect and artful the
metaphor using them. And the more distant, the more imperfect the excellence
of the metaphor. Imperfect metaphors are representations far removed from
what they represent, and they are to be shunned or rejected. For example, there
is the saying of the poet Imru'u 'l-Qais about a lean and bony mare: "Your
horse is like an old spear-handle." And his other saying: "When she comes
call her 'She-bear of fields covered by waves'; when she comes say 'Seductress,
there are no footprints in the water.' "[4] This saying is more apt than the first
because there is a certain amount of contrast in it.

Certain images represent concepts by sensible things when these things
have characteristics analogous to the concepts. Through these characteristics it
is possible for the concepts to be understood. For example there is the saying
about a favor: "It is a chain around your neck." And gifts: "'They are shackles
to the recipient." And as the poet al-Mutanabbi says: "The man who finds gifts
and favors finds shackles." A great many such metaphors are found among the
Arabs. And we should reject those metaphors which are inept and dispropor-
tionate and lack likeness. But this often is found in modern poems, especially
in the poetry of Abu Tammam, as in his saying, "Do not water me with the
water of reproach." Really, there is no relation between water and reproach.
And even less apt is his saying, "Death is curdled milk and milk freshly drawn."

Just as one should reject metaphors distant from the things to which
they are likened, so one should avoid metaphors based on ignoble things and
derive them from noble things. Sometimes, however, metaphors based on
noble things are used for base things, as in the poem of Abu Najm: "Now the
sun is setting and you have not yet finished; the sun half hidden on the
horizon is like a squinting eye or the orb of a one-eyed man." And as another
poet said in praise of king Saifu ad-Daulati:

Now the Romans knew—miserable and ill-starred as they were—
That you would confront them and their senate
And they were like mice hiding in the walls
And you were like a cat ready to pounce on them.

Aristotle says: There are other kinds of poetic expression which are
more proper for persuasion or creating belief than for arousing the imagination

or poetic representation, and they are closer to rhetorical example than metaphors and poetic representations. The kinds of poetic expression that Aristotle
mentions here occur frequently in the songs of al-Mutanabbi; for example, his
saying, "Blackening your eyes with antinomy dust is not the same as having
black eyes." And again, his saying: "When the sun has risen for you, you can
forget about Saturn." A charming example of this sort is the saying of the
poet Abu Firas al-Hamdani: "We men are not content with the mean./Either
we are at the heart of everything that goes on in the world,/Or we lie quiet in
our graves./To obtain glory we value our lives little/As a man little values
a rich dowry/When he is about to wed a lovely and honest woman."

Aristotle says: The third kind of representation is that which arouses
memories of someone. This is when the poet includes something in his poem
which makes someone recall someone else, so that when anyone reads what is
written about the other person he both remembers him and suffers and mourns
him if he is dead, or longs for him if he is alive. This is frequently found in
Arab poetry—as in the saying of the poet Mutammim ben Nuwaira:

> When someone objects: "Whatever the grave, you mourn,
> Renewing your sorrow at the grave of your friend—
> What end is there of the sorrow of graves?"
> To this I reply, "Common misfortunes recall private ones,
> Thus any grave recalls the grave of Malik
> And calls forth my own tears."

Many similar examples of commemorative songs are found among the
Arabs, when they want to arouse sad memories of the dead or express the
misfortunes and sorrows of lovers. And among the Arabs this sort of poetry
is most often used in elegies and laments.

Aristotle says: The fourth kind of representation or imitation—that is,
metaphoric "likeness"—is that which recalls that one person is like another of
the same sort. This sort of "likeness" is only used for deeds and character, as
when one says: "Lo, the second Plato approaches"—meaning that a Socrates
approaches, who is like Plato in character, in the opinion of the speaker. And
this is the kind of image used in the saying of the poet Imru'u 'l-Qais when
he remarks of a certain man: "You can recognize in him his father and his
father's whole character."

A statement of similarity is different from "likeness" based on metaphor.
Such "likeness" leaves a certain amount of doubt. But a statement or an open
assertion of similarity between two persons (that is, when one says, "this man
is like that one") is a true statement of the similarity between them and is like
the object of "accurate likening" [see above p. 351].

Aristotle says: The fifth kind is the one used by sophisticated poets and is hyperbole or lying exaggeration. This is frequently found in Arab poems. For example the saying of the poet an-Nabiga ad-Dubyani:

> He sent forth his ravening dog
> Swifter than the wind,
> And made a roaring fire
> On the stones of the street.

And again, the saying of the poet al-Mutanabbi: "Your enemy is scorned by every tongue;/The sun and the moon would be scorned/If they were your enemies." And his saying in the same work: "If your soul scorned the turning of the firmament,/Doubtless its turning would be somewhat impeded." A great many such hyperbolic expressions are found in Arab poems, but in the noblest book, that is the Koran, nothing like logical or sophistic expression occurs when this type of writing—that is, poetic writing—is being employed. However, this type of expression sometimes is put to good use in the work of poets who are learned and write about natural subjects, as one finds in the saying of al-Mutanabbi: "In the water where he watered the horses/There was no shallow place free of blood." And again, in another work:

> You do not cover yourselves in purples and silk
> For the sake of beauty.
> But to conceal your beauty within;
> You do not bind your hair for adornment
> But fearing the loss of the charms you have.

Aristotle says: The sixth kind is famous and widespread and the Arabs use it—that is, when the qualities of an animate thing are attributed to an inanimate one, like speech or reason. The Greeks call this figure *prosopopeia* [personification] that is, the invention of a new person, as when speech and the power to reply are ascribed to inanimate objects. For example, a certain poet,[5] mourning the inhabitants of a certain palace, says:

O noble house!
I am moved to tears, seeing your solitude.
And the palace trembled
Pitying me for my many tears.
I say to it: "Where, I beseech you, are those who once lived in you,
Leading a happy life, secure, and enjoying their time?"
And the building replies: "Those who live in time have passed away with time—
And they have left me and I will also pass away,
Some day, as time decides.
Nothing remains that flows with the current of time."

There are many examples of this figure used in various ways among the Arab poets. Aristotle also mentions this figure in the *Rhetoric* and says there that Homer himself often uses it.

Aristotle says: Direct representation of something being praised and "indirection" are only used for actions of the will. This technique is frequently found in the Koran—that is, praise of worthy actions of the will and blame of unworthy ones—but it is rarely found in Arab poetry. And the Koran prohibits reading of poetic fictions except some few songs that tend to satirize or rebuke vices, and tragic commendation of virtues and encouragement to practice them.

[Ch. XVII] Aristotle says: The excellence of poetic narration and what brings it to the fulfilling of its goal is when the poet in his stories and narratives writes so vividly that the audience considers what is narrated almost before its mind and eyes, so that it both understands what is narrated, and also does not fail simultaneously to understand things which are not narrated. This is frequently apparent in skilled and experienced poets. However, the techniques of making the thing vividly present to the imagination is not found in Arab poems except in elegaic songs which treat the actions or deeds of lovers, or when the poets wish only to achieve imaginative accuracy. For example, there is the song of the poet Imru'u l-Qais on the dialogue of two lovers:

> I burned for a flowing stream
> When I knew her husband was sleeping;
> But she, murmuring denial, said:
> "Do you wish to ruin me?"
> Do you not know that there are still people awake?
> I replied: "I am tormented by a fire
> Which I wish to extinguish."

Another example which employs only accuracy in the imaginative representation is the saying of the poet Du'r-Rumma describing a fire being kindled by striking flints:

> A glowing spark, glinting like an eye,
> Leaps forth as the blow is struck.
> I say: "Choose a nest for it to rest in.
> Supply dry tinder
> Summon the breath of the wind to rouse it.
> Hold your hand around it lest it go out."

The Arabs also use this technique in their poems when they narrate various events, such as wars and the like, where their stories can be tested. Mutanabbi the poet was best in this kind of representation, as is clear from his poems. It is said of him that he did not want to describe any deeds of king Saifu ad-Daulati, his master, that occurred when he himself was not present. He understood things that he witnessed for himself better than the things told him by others. Indeed, everyone does best in reporting those things that he has understood for himself and almost seen first-hand with all their accidents and circumstances. Such a man can best represent and express poetic figures—that is, through imaginative imitation and meter and melody.

Aristotle says: To list the kinds or modes of direct representation would be too long and take too much time. He means by this that there is a great diversity of the kind of poetry among the various nations and a great deal of it.

[Ch. XVIII] Aristotle says: Certain parts of every song of praise constitute the tying together, and certain parts the resolution. The thing that is closest to the parts of the Greek poems which constitute the "tying together" is the part of the song that we call "following" [see p. 361]. This is the part in which the elegiac section leads into the tragic section [i.e., the song of praise]. And, as has been said several times, this introduction has the nature of a prólogue to the other material of the song of praise so that the praise will seem more beautiful.

The resolution is the separation of one part from another; that is, it permits them to stand separately. The "tying together" is very frequent in modern poems, as can be seen in Abu Tammam:

> I have passed my year with camels
> In the boiling heat and caves of the desert.
> I have made a feast-day for the birds of the air
> With songs for dead animals.
> Far from me were the gardens of solace.
> Now, therefore, I have finally found rest
> Thinking of songs of praise.

After this prologue he begins the principal subject, extolling the man he intended to praise. Many examples of this sort are found among the Arabs.

The resolution, however, sometimes comes in without any preamble in connection with the principal subject of praise. This technique is frequently found among the Arabs.

Aristotle says: There are four species of poems of praise. There are simple ones, and there are the ones already discussed. The first is "indirectness"; the second is "directness"; the third is "passion" as they write about men in Hades, for there one finds continual sadness and inconsolable sorrow. The fourth is composed of two or all three of these. You should know that we do not find examples of those four species of poems of praise relating to acts of the will among the Arab poets. But they are frequent in holy writ—that is the Koran.

Aristotle says: Some poets are good at writing in long meters and some at writing short or brief meters. These are the forms that we call "curtailed." The reason is that a good and skilled poet should describe and delineate things according to their proper qualities and their true natures. These are varied according to the quantity and scarcity of the accidents and proper qualities pertaining to the things being treated. When the poet does this, the representation is good and apt, and the imaginative stimulation is not in excess of the qualities of the things and their true natures. And certain men are skilled by custom or nature at causing things to be imagined that have few proper qualities. Such poets make "curtailed" poems—not extended or lengthy ones.

Other poets have the opposite inclination. That is, they are excellent in meters of long lines. They are skilled by custom or nature at delineating things that have many accidents and proper qualities. Or it happens that both aids—that is, custom and nature—are joined in these poets.

Aristotle says: Certain representations and imaginative works are appropriate and adapted to lengthy meters and rhythms, and certain to short meters. At times, the meter or rhythm is appropriate and adapted to the subject and not to the imagery of the poem, and at times the reverse is true, and at times the meter and rhythm are inappropriate to both. Examples of these kinds of verse are difficult to find in Arab poems or cannot be found at all since the Arabs have only a few kinds of meter.

Aristotle says: Among the devices which accompany or relate to the basic materials of poetry are extrinsic ones like appearance, vocal inflections, and the rest which have already been mentioned. For the most part, poets employ these devices in songs involving passion. These are lamentations and other forms like those about men in Hades and in other similar situations.

[Ch. XIX] We have now discussed the parts of poems that are intrinsic and based on truth, which are the parts from which poems are composed and created. Therefore let us now discuss those extrinsic devices which add to the excellence of poems. Speaking generally, we say that these are types of gesture that are called for by those compositions called "poems of passion." Therefore when these devices are used, they should be used with this type of poetry. These types of gesture manifest the passions which the speech indicates, as though they most certainly happened.

You already know, from the *Rhetoric,* about speeches of passion [i.e. *pathos*] and the kinds of passion which these speeches use [cf. *Rhetoric* II]. These gestures are really more proper to the *Rhetoric* than to the *Poetics*. The passions expressed by rhetorical or poetic speech are fear, anger, love, hate, joy, and sadness, and the rest of these motions of the soul which are listed in the *Rhetoric*. It is clear that just as these kinds of speech induce these passions, likewise, the appearance and gestures of the speaker indicate the presence of the things arousing these passions and thereby arouse the passions themselves. The viewer or listener is therefore moved and perturbed and suffers. But one must not use these forms and gestures in poetry except in poetry of passion, either to exaggerate or diminish something or for sorrow or arousing fear—since the poetry of praise based on passionate speech employs these devices, as has already been said. They are used especially in passionate speeches that are not true—that is, which do not create vivid images. Passionate speeches that are vivid and imaginative and appropriate to the object of the speech do not need to use, in addition to speech, those things that enhance the poem extrinsically. Rather, they debase such speeches since they are only used in speeches that are too imperfect to achieve their objective unless extrinsic devices are added. They are defective and bad in themselves and without that efficacy that marked the speech of a certain poet[6] who wanted to stir up wrath in the soul of King Kortubi against a certain steward of his household. Before a great multitude of his people, he said to the king: "He through whom you reign and are exalted is considered a liar by your steward." Because this speech was effective in itself in arousing the wrath of the king, it does not need acting or gesturing on the part of the speaker.

Aristotle says: And sometimes the poet may use the extrinsic forms and figures in any sort of speech when he has been forced to do so by those who know the art of facial expression [i.e., actors]. I understand by figures of language or speech, the figures of declaration and of question and of petition and refusal. The figure of a man declaring something is different from that of one asking, and of one petitioning from one refusing. By this criterion, Aristotle can reject the figures that are extrinsic, since these make poetic speeches base. Therefore they should not be considered part of the art of poetry, but of some other art.

[Ch. XX] Aristotle says: Poetic speech consists of seven elements: syllable, copula or conjunction, disjunction, noun, verb, case, speech. The elements of syllables are indivisible—that is, letters. Not, however, all letters, but only those by nature fitted to the composition of syllables. This is the simplest of those elements from which speech is composed. Indeed, the cries or sounds of beasts cannot be divided into letters, and therefore we say that their cries are not composed of letters, nor is any part of their cry a letter.

The parts of a sound which form a syllable are the vowel and the consonant. There are two kinds of consonant—that which is not extended when spoken —like T in "TA" and "TE," and that which is extended, like R in "RE" and SC in "SCIN" and others, which are called semivowels. Vowels are sounds created by vibrations of the lips or teeth or some part of the throat or mouth. There is a vowel that is composite but inseparable. I understand by this that it is impossible to separate or detach the vowel from a consonant. And, I think, those letters are called vowels that among the Arabs are called "motives" and "letters of extension or protraction" and "liquid" or "soft" letters.

A semivowel is a letter that has a certain extension like a vowel but does not have an audible sound by itself. A consonant is a letter that makes a sound combined with a vowel but does not have an audible sound by itself. I understand here that it has an audible sound when it is joined to another and sounds along with it. And consonants have no sound except when joined to letters that sound, like *el* and *eb*. These consonants are what the Arabs call "quiet" and "mute" letters. They are varied according to the various configurations of the mouth and other places where they are produced and from which they come and according to short and long and acute and heavy, and generally according to the extremes and the means between them that are found in sounds and in rhymes and meters and the various poetic forms.

A syllable is a non-significant sound composed of vowels and consonants. What Aristotle says of letters is true. It is impossible to produce the sound of *el* or *em* with a single letter. Likewise the marks called *fatha* [f] and *damma* [d]; and no sound can be made except by joining both kinds of letter. However the existence of the sound *fatha* or *damma* is primary, and the vowel sound is secondary. In general, you should know that a sound is made up of two elements, one of which is, as it were, the matter—that is, the consonant—and the other the form—that is, the vowel. And those who speak Arabic call vowels "motive," "extensive," and "soft."

Aristotle says: A conjunction is a composite sound that does not mean anything by itself, like *and, then,* and *also,* and in general words of like meaning that are like the cords tying the parts of the statement together or else come at the beginning of a statement like *that* and *indeed*; and conditional expressions which establish continuity, like *if, when,* and the like.

Aristotle says: A disjunction is a composite sound that does not mean anything by itself and either separates words from each other, like *either* and *or,* and similar words; or indicates an exception, like *except, except for,* and similar words; or indicates contrast, like *but, however, but indeed,* and similar words. And these come either at the beginning or end or in the middle of the statement. Here, in our language, we understand by "a sound not meaningful by itself" simple sounds which have meaning when they are joined to other sounds— like particles of conjunction—not simple sounds like letters. For sounds that have meaning by themselves and are composed of several sounds—three or four or more—according to the rules of language are nouns and verbs. A noun is a sound or word that has meaning by itself and signifies a definite thing without an associated time concept. And none of the parts of a noun mean any of the separate parts of the thing. This applies to both simple and compound nouns. Nouns which are compounds of two nouns are not used so that one of their parts refers to some part of the thing to which the noun compounded from the two simple nouns refers—for example *equiferus* [*equi* + *ferus* = wild horse].

A verb is a sound or word that means something and includes the concept of the time related to what is meant. And none of its parts signifies any part of the thing meant. The temporal element of a verb distinguishes it from a noun. *Man* and *white* have no time concept; but *runs* and *ran* indicate present and past time.

Aristotle says: Case or inflection pertains to noun and to statement and to verb. An inflected noun is related to another noun as *of Socrates* or *to Socrates*. An inflected statement is, for example, one in the imperative or interrogative. And an inflected verb is past or future. An "upright" verb is one in the present tense. This is mostly proper to the Greek language. A statement is a composite expression each part of which has meaning by itself. It is called a "statement" according to one of two criteria. Either because it refers to a single thing or idea —like "man is an animal"—or because there is one factor binding it together —as we say that a syllogism is one statement and a rhetorical oration is one, and a poetical composition is one.

[Ch. XXI] Aristotle says: There are two kinds of noun: the simple, which is not composed of meaningful parts; and the compound, which is composed of meaningful parts although by them is meant a single thing that the nouns of which the word is composed do not mean—like *famulus solis* ["planet"] or *armiger* [knight].

Aristotle says: Every noun is either native to its language, or borrowed from another, or used metaphorically, or coined, or shortened [i.e. compressed], or extended [i.e. elongated], or altered. A native noun is common to its nation. A borrowed noun is one taken by poets and interpolated into their language from another, as happens in languages that are contiguous and exchange words with one another. A noun used metaphorically is when, for example, the word for the species is used for the genus—as when "slaughter" is called "death,"— or the genus is used for the species—as when "change" is called "motion"; or the name of the species is used for another—as when "robbery" is called "theft"; or when, in an analogy, that which is related to the second term is used for the third, or that which is related to the third is used for the fourth. [i.e., when, in the analogy *a* is to *b* as *c* is to *d*, *a* is used for *c*, or *b* is used for *d*.] For example, the ancients used to call "age" the "evening of life" and "evening" the "old age of the day." Clearly, the relation of old age to life is like the relation of evening to day.

A coined or made-up noun is one invented by the poet having its own special meaning, and the poet is the first one to use it. Such nouns are not found in Arabic. But they are found often in arts newly invented. And at times modern poets use them, basing their derivation on metaphor—as al-Mutanabbi did when speaking of a man prompt to do what he intended: "As soon as you think of a word in the present, you try to make it pass into the past." And at times they use an unorthodox inflexion, as when the impersonal verb *oportet* ["it is proper that . . ."] is used with a personal ending—*oporteo* ["I should"] or *oportuisti* ["you should have"].

Elongated and compressed words are not found among the Arabs.

An ornamental word is one whose parts are adorned by a special accent.

It has already been observed that by an "elongated word" Aristotle meant a word altered by addition or subtraction of a syllable. And although we have not remarked on the fact, Aristotle is referring to nouns that are difficult to pronounce. But it is evident from what Aristotle says that such nouns are composed by the Greeks from definite syllables. And a "compressed noun," in my opinion, is the kind that he called "varied." Also it seems from his discussion that this type is altered by cutting off a syllable—what we call *syncope*. "Altered" nouns, however, are metaphors based on resemblance—for example, the Greeks call a certain star "the vulture"—or else based on contrast—as when they call the sun "the dark orb"—or else on consequence as when they call a garland [*sepum* = ?*sertum*] "softness" and rain, "crops."

[Ch. XXII] Aristotle says: The speech that is easiest to understand is speech that is familiar and customary, which is not obscure to anyone. This is achieved by nouns that are familiar and from standard usage. The nouns that he refers to in his treatise are called "truthful" and "designative" and "standard." This is what you find in this poet and that. . . . I.e., poets who were famous among the Greeks. The reader should here refer to Arab poets in whose poems this kind of diction is found.

Aristotle says: Orations of moderate praise are composed of standard nouns and others—that is, metaphors and altered nouns and enigmas; for when a poem is wholly deprived of proper and standard words it becomes a riddle and an enigma. Riddles and enigmas are composed of borrowed and obscure—that is, metaphorical—nouns, and metaphors, and slang and analogies. An enigma is a speech that includes meanings which are impossible or difficult to reduce to a single sense. This is frequently found among Arab poets, especially in the poems of Duromati.

Noble poetic speech which is moderate or restrained is composed of nouns that are especially excellent according to usage and from the other kinds. And when the poet wants to say anything plainly and clearly he should use nouns that have a special clarity. And when he wants to present something as delightful and admirable he should use nouns of the other type. For this reason, we ridicule anyone who wants plainness and clarity and uses obscure nouns or slang or borrowed or coined ones. Likewise we ridicule anyone who wants to make anything delightful or admirable and uses words or nouns that are commonplace or trite, though a poet should beware the excessive use of unusual nouns. For he needs to make moderate use of enigmatic speech to prevent his speech from becoming wholly enigmatic. Also he should beware the excessive use of trite speech in order to avoid straying from the path of poetry into commonplace speech.

Aristotle says: The resemblance of certain words to certain others in quantity [i.e. sound] and the similar meanings of certain words, and their stress should be common to and involve all of the words that are in the poetic speech. And we find that some poets use "exact" words in places where they are ridiculous, but their poems do not lack the other two elements—that is accent and rhyme and likeness in quantity. This is emphatically true in all kinds of poetry. But poems that use a variety of kinds of nouns do this most obviously.

The resemblance of words in quantity which he mentions is the similarity of certain words in number of letters, whether they agree in respect to the ·vhole word or to a part. Poets of our time call this resemblance and kinship.

Resemblance, or rhyme, has many varieties. Either the resemblance is complete, as when a poet[7] says: "Don't you see *death*? / I know *death* spares no one." Or it is in a part of the word and a part of the meaning. Or it is in part of the word and in all of the meaning. Or it is in all of the word. Or it is in part of the word only. Or it is all of the meaning or it is part of the meaning only.

An example of resemblance in part of the word and part of the meaning is provided by different forms of the same stem, as in the poet al-Mutanabbi: "*Giving* GROWS to the GROWTH of the *giver;* and *givers* are multiplied by the GROWTH of *giving.*"

An example of resemblance in part of the word and in all of the meaning is the common expression, "*Strike,* and may the *striking* be hard." Analogous nouns are an example of resemblance in all the word and part of the meaning or significance. Poets often use these. And an example of resemblance in all the word only is when one says: "One dog with the troops *dines*; / Another in the stars *shines.*" [In Latin, *castris* and *astris*]. And an example of resemblance in part of the word only is the saying of Seneca: "What is born with me [*oritur*] dies with me [*moritur*]." And an example of resemblance in part of the meaning only is different words signifying the same thing according to different manners of speaking and different roots—like *homo* [man] and *anthropos* [man]. The etymology of homo is "*factus ex homo*" [made from earth]; of *anthropos, arbor inversa* [inverted tree]. Yet they are names of the same thing.

Rhyme among the Arabs is resemblance in quantity and in part of the word. It occurs in a single letter, the last, or two letters—and the moderns call this "consequence."

"Doubling" occurs in a speech in four ways. The first gives the thing and something like it, such as "sun and moon" or "night and day." The second gives the thing and something associated with its use, like "bow and arrow" or "horse and bridle." The third operates by analogy, like "king and god"—and an analogy pertains among four things. The poet al-Kumait is to be criticized in this respect in the poem praising his mistress for the serenity or calm of her face and the sweetness of her kiss, saying: "Complete in her face is serenity [serenit*as*] / Her kiss salivates so sweetly [suavit*as*]." For there is no similarity between serenity of face and sweetness of saliva.

And certain lines of Imru'u 'l-Qais to someone who criticized him are of this sort:

> As if a horse I had never ascended [*ascendissem*]
>   For the sake of pleasure;
> As if a girl I had never attended [*tenuissem*]
>   Adorned with bracelets;
> As if a barrel of strong wine
>   I had never upended [*salutassem*];
> As if a horse after many laps
>   Back to the race I had not remanded [*incitassem*].

Truly, the connection of these lines seems awkward. It is clear that the poet ought to have written in the reverse order. That is, the first two lines should have been the beginning of the second quatrain, and the two lines that begin the second quatrain should have come first.

A poem of al-Mutanabbi praising his master for self-control is of the same sort:

> You stayed, and your death was certain if you stayed
> As if you were in the eye of sleeping danger.
> Your brave soldiers passed by you, wounded and beaten;
> Because of your calm expression, they were encouraged.

As before, there would be metrical proportion in this, I think, if the first line came third and the third line came first. And the same thing has been said of the poetry of Omir-'l-Kaisi.

Aristotle says: Speech is changed or varied from truthful or standard speech when nouns are put in it that have resemblance in respect to accent and quantity, and that are borrowed, and that use the other devices of variation. A sign that poetic speech should be varied is that when truthful or standard speech is "varied" it is called a poem or poetic speech and it is found to have the effect of poetry. For example, one might say: "After we finished what needed doing in that place and the surveyor had measured the angles, we began to discuss what had recently happened to us. And the mules were sweating from the hardness of the journey."[8] This speech can be converted into a poem by avoiding standard diction through changing some of the words, as if one said: "We were conferring and we were arriving, and our carriers were sweating with effort."

Many similar speeches are found among the Arab poets. When you have carefully considered moving poems, you will find that they have elements of these kinds of ornament—that is, words rhyming together and meanings that clash or vice versa; and the other kinds of alteration, already mentioned, and metaphors and other figurative expressions and enigmatic obscurities, and the like. Speech that lacks these has nothing of a poetic nature except meter.

Variation from proper and standard speech is achieved by accents and rhyme and fitting metaphor and through "likeness" and, in general, through any sort of departure in language from standard usage—like addition and deletion of syllables, and inversions of syntax, and change from affirmation to negation and the reverse, and in general from a form to its opposite, and through all the techniques that fall under the heading of poetic license.

Examples of all of these devices are obvious enough, nor are you ignorant of the more obvious and common species, both simple and composite, included in the general categories. It would be extremely difficult to list all the species. Therefore Aristotle was content with a general summary.

The best of all styles is the one which is the most easy and clear and convincing. It is found only in the work of elegant and learned poets. Indeed, a sign of their skill is that they can use the techniques of style in a way that is convincing and clear. Then the poems are more readily accepted by the audience and the objects of the poetic speeches are understood; and they lead the soul of the audience wherever they want.

When the variation is emphatic, it leads to excellence in imagery and at the same time, a more complete understanding of the thing represented. And even among sluggish and stolid men, well proportioned variation produces moderate comprehension. For example, there is the saying from the Koran: "Until you can tell the black thread from the white." Certain readers thought that a real thread was being referred to until it was revealed further on that the reference should be understood as to the thread of dawn separating day from night.

Aristotle says: Compound nouns are proper for the meter in which the praises of good men of the past are sung, when the praise is directed to a specific individual. Compound nouns are rarely produced in the Arab language—as if one noun said "Abochemyn," deriving the noun from "Abus + chemzin."

Borrowed words or idioms—that is, words taken from foreign languages —are proper for the meter in which the poet foretells the future, or describes the delights of good men or the terrible misfortunes of bad ones.

These are two manners of poem known to the Greeks.

Metaphors are words used in a new sense and are appropriate for poems in which proverbs and wise maxims and famous and familiar histories are told.

[Ch. XXIII] Aristotle says: We have now sufficiently discussed the art of praise and the things common to the manners of poetry based on "likeness" and others. The procedure or method for historical poems in reference to the beginning, middle, and end is the same as the method of the parts of the art of praise. The same is true except when the representation is not of deeds themselves but of the historical periods in which they were done. In these historical poems one represents with historical accuracy the characters and conditions of men who preceded the moderns and the change of authority and kings and conditions and times.

Representation of this sort is rare in Arab literature. However, it is extremely frequent in the lawbooks. Aristotle mentions poets who were good at this sort of poetry, and praises Homer highly for his skill in the genre. Among the Arab poems that are commendable for this kind of writing is the song of al-Aswad ben Ya'fur about times gone by and the vicissitudes of those who were once glorious.

> What hope now that the family of Mauthairrikin
> Has left its home?
> Leaving the land of Egidin and Alkawarniky
> And Scedicy and Baraky
> And the fortress of Scendedin,
> They descended to Enkyratin
> Where the waters of the Euphrates
> Coming from Etwetin
> Descended over them.
> The winds flooded their dwellings
> Rushing over them as though from a sluice.
> I see now how the sweetness of life
> And all its joys
> Will one day
> Cease and perish.[9]

[Ch. XXIV] Aristotle says: The parts of this kind of poem are the parts of the art of moderate praise—"indirectness" and directness, and the composite form using both of them. And at times it uses passions, as happens in the art of moderate praise.

He mentions differences between the art of praise and other kinds of poetry among the Greeks and the special practices that the other kinds of poetry follow in respect to accents and parts and representation and length, and that certain poems have longer meters and greater capacity than others. And he says which poets are proficient in these matters and which not; and in all these matters he praises Homer. All these matters are proper to the Greeks and certain ones are not found among the Arabs, either because they are not common to all or most nations or because it happens that in these areas the Arabs are by nature untalented. This seems most likely. Indeed, Aristotle did not concentrate, in the *Poetics,* on what was peculiar to the Greeks, but on what was naturally common to all nations.

Aristotle says: That part of a poem which speaks for the poet should be like a short prologue and brief in comparison to the section of the poem in which the representation occurs—as Homer did. Homer delayed only a short time in giving his prologue, and afterwards spaciously and copiously treated the subject of the representation, although he did not include anything in this beyond what was usual. For extraordinary things are received badly.

He says this, I believe, because different nations have different customs in their "likenings" on account of subjects common to each and unknown to other nations, from which each draws metaphors. For example, there is the sandy desert called Zorabim where many snakes and lizards live. It seems to those who approach it from a distance to be a lake, and the snakes and lizards appear to be fish. Therefore the Arabs commonly say about someone deceived in a similar way, "You have seen the fish and water of Zorabim." The saying in the Koran is based on this: "Those who abandon a task they have undertaken are like viewers of Zorabim."

Aristotle says: When a speech is composed that has no variation or representation, then words of clear meaning should be used; that is, words that refer directly to the things themselves, not to the contraries of the things or to different things. Their composition or structure should have the familiar quality much admired among the Greeks and their pronunciation should be easy.

It seems that there are many poems of this type which have what we call "decorous style" in Arabic. The style is also decorous when the speech offers open truth and is clear. True speech which deserves critical favor uses little ornamentation and few poetic metaphors.

[Ch. XXV] Aristotle says: The poetic errors for which the poet must answer are six in number. The first is when his representation offers something that is not possible—or rather something that is impossible. There is an example of this in the work of Ibnu 'l-Hutazz describing a half moon and saying, "Look at her. She is like a little silver ship weighed down with a cargo of amber." This is indeed impossible. However, it is pleasing because of the strength of the simile, and because the poet does not intend it to impel the reader to do anything or to prevent him from doing something. Also, the representation should be through something that exists or people think exists—like the representation of bad men as demons—or through something where existence is possible, either for the greater part of the poem or on the average. The ways existence may be expressed are more proper to rhetoric than to poetics.

The second kind of poetic error is distorted representation, as happens when a painter adds a limb to the shape he is painting that does not fit it or puts it in an inappropriate place. For example, if anyone should paint the back legs of a quadruped on the front or the front on the back. Examples of this error in Arab poetry should be carefully examined. In my view, the diction of certain modern poets of Andalusia is close to this error, when they describe a wounded horse returning from battle with the line, "Over his ears was a third ear which the flashing sword had made."

The third error is to represent rational beings by irrational ones. This also can be answered. But, indeed, there is little truth in such representation and much falsehood unless the poet adds characteristics which rational beings have in common with irrational ones. And at times this is acceptable because of custom. As, for example, the Arab custom of comparing women to goats and wild cows and youths to young kids.

The fourth error is to compare a thing to its contrary or something resembling its contrary. For example the Arabs customarily say of women of modest demeanor that they have "sick eye-lids." They intend thereby to prove the beauty of the eyes and the modesty of the glance. Another example, close to this, is the Arab saying, "They stretched out in the evening like men sick from too much generosity."[10] And again, "His tunic was ragged and he entered the house like one sick from shame."[11] All these examples use words contrary to the fitting attributes, and yet they deserve favor because of customary forms of speech.

The fifth error is to use words having two different but equally common meanings—like *percussio* meaning both the act of striking a blow and the sensation of the man struck, and other similar cases which are frequent in various languages.

The sixth error is to abandon the poetic representation and employ rhetorical persuasion and speeches creating belief, and especially when the speech is of the humble style, for moderate persuasion. The poem of Imru'u 'l-Qais making excuses for his cowardice is of this sort, where he says, "My right-hand men did not flee because of fear, but because of longing for their home." At times this sort of writing is not improper when it has any degree of probability or truth. For example, there is the saying of another poet[12] making excuses for his flight from battle: "God knows that I did not leave the conflict until my horse was badly wounded by a poisoned arrow. I knew that by staying I would be destroyed and would die without hurting the enemy. / Thus I drew back from them hoping for a time of revenge on the day of their ruin." Here the expression is decorous, especially because of its direct truth, although there is a small amount of variation by metaphor in it. Because of such passages, there is that saying,

O people and society of Arabs—
You are wise in making any deed seem attractive.
You even know how to make flight from battle seem attractive.

Aristotle says: There are thus six kinds of error and an equal number of answers opposed to them. Therefore there are twelve kinds and topics pertaining to and proper to the poet—that is, six errors and six answers.

Examples of answers are not found among the Arabs, since our poets did not distinguish—in fact did not even know—those kinds of poetry.

This is the sum of what I, Averroes, have been able to understand of the subjects that Aristotle discusses in his poetic speeches common to all manners or kinds of poetry and especially of the art of praise, or tragedy. The rest of what he discusses in his book concerning the differences among the other Greek kinds of poetry and their differences from tragedy is proper to the Greeks. Moreover, we find nothing of certain matters which he mentioned in this book, as it has reached us. This means that the book was not completely translated and that it lacks discussion of the differences among many kinds of poetry which the Greeks wrote. Aristotle promised to speak of all these in the prologue of the *Poetics*. What is missing from the common kinds of poetry is a discussion of the art of reprehension or blame. However, the relevant points seem sufficiently obvious from what was said about the art of praise, since things can be known from their opposites.

You will see as you consider what I have written here that what writers in Arabic said about the rules of poetry is trivial and slight in comparison to what is found in this book of Aristotle and in his *Rhetoric*. As al-Farabi says about this, "It should not escape you how those rules were applied to the poems of the Greeks; and you should not fail to observe where the Greeks were right and where they were wrong in formulating their rules."

Here we bring our present task to an end.

The End. Thanks be to God. The year of our Lord 1256, the 17th day of March, in the noble city of Toledo.

GEOFFREY OF VINSAUF

(fl. ca. 1200)

INTRODUCTION

The *Poetria Nova* was written between 1200 and 1216. Its author was an Englishman. He was also the author of three other works: the *Documentum de Modo et Arte Dictandi et Versificandi*, the *Summa de Coloribus Rhetoricis*, and a short poem, the *Causa Magistri Guafredi Vinesauf*. From these works we learn that he studied at Paris, taught at Hampton in England, and at one point in his career made a trip to Rome. The *Poetria* has two dedications. The first is to Pope Innocent III, whom Geoffrey had obviously never met. The second, which occurs at the end of the work, is to a certain William, identified in two early manuscripts as (1) William of Wrotham, administrator of the navy and the stannaries, or (2) William, Bishop of London. Since this second dedication is chiefly an appeal for patronage, it implies no more familiarity with its recipient than the dedication to Innocent III.

Some fifty manuscripts of the *Poetria Nova* exist, twenty of them English. Evidently it was a popular textbook. In a well known passage in the *Nun's Priest's Tale* Chaucer salutes its author and refers to one of its more lugubrious set pieces, the "Lament" on the death of King Richard I:

> O Gaufred, deere maister soverayn,
> That whan thy worthy kyng Richard was slayn
> With shot, compleynedest his deeth so soore,
> Why ne hadde I now thy sentence and thy loore
> The Friday for to chide, as diden ye? (ll. 527–31)

Clearly, the reference is ironic. It suggests that the name of Geoffrey was familiar to Chaucer's readers. It also suggests that Geoffrey was regarded with amused contempt, perhaps as a kind of medieval Edgar Guest.

The *Poetria* is written in quantitative dactylic hexameter. The versification is hardly inspired, but it is sufficiently accurate for Geoffrey to make a little

123

joke in his dedication about the impossibility of fitting the name of Innocent III (Innŏcēns) into the meter. Geoffrey's *Documentum* covers much the same ground as the *Poetria* but is in prose. One's first impression is that we have here yet another example of the medieval practice of making verse redactions of prose works. However, the case is not quite this simple even if we could strain our credulity to the point of believing that Geoffrey would have versified the *Documentum* simply as an exercise. The *Documentum* is more down-to-earth than the *Poetria*. It lacks the dedication, the section comparing literary creation to architecture, the section on memory, and the epilogue. Its style is rather dry in comparison to the florid, discursive style of the *Poetria,* which is evidently designed to illustrate Geoffrey's principles about "serious" and "weighty" style; and its illustrations are brief. For example, it has nothing comparable to the long poem on Richard I illustrating the figures of amplification and the still longer poem to the Pope illustrating the figures of thought. On the other hand, there is important material in the *Documentum* that is not in the *Poetria*. The *Documentum* has an extensive treatment of transition (*prosecutio*) from the beginning of a work to its main body, which is balanced later by a section on endings. It also has a section on rules common to both the easy and difficult styles and discussions of how to treat "familiar matter," of inventing words, and of "humorous matter." Finally, there is a section on the low, middle, and elevated styles. In addition to this material, the *Documentum* uses much more quotation and citation than the *Poetria*. Horace's *Ars Poetica* is quoted or cited 22 times, Ovid 9 times, and Vergil, Statius, Juvenal, Sidonius, and Boethius one or more times. There are also allusions to Seneca, Lucan, Claudian, and Vegetius Renatus, a fourth-century authority on warfare.

This list of differences suggests several points about the two works. First, it suggests that the *Documentum* preceded the *Poetria*. Not only is it stylistically less ambitious, it is also less complete. The standard departments of rhetoric are invention, disposition, elocution, delivery, and memory. Assuming that the section of the *Poetria* comparing the conception of a work to the plan of a building refers generally to invention, the *Poetria* deals with all five departments. The *Documentum* has nothing which could be interpreted as referring to invention and lacks a discussion of memory.

Second, the *Documentum* relies more heavily on authority than the *Poetria*. In the *Documentum* Geoffrey quotes Horace's *Ars Poetica* frequently. This sometimes gives the *Documentum* greater range than the *Poetria* simply because Horace knew more about poetry than Geoffrey. But this advantage was probably not apparent to Geoffrey himself. In the *Poetria* we can detect at most two echoes of Horace. Beyond these, the discussion and examples are almost entirely Geoffrey's own, although, of course, his list of figures and their definitions come chiefly from the *Ad Herennium*, as do the same materials in the *Documentum*. Evidently, there was substantial assimilation of the *Ars Poetica* between the *Documentum* and the *Poetria*.

Third, if we add up the differences, it seems most likely that the *Documentum* should be understood as a general treatise intended for exercises in essay-writing and poetry, while the *Poetria* is a treatise intended specifically for aspiring poets. This would explain the large amount of technical matter in the *Documentum* on transitions, on the three styles, and on treating "familiar matter," as well as the more theoretical tone and florid style of the *Poetria.*

Neither the *Documentum* or the *Poetria* includes specific internal evidence on its placement in the trivium. The heavy reliance of both works on the *Ad Herennium* for treatment of the figures would suggest an allegiance with rhetoric rather than grammar. Moreover, the title *Poetria Nova* associates that work with the *Ad Herennium,* which was known during the Middle Ages as the *Rhetorica Nova,* in contrast to the *De Inventione,* known as the *Rhetorica Vetus.*

On the other hand, Horace's *Ars Poetica* was known as the *Poetria* during the Middle Ages, and it was generally understood as a treatise on poetry as it pertains to grammar. The extensive quotation from Horace in the *Documentum* and the title *Poetria Nova* suggest that the works should be associated with Horace and grammar rather than the rhetorical tradition in spite of their extensive use of rhetorical lore. The *Poetria* thus is Geoffrey's "New Art of Poetry" and is related to "reading the poets" rather than to rhetoric. Finally, there is the fact that the "theory of determinations" and "theory of conversions" found in both the *Documentum* and the *Poetria* have no precedent in the *Ad Herennium* and are clearly derived from grammar. While none of this evidence is conclusive, it supports the idea that the *Poetria* was intended for the grammar curriculum as a supplement to the *accessus* literature and the *artes metricae.*

The *Poetria Nova* has the following outline:

    I.   Dedication to Innocent III (lines 1–42)
   II.   Idea vs. subject matter in poetry (43–86)
  III.   Arrangement (87–201)
   IV.   Amplification and abbreviation (202–736)
    V.   Ornaments of style: difficult ornaments (737–1093)
   VI.   Easy ornaments (1094–1587)
  VII.   Theory of conversions (1588–1761)
 VIII.   Theory of determinations (1762–1841)
   IX.   Miscellaneous prescriptions; decorum (1842–1968)
    X.   Memory (1969–2031)
   XI.   Delivery (2032–2066)
  XII.   Epilogue (2067–2117)

The prominence given to amplification and abbreviation relates the *Poetria* to classical epideictic (or demonstrative) rhetoric. This branch of rhetoric was set aside for "praise and blame" according to a formula that appears as early as Aristotle's *Rhetoric* (I.3), and the figures of amplification and abbreviation—that is, heightening and diminution, or, occasionally, expansiveness and brevity—were always deemed especially appropriate to it. As legal and political oratory lost ground in the late classical period, and as ornamentation for its own sake became fashionable, epideictic rhetoric gained in favor. Its standard forms, particularly the encomium, epithalamium, and epicede (funeral oration), were taken over bodily as forms for occasional poetry, and its florid style was imitated assiduously by the poets.

To some degree the *Poetria* is a distant echo of that late classical fashion. The poetic strategies that it teaches are primarily for display, and its extended examples are clearly epideictic in nature—for example, the eulogy of Pope Innocent III, the lament for Richard and, later, for the Fall of Man, the generalized description of a beautiful woman, and the like. The basic devices are amplification and abbreviation, and the difficult and easy figures are subordinate to them. They are "ornaments" and "adornments" of the basic theme which enhance it like "a precious garment" (line 756), "a luminous mist" (1050), "blooms in the field" (1225), and the "colors" of a painter (*passim*). Although Geoffrey is not writing a treatise on epideictic rhetoric but a textbook for the grammar curriculum, praise and blame are never far from his mind. His first example of amplification is an example of "rebuke" (277). The theme of rebuke is repeated in references to "assailing" an adversary (433) and "rebuking" error (456). Conversely, we learn after the description of a banquet, "in this way you may celebrate the feasts of kings" (667), and that hyperbole "diminishes or heightens eulogy to a remarkable degree' (1020). Converting adjectives to nouns "intensifies or diminishes eulogy to a marked degree. Denunciation and panegyric offer suitable occasions for this technique" (1660–64). It is clear, incidentally, from the preceding quotation that amplification and abbreviation are understood by Geoffrey in their classical sense of heightening or diminishing a subject, and the fact that they make a poem longer or shorter is a secondary consideration.

If we stand back from the details, it is clear that a thematic motif runs through the *Poetria*. It is the motif of the primacy of the intellectual conception of the work over its materials. Geoffrey's artist is no Longinian genius excited to ecstasy and moved to utterance by a supernatural enthusiasm. In the ancient debate between the claims of genius (or inspiration) and craftsmanship, Geoffrey stands with Cicero and Horace: "Three things perfect a work: artistic theory by whose law you may be guided; experience, which you may foster by practice; and superior writers whom you may imitate. Theory makes the craftsman sure; experience makes him ready; imitation makes him versatile; the three together produce the greatest craftsman" (1705–9). Talent is needed, but without proper training and experience it will be useless. Geoffrey's artist is an artisan—an architect, to use his initial metaphor—rather than a vehicle for transcendent revelation: "The mind's hand shapes the entire house before the body's hand builds it. Its mode of being is archetypal before it is actual. Poetic art may see in this analogy the

law to be given to poets" (47ff.). The material is like wax made pliant by the
heat of the creative process: "If intense concentration enkindle native ability,
the material is soon made pliant by the mind's fire" (215ff.). Words have
internal and external qualities—meaning and sound—and the internal quality
must receive first consideration: "First examine the mind of a word, and only
then its face" (740). This does not mean that the adornments of the rhetorical
figures are without value. Rather, it sets up a concept of decorum according to
which the outer garment must suit the inner nature of the words in the composition: "There are judges of the proposed expression: let the mind be
the first judge, the ear the second, and usage the third and final one to conclude
the whole" (1967ff.). Finally, in reference to delivery: "The outward emotion
corresponds with the inward; outer and inner man are affected alike" (2046ff.).

How much emphasis should be placed on these remarks? Geoffrey does
not strike one as a creative or even very analytic thinker. The importance of
craftsmanship, the themes of art, exercise and imitation, the concept of ornamentation via the rhetorical figures—all these ideas can be traced to the *Ars
Poetica* and the *Ad Herennium* and are commonplace themes in medieval
criticism. On the other hand, the dichotomy of mind versus material and the
corollary emphasis on inner versus outer significance are too consistent and too
carefully worked out to be accidental.

We know that there were two related currents of thought during the
twelfth-century Renaissance. The first gave rise to the humanism of Bernard of
Chartres and John of Salisbury. It was grammatical with an overlay of rhetoric
derived chiefly from the *Ad Herennium* and Cicero's *De Inventione*, and it involved reading and imitation of the *auctores*. The second was more directly influenced by medieval Platonism as reflected in such works as Calcidius' translation and commentary on the *Timaeus*, Macrobius' commentary on the *Somnium
Scipionis*, and Boethius' *Consolation of Philosophy*, and as renewed in the works
of Dionysius the pseudo-Areopagite. Among the representatives of this school
were mystics like Bernard of Clairvaux and two highly significant literary
figures, Bernard Silvestris and Alanus de Insulis. Bernard Silvestris was particularly interested in literary theory. He evidently composed a treatise on the
art of poetry, perhaps the first in the series of twelfth- and thirteenth-century
artes exemplified here by the *Poetria Nova;* and his commentary on the first six
books of Vergil's *Aeneid* has survived. His *Megacosmus* and *Microcosmus* belong with Alanus' *De Planctu Naturae* and *Anticlaudianus* as the outstanding
examples for the twelfth-century Renaissance of the strain of Platonizing poetry
celebrating the harmony and beauty of the visible world. In this tradition, the
theme of what Alanus calls "God the elegant architect and golden maker of a
golden artifact" runs strong, as does the belief that Nature is the book of God
embodying invisible concepts in visible substances. Although the evidence is
indirect, it is most likely that Geoffrey of Vinsauf's poet—who plans his work

like an architect and embodies the ideas in material substance which must, however, always be treated in such a way as to reflect its inner meaning—is in the same tradition. Geoffrey is no mystic; if anything he is pedestrian. But in the *Poetria* he does seem to be reaching for a new poetic theory which improves on Horace precisely in its effort to shape the commonplaces of grammatical and rhetorical criticism with concepts derived from high medieval Platonism. The difference between Geoffrey's modest use of this material in what is essentially a textbook and an extended and more radical use of it can be estimated by a comparison of the *Poetria Nova* with the selections (below) from Boccaccio's *Genealogy of the Gentile Gods*.

The translation used here (and the notes) are by Margaret F. Nims, *The Poetria Nova of Geoffrey of Vinsauf* (Toronto: Pontifical Institute of Medieval Studies, 1967), by permission of the translator and of the President of the Pontifical Institute. The numbers inserted in the translation give the approximate location of every tenth line in the Latin text. For bibliography, see especially pp. 486–88.

from POETRIA NOVA

I. GENERAL REMARKS ON POETRY
Divisions of the Present Treatise

If a man has a house to build, his impetuous hand does not rush into action. The measuring line of his mind first lays out the work, and he mentally outlines the successive steps in a definite order. The mind's hand[1] shapes the entire house before the body's hand builds it. Its mode of being is archetypal before it is actual. Poetic art may see in this analogy the law to be given to poets: let the poet's hand not be swift to take up the pen, nor his tongue be impatient to speak; (50) trust neither hand nor tongue to the guidance of fortune. To ensure greater success for the work, let the discriminating mind, as a prelude to action, defer the operation of hand and tongue, and ponder long on the subject matter. Let the mind's interior compass first circle the whole extent of the material. Let a definite order[2] chart in advance at what point the pen will take up its course, or where it will fix its Cadiz.[3] As a prudent workman, construct the whole fabric within the mind's citadel; let it exist in the mind before it is on the lips.

When due order has arranged the material in the hidden chamber of the mind, (60) let poetic art come forward to clothe the matter with words. Since poetry comes to serve, however, let it make due preparation for attendance upon its mistress. Let it take heed lest a head with tousled locks, or a body in rumpled garments, or any final details[4] prove displeasing, and lest in adorning one part it should in some way disfigure another. If any part is ill-groomed, the work as a whole incurs censure from that one part. A touch of gall makes all the honey bitter; a single blemish disfigures the entire face. Give careful thought to the material, therefore, that there may be no possible grounds for reproach. (70)

Let the poem's beginning, like a courteous attendant, introduce the subject with grace. Let the main section, like a diligent host, make provision for its worthy reception. Let the conclusion, like a herald when the race is over, dismiss it honorably. In all of its parts let the whole method of presentation bring credit upon the poem, lest it falter in any section, lest its brightness suffer eclipse.

In order that the pen may know what a skillful ordering of material requires, the treatise to follow begins its course with a discussion of order. Since the following treatise begins its course with a discussion of order, its first concern is the path[5] that the ordering of material should follow. (80) Its second care: with what scales[6] to establish a delicate balance if meaning is to be given the weight appropriate to it. The third task is to see that the body of words is not boorishly crude but urbane. The final concern is to ensure that a well-modulated voice enters the ears and feeds the hearing, a voice seasoned with the two spices of facial expression and gesture.

II. ORDERING THE MATERIAL

The material's order may follow two possible courses: at one time it advances along the pathway of art, at another it travels the smooth road of nature. Nature's smooth road points the way when "things" and "words" follow the same sequence, and the order of discourse does not depart from the order of occurrence. (90) The poem travels the pathway of art if a more effective order presents first what was later in time, and defers the appearance of what was actually earlier. Now, when the natural order is thus transposed, later events incur no censure by their early appearance, nor do early events by their late introduction. Without contention, indeed, they willingly assume each other's place, and gracefully yield to each other with ready consent. Deft artistry inverts things in such a way that it does not pervert them; in transposing, it disposes the material to better effect. The order of art is more elegant than natural order, and in excellence far ahead, even though it puts last things first. (100)

The first branch of order has no offshoots; the second is prolific: from its marvelous stock, bough branches out into boughs, the single shoot into many, the one into eight. The air in this region of art may seem murky and the pathway rugged, the doors locked and the theory itself entangled with knots. Since that is so, the words that follow will serve as physicians for that disorder. Scan them well: here you will find a light to dispel the darkness, safe footing to traverse rugged ground, a key to unlock the doors, a finger to loose the knots. (110) The way is thrown open; guide the reins of your mind as the nature of your course demands.

Let that part of the material which is first in the order of nature wait outside the gates of the work. Let the end, as a worthy precursor, be first to enter and take up its place in advance, as a guest of more honorable rank, or even as master. Nature has placed the end last in order, but art respectfully defers to it, leads it from its humble position and accords it the place of honor.

The place of honor at the beginning of a work does not reserve its luster for the end of the material only; rather, two parts share the glory: the end of the material and the middle. (120) Art draws from either of these a graceful beginning. Art plays, as it were, the conjurer: causes the last to be first, the future to be present, the oblique to be straight, the remote to be near; what is rustic becomes urbane, what is old becomes new, public things are made private, black things white, and worthless things are made precious.

If a still more brilliant beginning is desired (while leaving the sequence of the material unchanged) make use of a proverb,[7] ensuring that it may not sink to a purely specific relevance, but raise its head high to some general truth. See that, while prizing the charm of the unusual, it may not concentrate its attention on the particular subject, (130) but refuse, as if in disdain, to remain within its bosom. Let it take a stand above the given subject, but look with direct glance towards it. Let it say nothing directly about the subject, but derive its inspiration therefrom.

This kind of beginning is threefold, springing up from three shoots. The shoots are the first, the middle, and the last parts of the theme. From their stem a sprig, as it were, bursts forth, and is thus wont to be born, one might say, of three mothers. It remains in hiding, however, and when summoned it refuses to hear. It does not as a rule come forward when the mind bids it; it is of a somewhat haughty nature, and does not present itself readily nor to all. (140) It is reluctant to appear, unless, indeed, it is compelled to do so.

Proverbs, in this way, add distinction to a poem. No less appropriately do exempla[8] occupy a position at the beginning of a work. The same quality, indeed, shines forth from exempla and proverbs, and the distinction conferred by the two is of equal value. In stylistic elegance, proverbs alone are on a par with exempla. Artistic theory has advanced other techniques [for the poem's beginning] but prefers these two; they have greater prestige. The others are of less worth and more recent appearance; the sanction of time favors the two forms mentioned. Thus the way that lies open is more restricted, its use more appropriate, its art superior, as we see both from artistic principle and from practice. . . . (150)

III. AMPLIFICATION AND ABBREVIATION

For the opening of the poem, the principles of art outlined above have offered a variety of paths. The poem's development now invites you onward. Keeping to our image, direct your steps further along the road's course.

The way continues along two routes: there will be either a wide path or a narrow, either a river or a brook. You may advance at a leisurely pace or leap swiftly ahead. You may report the matter with brevity or draw it out in a lengthy discourse. The footing on either path is not without effort; (210) if you wish to be wisely guided, entrust yourself to a reliable guide. Reflect upon the precepts below; they will guide your pen and teach the essentials for each path. The material to be molded, like the molding of wax, is at first hard to the touch. If intense concentration enkindle native ability, the material is soon made pliant by the mind's fire, and submits to the hand in whatever way it requires, malleable to any form. The hand of the mind controls it, either to amplify or curtail.

A. Amplification

REPETITION (*interpretatio, expolitio*). If you choose an amplified form, proceed first of all by this step: (220) although the meaning is one, let it not come content with one set of apparel. Let it vary its robes and assume different raiment. Let it take up again in other words what has already been said; let it reiterate, in a number of clauses, a single thought. Let one and the same thing be concealed under multiple forms—be varied and yet the same.

PERIPHRASIS (*circuitio, circumlocutio*). Since a word, a short sound, passes swiftly through the ears, a step onward is taken when an expression made up of a long and leisurely sequence of sounds is substituted for a word. In order to amplify the poem, avoid calling things by their names; use other designations for them. (230) Do not unveil the thing fully but suggest it by hints. Do not let your words move straight onward through the subject, but, circling it, take a long and winding path around what you were going to say briefly. Retard the tempo by thus increasing the number of words. This device lengthens brief forms of expression, since a short word abdicates in order that an extended sequence may be its heir. Since a concept is confined in one of three strongholds—in a noun, or a verb, or a combination of both—do not let the noun or verb or combination of both render the concept explicit, but let an amplified form stand in place of verb or noun or both. (240)

COMPARISON (*collatio*). A third step is comparison, made in accord with one of two laws—either in a hidden or in an overt manner. Notice that some things are joined deftly enough, but certain signs reveal the point of juncture. A comparison which is made overtly presents a resemblance which signs explicitly point out. These signs are three: the words *more, less, equally*. A comparison that is made in a hidden way is introduced with no sign to point it out. It is introduced not under its own aspect but with dissembled mien, as if there were no comparison there at all, (250) but the taking on, one might say, of a new form marvelously engrafted, where the new element fits as securely into the context as if it were born of the theme. The new term is, indeed, taken from elsewhere, but it seems to be taken from there; it is from outside and does not appear outside; it makes an appearance within and is not within; so it fluctuates inside and out, here and there, far and near; it stands apart, and yet is at hand. It is a kind of plant; if it is planted in the garden of the material the handling of the subject will be pleasanter. Here is the flowing water of a well-spring, where the source runs purer; here is the formula for a skillful juncture, where the elements joined flow together and touch each other as if they were not contiguous but continuous; (260) as if the hand of nature had joined them rather than the hand of art. This type of comparison is more artistic; its use is much more distinguished.

APOSTROPHE (*apostrophatio, exclamatio*). In order that you may travel the more spacious route, let apostrophe be a fourth mode of delay. By it you may cause the subject to linger on its way, and in it you may stroll for an hour. Take delight in apostrophe; without it the feast would be ample enough, but with it the courses of an excellent cuisine are multiplied. The splendor of dishes arriving in rich profusion and the leisured delay at the table are festive signs. (270) With a variety of courses we feed the ear for a longer time and more lavishly. Here is food indeed for the ear when it arrives delicious and fragrant and costly. Example may serve to complement theory: the eye is a surer arbiter than the ear. One example is not enough; there will be an ample number; from this ample evidence learn what occasion suitably introduces apostrophe, what object it addresses, and in what form.

Rise up, apostrophe, before the man whose mind soars too high in prosperity, and rebuke him thus:

Why does joy so intense excite your spirit? Curb jubilation with due restraint and extend not its limits beyond what is meet [appropriate]. O soul, heedless of misfortune to come, imitate Janus (280): look to past and to future; if your venture has prospered, regard not beginnings but issues. From the sun's setting appraise the day, not from its rising. To be fully secure, fear the future. When you think that you have done all, the serpent lurks in the grass. Keep in mind, as example, the sirens; learn from them in a happier time ever to beware an unhappy. There is nothing stable in things of this world: after honey comes poison; dark night brings the day to a close, and clouds end calm weather. Though happily all man's affairs are subject to change, (290) misfortune is wont to return with greater alacrity. . . .

DIGRESSION. If it is desirable to amplify the treatise yet more fully, go outside the bounds of the subject and withdraw from it a little; let the pen digress, but not so widely that it will be difficult to find the way back. (530) This technique demands a talent marked by restraint, lest the bypath be longer than decorum allows. A kind of digression is made when I turn aside from the material at hand, bringing in first what is actually remote and altering the natural order. For sometimes, as I advance along the way, I leave the middle of the road, and with a kind of leap I fly off to the side, as it were; then I return to the point whence I had digressed. Lest this matter of digression be veiled in obscurity, I offer the following example:

The bond of a single love bound together two hearts; a strange cause divided them one from the other. But before they were parted, lips pressed kisses on lips; (540) a mutual embrace holds and enfolds them both. From the fount of their eyes, tears flow down their cheeks, and sobs alternate with farewells. Love is a spur to grief, and grief a witness to the strength of love. Winter yields to spring. The air unclasps its robe of cloud, and heaven caresses the earth. Moist and warm, air sports with earth, and the feminine earth feels the masculine power of the air.[9] A flower, earth's child, bursts forth into the breeze and smiles at its mother. Their first foliage adorns the tips of the trees; seeds that were dead spring up into life; (550) the promise of harvest to come lives first in the tender blade. Now is the season in which birds delight. This hour of time found the lovers apart, who yet through their love were not parted.

DESCRIPTION, pregnant with words, follows as a seventh means of amplifying the work. But although the path of description is wide, let it also be wise, let it be both lengthy and lovely. See that the words with due ceremony are wedded to the subject. If description is to be the food and ample refreshment of the mind, avoid too curt a brevity as well as trite conventionality. Examples of description, accompanied by novel figures, will be varied, (560) that eye and ear may roam amid a variety of subjects.

If you wish to describe, in amplified form, a woman's beauty:

Let the compass of Nature first fashion a sphere for her head; let the color of gold give a glow to her hair, and lilies bloom high on her brow. Let her eyebrows resemble in dark beauty the blackberry, and a lovely and milk-white path separate their twin arches. Let her nose be straight, of moderate length, not too long nor too short for perfection. Let her eyes, those watch-fires of her brow, be radiant with emerald light, or with the brightness of stars. (570) Let her countenance emulate dawn: not red, nor yet white—but at once neither of those colors and both. Let her mouth be bright, small in shape—as it were, a half-circle. Let her lips be rounded and full, but moderately so; let them glow, aflame, but with gentle fire. Let her teeth be snowy, regular, all of one size, and her breath like the fragrance of incense. Smoother than polished marble let Nature fashion her chin—Nature, so potent a sculptor. Let her neck be a precious column of milk-white beauty, (580) holding high the perfection of her countenance. From her crystal throat let radiance gleam, to enchant the eye of the viewer and enslave his heart. Let her shoulders, conforming to beauty's law, not slope in unlovely descent, nor jut out with an awkward rise; rather, let them be gracefully straight. Let her arms be a joy to behold, charming in their grace and their length. Let soft and slim loveliness, a form shapely and white, a line long and straight, flow into her slender fingers. Let her beautiful hands take pride in those fingers. (590) Let her breast, the image of snow, show side by side its twin virginal gems. Let her waist be close girt, and so slim that a hand may encircle it. For the other parts I am silent—here the mind's speech is more apt than the tongue's. Let her leg be of graceful length and her wonderfully tiny foot dance with joy at its smallness.

So let the radiant description descend from the top of her head to her toe, and the whole be polished to perfection.

If you wish to add to the loveliness thus pictured an account of attire (600):

Let her hair, braided and bound at her back, bind in its gold; let a circlet of gold gleam on her ivory brow. Let her face be free of adornment, lovely in its natural hue. Have a starry chain encircle her milk-white neck. Let the border of her robe gleam with fine linen; with gold let her mantle blaze. Let a zone, richly set with bright gems, bind her waist, and bracelets enrich her arms. Have gold encircle her slender fingers, and a jewel more splendid than gold shed its brilliant rays. Let artistry vie with materials in her fair attire; (610) let no skill of hand or invention of mind be able to add aught to that apparel. But her beauty will be of more worth than richness of vesture. Who, in this torch, is unaware of the fires? Who does not find the flame? If Jupiter in those days of old had seen her, he would not, in Amphitryon's shape, have deluded Alcmena; nor assumed the face of Diana to defraud you, Callisto, of your flower; nor would he have betrayed Io in the form of a cloud, nor Antiope in the shape of a satyr, nor the daughter of Agenor as a bull, nor you, Mnemosyne, as a shepherd; nor the daughter of Asopo in the guise of fire; nor you, Deo's daughter, in the form of a serpent; nor Leda as a swan; nor Danae in a shower of gold. (620) This maiden alone would he cherish, and see all others in her. . . .

OPPOSITION (*oppositio, oppositum*). There remains yet another means of fostering the amplified style: any statement at all may assume two forms: one form makes a positive assertion, the other negates its opposite. (670) The two modes harmonize in a single meaning; and thus two streams of sound flow forth, each flowing along with the other. Words flow in abundance from the two streams. Consider this example: "*That young man is wise.*" Affirm the youthfulness of his countenance and deny its age: "*His is the appearance of youth and not of old age."* Affirm the maturity of his mind and deny its youthfulness: *"His is the mind of mature age and not of youth."* The account may perhaps continue along the same line: *"His is not the cheek of age but of youth;* (680) *his is not the mind of youth but of age."* Or, choosing details closely related to the theme, you may travel a rather long path, thus:

His face is not wrinkled, nor is his skin dry; his heart is not stricken with age, nor is his breath labored; his loins are not stiff, nor is his back bowed; physically he is a young man, mentally he is in advanced maturity.

In this way, plentiful harvest springs from a little seed; great rivers draw their source from a tiny spring; from a slender twig a great tree rises and spreads.

B. Abbreviation

If you wish to be brief, (690) first prune away those devices mentioned above which contribute to an elaborate style; let the entire theme be confined within narrow limits. Compress it in accordance with the following formula. Let *emphasis* be spokesman, saying much in few words. Let *articulus*, with staccato speech, cut short a lengthy account. The *ablative*, when it appears alone without a pilot, effects a certain compression. Give no quarter to *repetition*. Let skillful *implication* convey the unsaid in the said. Introduce no *conjunction* as a link between clauses—let them proceed uncoupled (*asyndeton*). Let the craftsman's skill effect a *fusion of many concepts in one,* (700) so that many may be seen in a single glance of the mind. By such concision you may gird up a lengthy theme; in this bark you may cross a sea. This form of expression is preferable for a factual account, in order not to enshroud facts discreetly in mist, but rather to clear away mist and usher in sunlight. Combine these devices, therefore, when occasion warrants: emphasis, articulus, ablative absolute, deft implication of one thing in the rest, omission of conjunctions between clauses, fusion of many concepts in one, avoidance of repetition. (710)   Draw on all of these, or at least on such as the subject allows. Here is a model of abbreviation; the whole technique is reflected in it:

Her husband abroad improving his fortunes, an adulterous wife bears a child. On his return after long delay, she pretends it begotten of snow.[10] Deceit is mutual. Slyly he waits. He whisks off, sells, and—reporting to the mother a like ridiculous tale—pretends the child melted by sun. . . .

IV. ORNAMENTS OF STYLE

Whether it be brief or long, a discourse should always have both internal and external adornment, but with a distinction of ornament reflecting the distinction between the two orders. First examine the mind of a word, and only then

its face; (740) do not trust the adornment of its face alone. If internal ornament is not in harmony with external, a sense of propriety is lacking. Adorning
the face of a word is painting a worthless picture: it is a false thing, its beauty
fictitious; the word is a whitewashed wall and a hypocrite, pretending to be
something whereas it is nothing. Its fair form conceals its deformity; it makes a
brave outward show, but has nothing within. It is a picture[11] that charms one
who stands at a distance, but displeases the viewer who stands at close range.
Take care, then, not to be hasty, but be Argus in relation to what you have said,
and, Argus-eyed, examine the words in relation to the meaning proposed.
(750) If the meaning has dignity, let that dignity be preserved; see that no
vulgar word may debase it. That all may be guided by precept: let rich meaning
be honored by rich diction, lest a noble lady blush in pauper's rags.

In order that meaning may wear a precious garment, if a word is old, be
its phsyician and give to the old a new vigor. Do not let the word invariably
reside on its native soil[12]—such residence dishonors it. Let it avoid its natural
location, (760) travel about elsewhere, and take up a pleasant abode on the
estate of another. There let it stay as a novel guest, and give pleasure by its very
strangeness. If you provide this remedy, you will give to the word's face a new
youth.

Difficult Ornament

METAPHOR (*translatio*). The method suggested above affords guidence in
the artistic transposition of words. If an observation is to be made about man,
I turn to an object which clearly resembles man [in the quality or state of being
I wish to attribute to him]. When I see what that object's proper vesture is, in
the aspect similar to man's, I borrow it, and fashion for myself a new garment in
place of the old. For example, taking the words in their literal sense, (770) gold
is said to be yellow; milk, white; a rose, very red; honey, sweet-flowing; flames,
glowing; snow, white. Say therefore: *snowy* teeth, *flaming* lips, *honied* taste, *rosy*
countenance, *milky* brow, *golden* hair. These word-pairs are well suited to each
other: teeth, snow; lips, flames; taste, honey; countenance, rose; brow, milk;
hair, gold. And since here the linking of aspects that are similar sheds a pleasing
light, if the subject of your discourse is not man, turn the reins of your mind
to the human realm. With artistic tact, transpose a word which, in its literal
sense, applies to man in an analogous situation. (780) For example, if you
should wish to say: "Springtime makes the earth beautiful; the first flowers
grow up; the weather turns mild; storms cease; the sea is calm, its motion without violence; the vales are deep, the mountains lofty"; consider what words, in
a literal sense, express the analogous situation in our human life. When you
adorn something, you *paint*; when you enter on existence, you *are born*; affable
in discourse, you *placate*; withdrawing from all activity, you *sleep*; motionless,

you *stand on fixed foot;* sinking down, you *lie;* lifted into the air, you *rise.* (790) The wording is a source of pleasure, then, if you say:

Springtime paints the earth with flowers: the first blossoms are born; the mild weather soothes; storms, dying down, slumber; the sea stands still, as if without movement; the valleys lie deep; the mountains rise aloft. . . .

Art has woven other garments of less price, yet they, too, have a dignified and appropriate use. There are in all ten[13] tropes, six in this group, four [in addition to metaphor, onomatopoeia, antonomasia, and allegory] mentioned above. (960) This decade of figures adorns expression in a way we term *difficult* in that a word is taken only in its figurative and not in its literal sense. All the tropes are of one general class, distinguished by the figurative status of the words and the uncommon meaning assigned them. Lest understanding be uncertain and hesitant here, the following examples will ensure confidence.

METONYMY (*denominatio*). Consider a statement of this kind: *The sick man seeks a physician; the grieving man, solace; the poor man, aid.* Expression attains a fuller flowering in this trope: *Illness is in need of a physician; grief is in need of solace; poverty is in need of aid.* (970) There is a natural charm in this use of the abstract for the concrete, and so in the change of *sick man* to *sickness, grieving man* to *grief, poor man* to *poverty.*

What does fear produce? Pallor. What does anger cause? A flush. Or what, the vice of pride? A swelling up. We refashion the statement thus: *Fear grows pale, anger flushes; pride swells.* There is greater pleasure and satisfaction for the ear when I attribute to the cause what the effect claims as its own.

Let the comb's action groom the hair after the head has been washed. Let scissors trim away from the hair whatever is excessive, (980) and let a razor give freshness to the face. In this way, art teaches us to attribute to the instrument, by a happy turn of expression, what is proper to the one who uses it. So from the resources of art springs a means of avoiding worn-out paths and of travelling a more distinguished route.

Again, a statement expressed in the following way adds luster to style: *We have robbed their bodies of steel, their coffers of silver, their fingers of gold.* The point here is not that zeugma adorns the words with its own figure of speech, but that when I am about to mention something, I withhold its form completely and mention only the material. Whereas a less elegant style mentions both, art is silent about one, and conveys both by a single term. This device brings with it three advantages (990): it curtails the number of words required, it constitutes a poetic adornment, and it is helpful to the meter. It curtails the number of words in that a single term is more succinct than a word-group; it constitutes a poetic adornment in that an expression of this kind is artistically more skillful; and it is helpful to the meter if an oblique case, whose form the meter rejects, requires such help. This is clear from the following example: *The finger rejoices in gold. Gold* is a shorter sound, *a ring of gold* is longer; the latter form names the object itself, the former conveys it more artfully; in the former [*aurum*] the meter admits of oblique cases, in the latter [*annulus auri*] it rejects them. (1000)

Instead of the thing contained, name that which contains it, choosing the word judiciously whether it be noun or adjective. Introduce a noun in this way: *tippling England; weaving Flanders; bragging Normandy.* Try out an adjective thus: *clamorous market-places; silent cloisters; lamenting prison; jubilant house; quiet night; laborious day.* Seek turns of expression like the following: *In time of sickness Salerno, with its medical skill, cures those who are ill. In civil causes Bologna arms the defenceless with laws. Paris, in the arts, dispenses bread to feed the strong.* (1010) *Orleans, in its cradle, rears tender youth on the milk of the authors.*

HYPERBOLE (*superlatio*). Give hyperbole rein, but see that its discourse does not run ineptly hither and yon. Let reason keep it in check, and its moderate use be a source of pleasure, that neither mind nor ear may shrink from excess. For example, employing this trope: *A rain of darts lashes the foe like hail; the shattered array of spears resembles a forest; a tide of blood flows like a wave of the sea, and bodies clog the valleys.* This mode of expression diminishes or heightens eulogy to a remarkable degree; (1020) and exaggeration is a source of pleasure when both ear and good usage commend it.

SYNECDOCHE (*intellectio*). If you intend to say: *I studied for three years,* you may, with happier effect, adorn the statement. The wording above is inelegant and trite; you may refine the inelegant, your file may renew the trite in this way: *The third summer came upon me in study; the third autumn found me engaged; the third winter embroiled me in cares; in study I passed through three spring times.* I word the statement more skillfully when, suppressing the whole, I imply that whole from the parts, in the way just exemplified. Part of the year may be wet. *The year is wet;* (1030) part may be dry: *The year is dry;* part may be hot. *The year is hot;* part may be mild: *The year is mild.* I attribute to the whole what characterizes a part of it. By this same mode of reckoning, you, Gion, will be accounted turbid and clear, narrow and broad, brackish and sweet, because of some varied part of your course. Again, by the same figure, a day is to be accounted dry and yet rainy because of a part of it. Since both forms of this figure are pleasing, you may give pleasure by either form.

CATACHRESIS (*abusio*). There is likewise an urbane imprecision of diction when a word is chosen which is neither literal nor precise in its context, but which is related to the literal word. For example, if one proposes to say: (1040): *The strength of the Ithacan is slight, but yet he has a mind of great wisdom,* let catachresis alter the wording thus: *Strength in Ulysses is short, wisdom in his heart is long,* for there is a certain affinity between the words *long* and *great,* as between *short* and *slight.*

In the figures given above there is a common element of adornment and weightiness, arising from the fact that an object does not come before us with unveiled face, and accompanied by its natural voice; rather, an alien voice attends it, and so it shrouds itself in mist, as it were, but in a luminous mist. (1050)

HYPERBATON (*transgressio*). A certain weightiness of style results also from the order of words alone, when units grammatically related are separated by their position, so that an inversion of this sort occurs (anastrophe [*perversio*]):*rege sub ipso; tempus ad illud; ea de causa; rebus in illis* [under the king himself; up to that time; for this reason; in those matters]; or a transposed order of this sort (transposition [*transjectio*]): *Dura creavit pestiferam fortuna famen* [harsh fortune produced a pestilent famine]; *Letalis egenam gente fames spoliavit humum* [deadly famine robbed the destitute soil of produce]. Here words related grammatically are separated by their position in the sentence. Juxtaposition of related words conveys the sense more readily, but their moderate separation sounds better to the ear and has greater elegance. . . . (1060)

Easy Ornament

If a mode of expression both easy and adorned is desired, set aside all the techniques of the dignified style and have recourse to means that are simple, but of a simplicity that does not shock the ear by its rudeness. . . .

Figures of thought. There are other figures [besides those of speech] to adorn the meaning of words. (1230) All of these I include in the following brief treatment: when meaning is adorned, this is the standard procedure. *Distributio* assigns specific roles to various things or among various persons. At times, *licentia,* fairly and lawfully, chides masters or friends, offending no one with its words. At times, *diminutio* implies more in the subject than is expressed in words, and makes its point by understatement, though with moderation. So, too, *descriptio* presents consequences, and the eventualities that can ensue from a given situation. It gives a full and lucid account with a certain dignity of presentation. (1240) Or again, *disjunctio* distinguishes alternatives, accompanying each with a reason, and bringing both to a conclusion. Or single details are brought together, and *frequentatio* gathers up points that had been scattered through the work. *Expolitio.* By turning a subject over repeatedly and varying the figure, I seem to be saying a number of things whereas I am actually dwelling on one thing, in order to give it a finer polish and impart a smooth finish by repeated applications of the file, one might say. This is done in two ways: either by saying the same thing with variations, or by elaborating upon the same thing. We may say the same thing with variations in three ways; we may elaborate upon the same thing with variations in seven ways. (1250) You may read about all of these at greater length in Cicero. [By *commoratio*] I go deeply into one point and linger on in the same place; or [by *contentio*] I institute a comparison in which the positions set forth are antithetical to each other. *Similitudo.* Often from an object basically dissimilar I draw forth a point of resemblance. Or I present as exemplum, with the name of a definite authority, some statement he has made or some deed he has performed. *Imago.* Or I pass over the figures just mentioned, and, as another figure comes to the fore, I introduce a comparison of one thing with a similar thing by means of an appropriate image. *Effictio.* Or there is a figure allied to this last one, (1260) whereby I depict or represent corporeal appearance, in so far as is requisite. *Notatio.* Again, I set down certain distinguishing marks—very definite signs, as it were—by which I describe clearly the character of a man; this is a better and more effective figure. *Sermocinatio.* There is another figure whereby a speech is adapted to the person speaking, and what is said gives the very tone and manner of the speaker. *Conformatio.* Again, adorning the subject with a different kind of freshness, at one time I fashion a new person by giving the power of speech where nature has denied it. *Significatio.* At another, I leave to suspicion more than I actually put into words. (1270) *Brevitas.* Again, I compress the entire subject into a few words—those which are essential to it and no others. *Demonstratio.* At another time the subject is revealed so vividly that it seems to be present to the eyes; this effect will be perfectly achieved by five means: if I show what precedes, what constitutes, and what follows the event itself, what circumstances attend it, and what consequences follow upon it. . . .

UNDERSTATEMENT. If this statement is proposed: *My power is not slight, my dignity not insignificant,* I am implying more than I say, and the actual situation is of greater consequence than the words indicate. If I happen to be speaking on behalf of my friends, or on my own behalf, this manner of speech is in good taste, and I show becoming modesty in employing such an expression. In this way, the meaning makes its appearance veiled; the true situation is not clearly apparent; there is more consequence in the actual fact than the expression of it indicates.

HYPERBOLE. *From the numerous and great resources left by his father, the squanderer of wealth has not enough to conceal his poverty with a covering, nor even an earthen jug in which to beg a fire.* (1540) Here I speak in excessive terms about a thing that is in itself excessive. I chide immoderately what is not moderate; there is moderation neither in the actual situation nor in my expression of it. If the situation is more moderate than my words, still the excessive language does suggest that there is less excess in the fact itself.

AMBIGUITY. *That peerless man:* the word means *most excellent;* but *most vicious* glances at us obliquely: this is its meaning. The word belies its appearance, or else our perception errs. In such ambiguities, the actual fact is veiled and the mockery is obvious.

CONSEQUENCE. *The boy's ruddy color fled his cheeks when he saw the rods, and his countenance was bloodless.* (1550) Such pallor indicates that he was afraid. *A blush had spread over the maiden's face;* her appearance indicates that she was ashamed. *The stroller went sauntering on with hair adorned;* the manner of expression suggests dissolute conduct. Note the signs that accompany a given circumstance. Present the facts, but do not present them as such; rather, reveal only signs of the facts: show fear by pallor, sensuality by adornment, and shame by a sudden blush; show the thing itself by its definite signs, what is prior by what is consequent upon it: this complexion, this sex, this age, that form.

APOSIOPESIS. *Recently in another's chamber . . . but I will not say it.* (1560) In this way I break off my words, and I do not say *that man,* but *a man of such-and-such an age,* or *of a certain appearance.*

ANALOGY. *You are great, and the world supplicates you on bent knee. Although you have power to vent your rage, do not do so; remember Nero.* After introducing an analogy in this way, I add nothing further. . . .

Various Prescriptions

If you heed the directives carefully and suit words to content, you will speak with precise appropriateness in this way. If mention has perhaps arisen of an object, sex, age, condition, event, place, or time, it is regard for its distinctive quality that the object, sex, age, condition, event, time, or place claims as its due. Felicity in this matter is an admirable thing, for when I make an apt use of qualifying words [*determino*] I give the whole theme a finished completeness [*termino*]. An object described [*condita*] in its entirety is a dish well-seasoned [*condita*]. Note this prescription and heed its tenor; (1850) it is a prescription that is valid for prose as well as for verse. The same principle of art holds good for both, although in a different way.

Meter is straitened by laws, but prose roams along a freer way, for the public road of prose admits here and there wagons and carts, whereas the narrow path of a line of verse does not allow of things so inelegant. Verse wishes its very words to be graceful in appearance, lest the rustic form of a word embarrass by its ungainliness, and bring shame to the line. Meter desires to appear as a handmaid with hair adorned, with shining cheek, slim body, and peerless form. (1860) The charming gracefulness of verse cannot find a group of words of equal sweetness to the ear. A line of prose is a coarser thing; it favors all words, observing no distinction except in the case of those which it keeps for the end of periods: such words are those whose penultimate syllable carries the accent. It is not desirable that other words hold this final position. Aulus Gellius reaches the same conclusion and subjoins his reason: lest otherwise the number of syllables be weak and insufficient to bring the line to a close. If the last word of a period should be, as it frequently is, of a different cursus, (1870) nevertheless the one suggested above is preferable in as much as sounder opinion supports it —and my authority here is Aulus Gellius.[14] For the rest, the method of prose and verse does not differ; rather, the principles of art remain the same, whether in a composition bound by the laws of meter or in one independent of those laws, although what depends upon the principles of art is not always the same. In both prose and verse see that diction is controlled in such a way that words do not enter as dry things, but let their meaning confer a juicy savor upon them, and let them arrive succulent and rare. Let them say nothing in a childish way; see that they have dignity but not pomposity, lest what should be honorable becomes onerous. (1880) Do not let them enter with unsightly mien; rather, see that there is both internal and external adornment. Let the hand of artistic skill provide colors of both kinds. . . .

V. MEMORY

If you wish to remember all that reason invents, or order disposes, or adornment refines, (1970) keep in mind this counsel, valuable though brief: the little cell that remembers is a cell of delights, and it craves what is delightful, not what is boring. Do you wish to gratify it? Do not burden it. It desires to be treated kindly, not hard pressed. Because memory is a slippery thing, and is not capable of dealing with a throng of objects, feed it in the following way. When you appease hunger, do not be so sated with food that you can have nothing further set before you. Be more than half, but less than fully satisfied. Give to your stomach not as much as it can hold, but as much as is beneficial; (1980) nature is to be nourished, not overburdened. To remain between satiety and hunger is the wiser practice. So, too, in drinking, you moderate drink in accordance with reason. Sip, do not swill; let drink be taken in an honorable [honori], not an onerous [oneri] fashion. Drink as a temperate man, not a tippler. The abstemious man arraigns wine with better grace than the drunkard refutes him.[15] Knowledge, which is the food and drink of the mind, should be tasted in accordance with the same rule. Let it feed the mind in such a way that it is offered as a delight, not a burden to it. Suppose you are to learn this entire discourse: divide it into very small parts. (1990) Do not take several at once; rather, take one at a time, a very short section, much shorter than your shoulders are capable and desirous of bearing. In this way there will be pleasure, and nothing burdensome in the burden. Let practice come as companion; while the matter is fresh and new go over it frequently and repeat it; then stop, rest for a little while, take a breathing space. After a short delay has intervened, another piece may be summoned up; when it has been memorized in the same way, let practice join both parts together in the cell mentioned above, let it consolidate them and cement them together. (2000) Join a third part to these two with a similar bond, and a fourth part to the other three. But, in following through these steps, you make a mistake if you do not consistently proceed in such a way that you stop short of weariness. This advice holds good for all the faculties of sense; it sharpens those that are dull, makes pliable those that are rigid, and raises to greater heights of excellence those that are acute and flexible. Whatever attempts more than these precepts accomplishes less. Therefore let this sound principle adapt to each man the weight he can bear, and be the one model for all.

To these methods add others which I make use of—and which it is expedient to use. When I wish to recall things I have seen, or heard, (2010) or memorized before, or engaged in before, I ponder thus: I saw, I heard, I considered, I acted in such or such a way, either at that time or in that place: places, times, images, or other similar signposts are for me a sure path which leads me to the things themselves. Through these signs I arrive at active knowledge. Such and such a thing was so, and I picture to myself such and such a thing.

Cicero relies on unusual images as a technique for training the memory; but he is teaching himself; and let the subtle teacher, as it were in solitude, address his subtlety to himself alone. But my own subtlety may be pleasing to me and not to him. (2020) It is beneficial to one whom it suits, for enjoyment alone makes the power of memory strong. Therefore have no faith in these or in other signposts if they are difficult for you, or if they are unacceptable. But if you wish to proceed with greater security, fashion signs for yourself, whatever kind your own inclination suggests. As long as they give you pleasure, you may be taught through their means. There are some men who wish to know, but not to make an effort, nor to endure the concentration and pain of learning. That is the way of the cat; it wants the fish, but not the fishing. I am not addressing myself to such men, but to those who delight in knowing, and also in the effort of acquiring knowledge. (2030)

VI. DELIVERY

In reciting aloud, let three tongues speak: let the first be that of the mouth, the second that of the speaker's countenance, and the third that of gesture. The voice has its own laws, and you should observe them in this way: the period that is spoken should observe its natural pauses, and the word its accent. Separate those words which the sense separates, join those that sense joins. Modulate your voice in such a way that it is in harmony with the subject; and take care that voice does not advance along a path different from that which the subject follows. Let the two go together; let the voice be, as it were, a reflection of the subject. As the nature of your subject is, so let your voice be when you rehearse it: let us recognize them as one. (2040)

Anger, child of fire and mother of fury, springing up from the very bellows, poisons the heart and soul. It stings with its bellows, sears with its fire, convulses with its fury. Under its emotion, a caustic voice speaks; an inflamed countenance and turbulent gestures accompany it. The outward emotion corresponds with the inward; outer and inner man are affected alike. If you act the part of this man, what, as reciter, will you do? Imitate genuine fury, but do not be furious. Be affected in part as he is, but not deeply so. (2050) Let your manner be the same in every respect, but not so extreme; yet suggest, as is fitting, the emotion itself. You can represent the manner of a rustic and still be graceful: let your voice represent his voice; your facial expression, his own; and your gesture his gesture—by recognizable signs. This is a carefully tempered skill; this method is attractive in the tongue that recites, and this food is a delight to the ear. Therefore, let a voice controlled by good taste, seasoned with the two spices of facial expression and gesture, be borne to the ears to feed the hearing. Strength issues from the tongue, for death and life depend upon the powers of the tongue, (2060) if haply it is aided by the tempering principles of facial expression and gesture. So, then, let all be in harmony: suitable invention, flowing expression, polished development, firm retention in memory. If discourses are delivered ineptly, they are no more to be praised than is a recitation charmingly delivered but without the other requirements mentioned.

DANTE

(1265–1321)

INTRODUCTION

Dante's *Divine Comedy* is usually considered the culmination of medieval poetry. His critical works are in the same sense a culmination of medieval poetics. Unlike most medieval critical works, they are highly original. They show an awareness of tradition, particularly scholastic tradition, but Dante was not a compiler or redactor like Vincent of Beauvais or Geoffrey of Vinsauf. He depended on his own direct experience as a poet for much of his knowledge, supplementing this with deduction based on forms of scholastic logic. His three major treatises are the *De Vulgari Eloquentia*, the *Convivio*, and the thirteenth of his *Epistles*, which is an exposition of the *Divine Comedy*. The first two works are incomplete. They were probably begun in 1304–6, during Dante's residence in Bologna in the years following his exile from Florence (1301) after the triumph of the "Black" party led by Gabrielli da Gubbio. The *De Vulgari* was planned in four books but it breaks off in the middle of Chapter 14 of Book II. The *Convivio* was planned as an encyclopedic work of fifteen books. The materials were to evolve naturally in the course of a detailed commentary by Dante on fourteen of his own *canzoni*. Only four books were completed. *Epistle XIII* is addressed to Can Grande della Scala and dedicates the *Paradiso* to him. If it is genuine, internal evidence suggests a date of around 1316–19. However, its genuineness has long been doubted. It is first mentioned around 1390, long after Dante's death; and it is a tissue of critical formulas. If not genuine, it remains an important document for the light it casts on the *Comedy* and for the summation it provides of medieval thought on allegory, literary genres, the system of styles, and related objects.

The *Convivio* is the least easy of Dante's critical works to "place" in medieval tradition. The title *Convivio*—or "banquet"—relates it ultimately to Plato's *Symposium*, and more proximately to such informal miscellanies as the *Noctes Atticae* of Aulus Gellius and the *Saturnalia* of Macrobius; but it is more formal than either of these. It is not a dialogue but a group of formal essays divided into chapters. Its approach is philosophical rather than grammatical or rhetorical, and the philosophy is deduced by allegorical readings of the poems under consideration. In this respect, it is close to the *De Continentia* of Fulgentius and the Vergil commentary of Bernard Silvestris. The immediate source for the work, apart from Dante's wish to justify himself and express his thoughts about an ideal society, seems to have been Brunetto Latini's *Tesoretto*.

The most interesting sections of the *Convivio* are the first book, which contains a lengthy discussion of Dante's reasons for choosing the vernacular rather than Latin, and the first Chapter of Book II, which is a little essay on the various allegorical senses to be found in a literary work. The consideration of the vernacular overlaps the *De Vulgari* and need not be taken up here. The discussion of allegory is the most detailed treatment of the subject which we have from Dante. If the *Epistle to Can Grande* is spurious, the discussion in the *Convivio* is the only extended treatment. Dante begins by distinguishing the literal from the other senses. The first non-literal sense is called "allegorical" since it presents meanings "hidden under the veil of the fables, and it is a truth concealed in a beautiful lie." Ovid, for example, relates that Orpheus charmed wild animals and moved stones and trees with his music. This is an allegory of the fact that the wise man can charm the hearts of ignorant and unruly men. Dante adds, "Indeed, the theologians understand this [allegorical] sense differently from the poets; but because my intention is to follow the fashion of the poets here, I take the allegorical sense in the way that it is used by the poets." The distinction between poetic and theological allegory is important and has been discussed frequently. Dante probably made it to placate the conservative theologians of the day who mistrusted and attacked the divine pretentions of the humanistic poetics—the claim that poetry is divinely inspired, that the poet is a *vates*—a prophet, and that poetry is a kind of revelation.

In context, the distinction between theological and poetic allegory is related to Dante's use of the term *favola,* which, in the later Middle Ages, almost always meant a fictional (i.e., lying) story. If they write *favole,* poets are in some sense committed to falsehood rather than truth. As Conrad of Hirsau put it, a poet is "a maker or former, because he says false things rather than true ones or mixes truth from time to time with his falsehoods." But the *favola* is only the "literal" level of secular poetry. Its higher senses may be both true and morally edifying. This provides the basis for Dante's distinction between theology and poetry. Essentially, theology is true in all senses—literal as well as allegorical— whereas poetry is false in its literal sense and true only in its higher meanings: "The subject of sacred [theology] is divine virtue; the ancient poets treat the Gods of the Gentiles as men. Theology and poetry are contradictory insofar as theology brings forward from the beginning nothing unless it is true; poetry brings forward things as true that are wholly false."

The second non-literal sense is defined as moral. It teaches useful lessons. Scripture is especially rich in this kind of allegory. The third is anagogical or spiritual. When David, for example, speaks of the exodus of the Israelites from Egypt, he not only refers to an historical event but also, anagogically, to the freeing of the spirit from a state of sin. Dante stresses the fact that the literal sense is important; it is the "outside" and one cannot come to the "inside" of a thing without passing through its "outside." His point is significant. Most obviously, he is saying that one cannot proceed immediately in criticism to the inner or higher sense of a work ignoring its "outside." One must begin with what it is, its surface texture, its story and language. By implication, the passage is an assertion of the unity of any work of art. A poem cannot any more be separated into "meaning" and "content" than the "inside" of something can be separated from the "outside." After further argument along this line, Dante ends with a statement of the critical method to be used in analyzing the *canzoni* to be considered in the later books of the *Convivio*: "Therefore, for this reason, I will regularly analyze the literal sense of each *canzone* first, and after that I will analyze the allegory, that is, what is the hidden truth, and from time to time I will touch on the other senses in passing, as time and place permit."

II

The *Epistle to Can Grande della Scala* is in every way a more mechanical piece of work than the *Convivio*. It is heavily scholastic and heavily "Aristotelian" in the negative sense of being dominated by nice logical distinctions and formal definitions. Based on the *accessus* (list of authors) tradition, it tells us, essentially, that the *Divine Comedy* is an allegory having the four levels of biblical allegory. If the work is genuine, Dante has either forgotten the distinction in the *Convivio* between poetic and theological allegory, or he is making a bolder claim for the *Comedy* than he was willing to make for his *canzoni*. We learn further that the subject and form of the poem are both double. On the literal level the subject of the *Comedy* is the state of souls after death; allegorically, the consequences of virtuous and sinful choices. The definition of the form of the poem is particularly redolent of scholastic method: "The form or mode of treatment is poetic, fictitious, descriptive, digressive, transumptive [metaphorical], and, with all, definitive, divisive, probative, improbative, and exemplary."

The *accessus* formula calls for an explanation of the work's title. Dante explains the word *comedy* in a substantial passage based directly or indirectly on the treatises on tragedy and comedy ascribed to Donatus. He further points out that the department of philosophy to which the poem belongs is ethics—an echo of medieval didacticism, although less ambitious than Boccaccio's claim that Dante wrote as a theologian. All of this is most useful to reader of the *Divine*

Comedy, but it is so stylized as to be impersonal, and it contributes much less than the *Convivio* and the *De Vulgari* to our sense of Dante as a literary critic.

III

Written at approximately the same time as the *Convivio, De Vulgari Eloquentia* is both more traditional and more radical. Its subject matter relates it to the mass of grammatical literature dealing with the *ars metrica* collected in Volume VI of Keil's *Grammatici Latini* and—for the late Middle Ages—in Giovanni Mari's *I trattati medievali di ritmica latina* (Milan, 1899). Mari's *Trattati* deal with accentual Latin meters, and rhymes and stanza forms, and presumably reflect the tradition that led to manuals on vernacular poetry. They anticipate the chapters in Book II of the *De Vulgari* that give the rules for writing *canzoni.* But concern for prosody and rhyme are all they have in common with Dante. They are derivative for the most part and offer no precedent whatever for the wide-ranging philosophical analysis of language which occupies Book I and the earlier chapters of Book II.

Dante was conscious of the originality of his work. He begins with the statement that "we do not find that anyone before us has treated the science of vernacular language," and later he remarks (I.10), "our purpose is to investigate matters in which we are supported by the authority of none"—a remarkable statement for an age almost supinely dependent on authority.

Several general themes of great interest run through the work. Speech is considered an innate faculty correlative to man's status as a rational being, but, at the same time, a divine gift, "inspired by the vivifying power" (I.5). The purpose of speech is social, for rational beings must have a medium for the "intercommunication" of their thoughts (I.3). Dante now moves from hypothesis to the record of history as he understood it. During the first age, from Adam to Nimrod, there was only one language with a single form: "And I say 'a form,' both in respect of words and their construction and of the utterance of this construction; and this form every tongue of speaking men could use, if it had not been dissipated by the fault of man's presumption" (I.6). That there was originally only one language and that this was Hebrew follows both from the Bible and from the fact that God intended language for "intercommunication." The primitive unity of man was soon destroyed, however, by the vanity that created the Tower of Babel. Since then, the number of languages has multiplied. "Intercommunication" has given way to lack of communication. And the process is continuing. Dante points out that in Italy alone there are some fourteen dialects with innumerable local variations (I.10) and that changes are still going on: "since man is a most unstable and changeable animal, no human language can be lasting and continuous, but must needs vary like other properties of ours, as for instance our manners and our dress" (I.9). Dante revised and deepened his view of language in human affairs later in his life (see *Paradiso* XXVI). His later view suggests an attitude toward linguistic change that anticipates what is today called "historicism."

The image which Dante's history gives us is partly anthropological, partly psychological. Language is the vehicle of human society and man finds fulfillment in it. It is bestowed on men by a loving God, but man frustrates God's wishes—and his own needs as a spiritual being—by vanity. As languages multiply and become ever more distinct, men grow more and more isolated from one another.

There are two remedies for this. The first is grammar, which attempts to formulate universal principles of language: "Hence were set in motion the inventors of the art of grammar, which is nothing else but a kind of unchangeable identity of speech in different times and places. This, having been settled by the common consent of many peoples, seems exposed to the arbitrary will of none in particular, and consequently cannot be variable. They therefore invented grammar in order that we might not, on account of the variation of speech fluctuating at the will of individuals, either fail altogether in attaining, or at least attain but a partial knowledge of the opinions and exploits of the ancients, or of those whom difference of place causes to differ from us" (I.9).

Dante's emphasis on community, the original function of speech, is reasserted here in the opposition of "common consent" to "arbitrary will" and the "will of individuals." Grammar enables us to move, even though the movement may be slight, away from diversity and toward the unity that was our primitive birthright.

The second way is the way of the poet. It forms the burden of the remainder of Book I. As an Italian who had self-consciously chosen the path of vernacular rather than Latin poetry, Dante was primarily interested in his own language. His survey of Italian dialects (I.10) shows that he was thoroughly aware of how numerous and how diverse they were. On the one hand, this poses an aesthetic problem: "As the Italian vernacular has so very many discordant varieties, let us hunt after a more fitting and an illustrious Italian language" (I.11). On the other hand, and perhaps more deeply, we have seen that for Dante variation in language is a movement away from divinely ordained unity. The aesthetic problem cannot be separated from a social one. The Florentine exile and later, in the *De Monarchia,* the apostle of secular unity through world government, could hardly have been unaware of the practical and at the same time politically radical implications of calling for a single "fitting and illustrious Italian tongue" sanctioned by poets and used in the great affairs of state: "if we Italians had a court it would be spoken at court. For if a court is a common home of all the realm and an august ruler of all parts of the realm, it is fitting that whatever is of such a character as to be common to all [parts] without being peculiar to any, should frequent this court and dwell there . . . hence it is that those who frequent all royal palaces always speak the illustrious vernacular. Hence also it is that our illustrious language wanders about like a wayfarer, and is welcomed in humble shelters, seeing we have no court" (I.18).

The language that Dante seeks will be "illustrious, cardinal, courtly, and curial" (I.16). His method of deducing it constitutes the first empirical linguistic survey ever made of a modern European language and anticipates the efforts of the Accademia della Crusca and the Académie Française by almost three hundred years. Dante's metaphor for the project, which conveys some of its excitement, is that of the hunt (I.xi.16). In considering each dialect, Dante seeks elements common to all. In other words, he is seeking (in terms of the hunt metaphor, attempting to "track down") something like the underlying "form of speech" which was instilled by God in the first soul (I.6) and which is revealed in the analytic studies of the grammarians (I.9). Certain dialects have little to offer grammarians. This is proven by the fact that poets to whom these dialects were native abandoned them for a higher kind of speech in their poems. The point is charming and persuasive, and it has a serious meaning. The poet depicted in the De Vulgari is a man especially sensitive to language. Whether by instinct or design the great Italian poets of the past have pointed the way to the "illustrious vernacular"; and future poets will insure its greatness when it has been fully revealed. We are far, here, from the divinely inspired seer of Boccaccio, but nearer, perhaps, to an understanding of the poet's social role which a twentieth-century critic could accept.

Three dialects particularly interest Dante. Sicilian itself is defective, but the language of the poets of the court of Frederick and Manfred "differs in nothing from that language which is the most worthy of praise" (I.12). This association of the best language with a noble and gracious court is presented in an empirical observation in Chapter 12, but it reappears as an integral part of Dante's definition in the requirement that the best language be "illustrious" and "courtly" (I.16).

In Chapter 16 Dante announces that the hunt—i.e., the empirical survey —is over, and that the next step will be logical analysis. All members of the same genus may be compared because of certain common properties. It is these common properties that constitute the language "whose fragrance is in every town, but whose lair is in none." The analysis ends with the famous definition, which establishes the "form of speech" of the ideal vernacular:

> We declare the illustrious, cardinal, courtly and curial vernacular language in Italy to be that which belongs to all the towns in Italy but does not appear to belong to any one of them, and by which all the municipal dialects of the Italians are measured, weighed, and compared. (I.16)

In this definition "illustrious" refers to the fact that the language "shines forth" from the surrounding dross. This has been demonstrated in its use by the many poets, nurtured on different dialects, cited by Dante in the preceding chapters. It also "illuminates" those who use it, in the sense of exerting a noble and refining power. Again we are reminded of Dante's conception of language as a vehicle of culture. It not only permits communication. When properly constituted, it elevates and liberates those who use it. Poetry was a cause as well as a manifestation of the greatness of King Frederick's court. Social cannot be separated from aesthetic considerations.

The term "cardinal" (Lat. *cardo*-hinge) is a description of the centrality of the ideal language among the multitude of dialects. "Courtly" refers to its appropriateness to educated society with the hint, perhaps, that it may have a unifying effect on Italy similar to that of a royal court. "Curial" (Lat. *curia*, a court of justice) alludes to the fact that the illustrious language has been judged proper by the "gracious light of reason" (I.18) which is the Italian equivalent of the German imperial court.

Book II may be treated summarily. Dante continues the analytic method initiated in the closing chapters of Book I. He shows that the illustrious language is suited only to noble men and worthy objects. The worthiest objects (II.2) are arms, love, and virtue, the objectives respectively of the vegetable, animal, and rational souls. The worthiest form of poetry is the *canzone* which "embraces the art of poetry" much as the illustrious vernacular is common to all dialects. Among styles, the tragic is the most worthy (II.4), and among standard Italian lines, the eleven-syllable line is superior, although lines of three, five, and seven syllables may also be used (II.5). In vocabulary, words which are "combed out," "glossy," and "shaggy," and "rumpled" will be most appropriate (II.7). The discussion is of interest to the history of style since it echoes the ancient distinction between the three styles (*humilis, mediocris, nobilis*) and the tradition linking these styles to literary types (for Dante, elegy is humble, comedy, middle, and tragedy, elevated). Dante's selection of the hendeca syllabic is not only appropriate for Italian, but echoes for the vernacular the standard preference of the *artes metricae* for the dactylic hexameter, the longest of regular Latin quantitative lines. His stylistic terms are unique to the *De Vulgari*, but the fondness of late classical and medieval authors for adjectives suggesting different stylistic ideals has been amply documented by de Bruyne in his discussion of the Attic-Asiatic controversy between the fifth and the ninth centuries. The remainder of Book II is more technical. Although Dante continues to work deductively, his prescriptions are really a summary of the rules that he and his fellow poets regularly followed.

In spite of being unfinished, the *De Vulgari* is the only medieval critical essay that ranks with the great classical and modern critical essays. Its assumption of the fundamental unity of man, its view of language as both an innate faculty and a creator of culture, its vision of the poet as a supreme master of language who uses his genius and skill to further the ends of language, and its consistent linking of social and cultural matters are ideas which remain worthy of respect in the twentieth century. But the *De Vulgari* is more than an expression of critical ideals. It is also a brilliant essay in speculative anthropology, an informed survey of Italian dialects, and the only medieval treatise dealing with prosody that breaks away from the tired stereotypes of the *artes rithmicae* and the *artes poeticae*.

The translation, here slightly modernized, and the notes are from A. G. Ferrers Howell and Philip H. Wicksteed, *A Translation of the Latin Works of Dante Alighieri* (London: Dent, 1904). For bibliography, see especially pp. 489–90. For a recent discussion of Dante's authorship of the *Epistle to Can Grande della Scala,* see Allan H. Gilbert, "Did Dante Dedicate the *Paradiso* to Can Grande?" *Italica,* XLII (1966), 100–24.

DE VULGARI ELOQUENTIA

BOOK I
I

Since we do not find that any one before us has treated of the science of the vernacular language, while in fact we see that this language is highly necessary for all, inasmuch as not only men, but even women and children, strive, in so far as nature allows them, to acquire it; and since it is our wish to enlighten to some little extent the discernment of those who walk through the streets like blind men, generally fancying that those things which are [really] in front of them are behind them, we will endeavor, the Word aiding us from heaven, to be of service to the vernacular speech; not only drawing the water of our own wit for such a drink, but mixing with it the best of what we have taken or compiled from others, so that we may thence be able to give draughts of the sweetest hydromel.[1] But because the business of every science is not to prove but to explain its subject, in order that men may know what that is with which the science is concerned, we say (to come quickly to the point) that what we call the vernacular speech is that to which children are accustomed by those who are about them when they first begin to distinguish words; or to put it more shortly, we say that the vernacular speech is that which we acquire without any rule, by imitating our nurses. There further springs from this another secondary speech, which the Romans called grammar. And this secondary speech the Greeks also have, as well as others, but not all. Few, however, acquire the use of this speech, because we can only be guided and instructed in it by the expenditure of much time, and by assiduous study. Of these two kinds of speech also, the vernacular is the nobler, as well because it was the first employed by the human race, as because the whole world makes use of it, though it has been divided into forms differing in pronunciation and vocabulary. It is also the nobler as being natural to us, whereas the other is rather of an artificial kind; and it is of this our nobler speech that we intend to treat.

II

This [then] is our true first speech. I do not, however, say "our" as implying that any other kind of speech exists beside man's; for to man alone of all existing beings was speech given, because for him alone was it necessary. Speech was not necessary for the angels or for the lower animals, but would have been given to them in vain, which nature, as we know, shrinks from doing. For if we clearly consider what our intention is when we speak, we shall find that it is nothing else but to unfold to others the thoughts of our own mind. Since, then, the angels have, for the purpose of manifesting their glorious thoughts, a most ready and indeed ineffable sufficiency of intellect, by which one of them is known in all respects to another, either of himself, or at least by means of that most brilliant mirror in which all of them are represented in the fulness of their beauty, and into which they all most eagerly gaze, they do not seem to have required the outward indications of speech. And if an objection be raised concerning the spirits who fell, it may be answered in two ways. First we may say that inasmuch as we are treating of those things which are necessary for well-being, we ought to pass over the fallen angels, because they perversely refused to wait for the divine care.[2] Or secondly (and better), that the devils themselves only need, in order to disclose their perfidy to one another, to know, each of another, that he exists, and what is his power: which they certainly do know, for they had knowledge of one another before their fall.

The lower animals also, being guided by natural instinct alone, did not need to be provided with the power of speech, for all those of the same species have the same actions and passions; and so they are enabled by their own actions and passions to know those of others. But among those of different species not only was speech unnecessary, but it would have been altogether harmful, since there would have been no friendly intercourse between them.

And if it be objected concerning the serpent speaking to the first woman, or concerning Balaam's ass, that they spoke, we reply that the angel in the latter, and the devil in the former, wrought in such a manner that the animals themselves set their organs in motion in such wise that the voice thence sounded clear like genuine speech; not that the sound uttered was to the ass anything but braying, or to the serpent anything but hissing.

But if any one should argue in opposition, from what Ovid says in the fifth book of the *Metamorphoses*[3] about magpies speaking, we reply that he says this figuratively, meaning something else. And if any one should rejoin that even up to the present time magpies and other birds speak, we say that it is false, because such action is not speaking, but a kind of imitation of the sound of our voice, or in other words, we say that they try to imitate us in so far as we utter sounds, but not in so far as we speak. If accordingly any one were to say expressly "Pica" [magpie], and "Pica" were answered back, this would be but a copy or imitation of the sound made by him who had first said the word.

And so it is evident that speech has been given to man alone. But let us briefly endeavor to explain why this was necessary for him.

III

Since, then, man is not moved by natural instinct but by reason, and reason itself differs in individuals in respect of discernment, judgment, and choice, so that each one of us appears almost to rejoice in his own species, we are of opinion that no one has knowledge of another by means of his own actions or passions, as a brute beast; nor does it happen that one man can enter into another by spiritual insight, like an angel, since the human spirit is held back by the grossness and opacity of its mortal body. It was therefore necessary that the human race should have some sign, at once rational and sensible, for the intercommunication of its thoughts, because the sign, having to receive something from the reason of one and to convey it to the reason of another, had to be rational; and since nothing can be conveyed from one reason to another except through a medium of sense, it had to be sensible; for, were it only rational, it could not pass [from the reason of one to that of another]; and were it only sensible it would neither have been able to take from the reason of one nor to deposit in that of another.

Now this sign is that noble subject itself of which we are speaking; for in so far as it is sound, it is sensible, but in so far as it appears to carry some meaning according to the pleasure [of the speaker] it is rational.

IV

Speech was given to man alone, as is plain from what has been said above. And now I think we ought also to investigate to whom of mankind speech was first given, and what was the first thing he said, and to whom, where, and when he said it; and also in what language this first speech came forth. Now, according to what we read in the beginning of Genesis, where the most sacred Scripture is treating of the origin of the world, we find that a woman spoke before all others, I mean that most presumptuous Eve, when in answer to the inquiry of the devil she said, "We eat of the fruit of the trees which are in Paradise, but of the fruit of the tree which is in the midst of Paradise God has commanded us not to eat, nor to touch it, lest peradventure we die." But though we find it written that the woman spoke first, it is, however, reasonable for us to suppose that the man spoke first; and it is unseemly to think that so excellent an act of the human race proceeded even earlier from woman than from man. We therefore reasonably believe that speech was given to Adam first by him who had just formed him.

Now I have no doubt that it is obvious to a man of sound mind that the first thing the voice of the first speaker uttered was the equivalent of God, namely *El,* whether in the way of a question or in the way of an answer. It seems absurd and repugnant to reason that anything should have been named by man before God, since man had been made by him and for him. For as, since the transgression of the human race, every one begins his first attempt at speech with a cry of woe, it is reasonable that he who existed before that transgression should begin with joy; and since there is no joy without God, but all joy is in God, and God himself is wholly joy, it follows that the first speaker said first and before anything else "God." Here also this question arises from our saying above that man spoke first by way of answer: If an answer, was it addressed to God? For if so it would seem that God had already spoken, which appears to make against what has been said above. To which we reply that he might well have made answer when God questioned him; but it does not follow from this that God uttered what we call speech. For who doubts that whatsoever is can be bent according to the will of God? For by him all things were made, by him they are preserved, and by him also they are governed. Therefore since the air is made to undergo such great disturbances by the ordinance of that lower nature which is the minister and workmanship of God, that it causes the thunder to peal, the lightning to flash, the water to drop, and scatters the snow and hurls down the hail, shall it not be moved to utter certain words rendered distinct by him who has distinguished greater things? Why not? Wherefore we consider that these observations are a sufficient answer to this difficulty, and to some others.

V

Thinking then (not without reason drawn as well from the foregoing considerations as from those which follow) that the first man directed his speech first of all to the Lord himself, we may reasonably say that this first speaker at once, after having been inspired by the vivifying power, spoke without hesitation.

For in man we believe it to be more characteristic of humanity to be heard than to hear, provided he be heard and hear as a man. If, therefore, that workman and origin and lover of perfection by his breath made the first of us complete in all perfection, it appears to us reasonable that this most noble of animals did not begin to hear before he began to be heard. But if any one raises the objection that there was no need for him to speak, as he was, so far, the only human being, whilst God discerns all our secret thoughts without any words of ours, even before we do ourselves, we say with that reverence which we ought to use in judging anything respecting the eternal will, that though God knew, nay, even fore-knew (which is the same thing in respect of God) the thought of the first man who spoke, without any words being said, still he wished that the man should also speak, in order that, in the unfolding of so great a gift, he himself who had freely bestowed it might glory. And therefore it is to be believed that it is by God's appointment that we rejoice in the well-ordered play of our emotions.

Hence also we can fully determine the place where our first speech was uttered; for if man was inspired with life outside Paradise, he first spoke outside; but if within, we have proved that the place of his first speech was within.

VI

Since human affairs are carried on in very many different languages, so that many men are not understood by many with words any better than without words, it is appropriate for us to make investigation concerning that language which that man who had no mother, who was never suckled, who never saw either childhood or youth, is believed to have spoken. In this as in much else Pietramala is a most populous city, and the native place of the majority of the children of Adam. For whoever is so offensively unreasonable as to suppose that the place of his birth is the most delightful under the sun, also rates his own vernacular (that is, his mother-tongue) above all others, and consequently believes that it actually was that of Adam. But we, to whom the world is our native country, just as the sea is to the fish, though we drank of Arno before our teeth appeared, and though we love Florence so dearly that for the love we bore her we are wrongfully suffering exile—we rest the shoulders of our judgment on reason rather than on feeling. And although as regards our own pleasure or sensuous comfort there exists no more agreeable place in the world than Florence, still, when we turn over the volumes both of poets and other writers in which the world is generally and particularly described, and take account within ourselves of the various situations of the places of the world and their arrangement with respect to the two poles and to the equator, our deliberate and firm opinion is that there are many countries and cities both nobler and more delightful than Tuscany and Florence of which we are a native and a citizen, and also that a

great many nations and races use a speech both more agreeable and more service-
able than the Italians do. Returning therefore to our subject, we say that a certain
form of speech was created by God together with the first soul. And I say "a
form," both in respect of words and sentences and of the utterance of sentences;
and this form every tongue of speaking men would use, if it had not been dissipated by the fault of man's presumption, as shall be shown further on.

In this form of speech Adam spoke; in this form of speech all his
descendants spoke until the building of the Tower of Babel, which is by interpretation the tower of confusion; and this form of speech was inherited by the
sons of Heber, who after him were called Hebrews. With them alone did it
remain after the confusion, in order that our Redeemer (who was, as to his
humanity, to spring from them) might use, not the language of confusion, but
of grace. Therefore Hebrew was the language which the lips of the first speaker
formed.

VII

It is, alas! with feelings of shame that we now recall the ignominy of the
human race. But since it is impossible for us to avoid passing through it, we will
hasten through it, though the blush of shame rises to our cheeks and our mind
recoils. O thou our human nature, ever prone to sin! O thou, full of iniquity
from the first and ever afterwards without cessation! Did it suffice for thy cor-
rection that, deprived of light through thy first transgression, thou wast banished
from thy delightful native land? Did it suffice, did it suffice that through the
universal lust and cruelty of thy family, one house alone excepted, whatsoever
was subject to thee had perished in the Flood, and that the animals of earth and
air had already been punished for what thou hadst committed? Certainly this
should have been enough! But as men are wont to say in the proverb, "Thou
shalt not ride on horseback before the third time," thou, wretched one, didst
choose rather to come to a wretched steed.

See, reader, how man, either forgetting or despising his former discipline,
and turning aside his eyes from the marks of the stripes which had remained,
for the third time provoked the lash by his stupid and presumptuous pride! For
incorrigible man, persuaded by the giant, presumed in his heart to surpass by
his own skill not only nature, but even the very power that works in nature, who
is God; and he began to build a tower in Sennear, which was afterwards called
Babel, that is, confusion, by which he hoped to ascend to heaven; purposing in
his ignorance, not to equal, but to surpass his Maker. O boundless clemency of
the heavenly power! Who among fathers would bear so many insults from a
son? But he arose, and, with a scourge which was not hostile but paternal and
had been wont at other times to smite, he chastised his rebellious son with cor-
rection at once merciful and memorable. For almost the whole human race had

come together to the work of wickedness. Some were giving orders, some were acting as architects, some were building the walls, some were adjusting the masonry with rules, some were laying on the mortar with trowels, some were quarrying stone, some were engaged in bringing it by sea, some by land; and different companies were engaged in different other occupations, when they were struck by such confusion from heaven, that all those who were attending to the work, using one and the same language, left off the work on being estranged by many different languages and never again came together in the same intercourse. For the same language remained to those alone who were engaged together in the same kind of work; for instance, one language remained to all the architects, another to those rolling down blocks of stone, another to those preparing the stone; and so it happened to each group of workers. And the human race was accordingly then divided into as many different languages as there were different branches of the work; and the higher the branch of work the men were engaged in, the ruder and more barbarous was the language they afterwards spoke.

But those to whom the hallowed language remained were neither present, nor countenanced the work; but utterly hating it, they mocked the folly of those engaged in it. But these, a small minority, were of the seed of Shem (as I conjecture), who was the third son of Noah; and from them sprang the people of Israel, who made use of the most ancient language until their dispersion.

VIII

On account of the confusion of tongues related above we have no slight reason for thinking that men were at that time first scattered through all the climates of the world, and the habitable regions and corners of those climates. And as the original root of the human race was planted in the regions of the East, and our race also spread out from there on both sides by a manifold diffusion of shoots, and finally reached the boundaries of the West, it was then perhaps that rational throats first drank of the rivers of the whole of Europe, or at least of some of them. But whether these men then first arrived as strangers, or whether they came back to Europe as natives, they brought a threefold language with them, and of those who brought it some allotted to themselves the southern, others the northern part of Europe, while the third body, whom we now call Greeks, seized partly on Europe and partly on Asia.

Afterwards, from one and the same idiom received at the avenging confusion, various vernaculars drew their origin, as we shall show farther on. For one idiom alone prevailed in all the country which from the mouths of the Danube, or marshes of Mæotis to the western boundary of England, is bounded by the frontiers of Italy and France and by the ocean; though afterwards through the Slavs, Hungarians, Teutons, Saxons, English, and many other nations it was drawn off into various vernaculars, this alone remaining to almost all of them as a sign of their common origin, that nearly all the above-named answer in affirmation *io*.

Starting from this idiom, that is to say eastward from the Hungarian frontier, another language prevailed over all the territory in that direction comprised in Europe, and even extended beyond. But a third idiom prevailed in all that part of Europe which remains from the other two, though it now appears in a threefold form. For of those who speak it, some say in affirmation *oc*,[4] others *oïl*, and others *sì*, namely the Spaniards, the French, and the Italians. Now the proof that the vernaculars of these nations proceed from one and the same idiom is obvious, because we see that they call many things by the same names, as *Deum, celum, amorem, mare, terram, vivit, moritur, amat,* and almost all other things. Now those of them who say *oc* inhabit the western part of the South of Europe, beginning from the frontier of the Genoese; while those who say *sì* inhabit the country east of the said frontier, namely that which extends as far as that promontory of Italy where the Gulf of the Adriatic Sea begins, and Sicily. But those who say *oïl* lie in some sort to the north of these last; for they have the Germans on their east and north; on the west they are enclosed by the English sea, and bounded by the mountains of Aragon; they are also shut off on the south by the inhabitants of Provence, and the precipices of the Apennines.

IX

We must now put whatever reason we possess to the proof, since it is our purpose to investigate matters in which we are supported by the authority of none, namely, the change which has passed over a language which was originally of one and the same form. [And] because it is safer as well as quicker to travel by known paths, let us proceed with that language alone which belongs to us, neglecting the others. For that which we find in one appears by analogy to exist in the others also.

The language, then, which we are proceeding to treat of is threefold, as has been mentioned above; for some of those who speak it say *oc*, others *sì*, and others *oïl*. And that this language was uniform at the beginning of the confusion (which must first be proved) appears from the fact that we agree in many words, as eloquent writers show, which agreement is repugnant to that confusion which expiated the crime [committed] in the building of Babel.

The writers of all three forms of the language agree, then, in many words, especially in the word *Amor*. Giraut de Borneil says: *"Sim sentis fezelz amics / per ver encusera Amor."*[5] The King of Navarre: *"De fine amor si vient sen et bonté."*[6] Messer Guido Guinizelli: *"Nè fa amor prima che gentil core / nè gentil cor prima che amor natura."*[7] Let us now inquire why it is that this language has varied into three chief forms, and why each of these variations varies in itself; why, for instance, the speech of the right side of Italy varies from that of the left (for the Paduans speak in one way and the Pisans in another); and also why those who live nearer together still vary in their speech, as the Milanese and Veronese, the Romans and the Florentines, and even those who have the same national designation, as the Neapolitans and the people of Gaeta, those of Ravenna and those of Faenza, and what is stranger still, the inhabitants of the same city, like the Bolognese of the Borgo S. Felice and the Bolognese of the Strada Maggiore. One and the same reason will explain why all these differences and varieties of speech occur.

We say, therefore, that no effect as such goes beyond its cause, because nothing can bring about that which itself is not. Since therefore every language of ours, except that created by God with the first man, has been restored at our pleasure after the confusion, which was nothing else but forgetfulness of the former language, and since man is a most unstable and changeable animal, no human language can be lasting and continuous, but must needs vary like other properties of ours, as for instance our manners and our dress, according to distance of time and place. And so far am I from thinking that there is room for doubt as to the truth of our remark that speech varies "according to difference of time," that we are of opinion that this is rather to be held as certain. For, if we consider our other actions, we seem to differ much more from our fellow-countrymen in very distant times than from our contemporaries very remote in place. Wherefore we boldly affirm that if the ancient Pavians were to rise from the dead they would talk in a language varying or differing from that of the modern Pavians. Nor should what we are saying appear more wonderful than to observe that a young man is grown up whom we have not seen growing. For the motion of those things which move gradually is not considered by us at all; and the longer the time required for perceiving the variation of a thing, the more stable we suppose that thing to be. Let us not therefore be surprised if the opinions of men who are but little removed from the brutes suppose that the citizens of the same town have always carried on their intercourse with an unchangeable speech, because the change in the speech of the same town comes about gradually, not without a very long succession of time, whilst the life of man is in its nature extremely short.

If, therefore, the speech of the same people varies (as has been said) successively in course of time, and cannot in any wise stand still, the speech of people living apart and removed from one another must needs vary in different ways; just as manners and dress vary in different ways, since they are not rendered stable either by nature or by intercourse, but arise according to men's inclinations and local fitness. Hence were set in motion the inventors of the art of grammar, which is nothing else but a kind of unchangeable identity of speech in different times and places. This, having been settled by the common consent of many peoples, seems exposed to the arbitrary will of none in particular, and consequently cannot be variable. They therefore invented grammar in order that we might not, on account of the variation of speech fluctuating at the will of in-dividuals, either fail altogether in attaining, or at least attain but a partial knowl-edge of the opinions and exploits of the ancients, or of those whom difference of place causes to differ from us.

X

Our language being now spoken under three forms (as has been said above), we feel, when comparing it with itself, according to the three forms that it has assumed, such great hesitation and timidity in placing [its different forms] in the balances, that we dare not, in our comparison, give the preference to any one of them, except in so far as we find that the founders of grammar have taken *sic* as the adverb of affirmation, which seems to confer a kind of precedence on the Italians, who say *sì*. For each of the three divisions [of our language] defends its pretensions by copious evidence. That of *oïl*, then, alleges on its behalf that because of its being an easier and pleasanter vernacular language, whatever has been translated into or composed in vernacular prose belongs to it, namely, the compilations of the exploits of the Trojans and Romans, the exquisite legends of King Arthur, and very many other works of history and learning. Another, namely that of *oc*, claims that eloquent speakers of the ver-nacular first employed it for poetry, as being a more finished and sweeter lan-guage, for instance Peter of Auvergne and other ancient writers. The third also, which is the language of the Italians, claims pre-eminence on the strength of two privileges: first, that the sweetest and most subtle poets who have written in the vernacular are its intimate friends and belong to its household, like Cino of Pistoia and his friend[8]; second, that it seems to lean more on grammar, which is common: and this appears a very weighty argument to those who examine the matter in a rational way.

We, however, decline to give judgment in this case, and confining our treatise to the vernacular Italian, let us endeavor to enumerate the variations it has received into itself, and also to compare these with one another. In the first place, then, we say that Italy has a twofold division into right and left. But, if any should ask what is the dividing line, we answer shortly that it is the ridge of the Apennines, which like the ridge of a tiled roof discharges its droppings in different directions on either side, and pours its waters down to either shore alternately through long gutter-tiles, as Lucan describes in his second book. Now the right side has the Tyrrhenian Sea as its basin, while the waters on the left fall into the Adriatic. The districts on the right are Apulia (but not the whole of it), the Duchy [of Spoleto], Tuscany, and the March of Genoa. Those on the left are part of Apulia, the March of Ancona, Romagna, Lombardy, and the March of Treviso with Venetia. Friuli and Istria cannot but belong to the left of Italy, and the islands of the Tyrrhenian Sea, namely Sicily and Sardinia, must belong to, or be associated with the right of Italy. Now in each of these two sides, and those districts which follow them, the languages of the inhabitants vary, as for instance the language of the Sicilians as compared with that of the Apulians, of the Apulians with that of the Romans, of the Romans with that of the Spoletans, of these with that of the Tuscans, of the Tuscans with that of the Genoese, of the Genoese with that of the Sardinians; also of the Calabrians with that of the people of Ancona, of these with that of the people of Romagna, of the people of Romagna with that of the Lombards, of the Lombards with that of the Trevisans and Venetians, and of these last with that of the Aquileians, and of them with that of the Istrians; and we do not think that any Italian will disagree with us in this statement. Whence it appears that Italy alone is diversified by fourteen dialects at least, all of which again vary in themselves: as for instance in Tuscany the Sienese differ in speech from the Aretines; in Lombardy the Ferrarese from the Placentines; in the same city also we observe some variation, as we remarked above in the last chapter. Wherefore if we would calculate the primary, secondary, and subordinate variations of the vulgar tongue of Italy, we should find that in this tiny corner of the world the varieties of speech not only come up to a thousand but even exceed that figure.

XI

As the Italian vernacular has so very many discordant varieties, let us hunt after a more fitting and an illustrious Italian language; and in order that we may be able to have a practicable path for our chase, let us first cast the tangled bushes and brambles out of the wood. Therefore, as the Romans think that they ought to have precedence over all the rest, let us in this process of uprooting or clearing away give them (not undeservedly) precedence, declaring that we will have nothing to do with them in any scheme of a vernacular language. We say, then, that the vulgar tongue of the Romans, or rather their hideous jargon, is the ugliest of all the Italian dialects; nor is this surprising, since in the depravity of their manners and customs also they appear to stink worse than all the rest. For they say *"Mezzure, quinto dici?"*[9] After them, let us get rid of the inhabitants of the March of Ancona, who say, *"Chignamente scate sciate?"*[10] with whom we reject the Spoletans also. Nor must we forget that a great many canzoni have been written in contempt of these three peoples, among which we have noticed one correctly and perfectly constructed, which a certain Florentine named Castra had composed. It began: *"Una fermana scopai da Casciòli / Cita cita sen gia'n grande aina."*[11] And after these let us weed out the people of Milan and Bergamo with their neighbors, in reproach of whom we recollect that some one has sung: *"Enti l'ora del vesper, / Ciò fu del mes d' ochiover."*[12] After them let us sift out the Aquileians and Istrians, who belch forth with cruelly harsh accents, *"Ces fastu?"*[13] And with these we cast out all the mountainous and rural dialects, as those of Casentino and Prato, which by the extravagance of their accent always seem discordant to the citizens dwelling in the midst of the towns. Let us also cast out the Sardinians, who are not Italians, but are, it seems, to be associated with them; since they alone seem to be without any vulgar tongue of their own, imitating Latin as apes do men: for they say, *"Domus nova"*[14] and *"dominus meus."*[15]

XII

Having sifted, so to speak, the Italian vernaculars, let us, comparing together those left in our sieve, briefly choose out the one most honorable and conferring most honor. And first let us examine the genius of the Sicilian, for the Sicilian vernacular appears to arrogate to itself a greater renown than the others, both because whatever poetry the Italians write is called Sicilian, and because we find that very many natives of Sicily have written weighty poetry, as in the canzoni, *"Ancor che l'aigua per lo focho lassi,"*[16] and *"Amor che lungiamente m'ài menato."*[17] But this fame of the land of Trinacria[18] appears, if we rightly examine the mark to which it tends, only to have survived by way of a reproach to the princes of Italy, who, not in a heroic but in a plebeian manner, follow pride. But those illustrious heroes Frederick Cæsar[19] and his happy-born son Manfred, displaying the nobility and righteousness of their character, as long as fortune remained favorable, followed what is human, disdaining what is bestial; wherefore those who were of noble heart and endowed with graces strove to attach themselves to the majesty of such great princes; so that in their time, whatever the best Italians attempted first appeared at the court of these mighty sovereigns. And from the fact that the royal throne was Sicily it came to pass that whatever our predecessors wrote in the vulgar tongue was called Sicilian; and this name we also retain, nor will our successors be able to change it. Racha, racha![20] what is the sound now uttered by the trumpet of the latest Frederick?[21] What is that uttered by the bell of Charles II.? What is that uttered by the horns of the powerful Marquises John and Azzo? What is that uttered by the flutes of the other magnates? What but "Come, ye murderers; come, ye traitors; come, ye followers of avarice."

But it is better to return to our subject than to speak in vain: and we declare that if we take the Sicilian dialect, that namely spoken by the common people, out of whose mouths it appears our judgment should be drawn, it is in nowise worthy of preference, because it is not uttered without drawling, as for instance here: *"Tragemi d'este focora, se t'este a boluntate."*[22] If, however, we choose to take the language as it flows from the mouths of the highest Sicilians, as it may be examined in the canzoni quoted before, it differs in nothing from that language which is the most worthy of praise, as we show further on.

The Apulians also, because of their own harshness of speech, or else because of their nearness to their neighbors who are the Romans and the people of the March [of Ancona], make use of shameful barbarisms, for they say, "*Volzera che chiangesse lo quatraro.*"[23]

But though the natives of Apulia commonly speak in a hideous manner, some of them have been distinguished by their use of polished language, inserting more *curial* words into their canzoni, as clearly appears from an examination of their works, for instance, "*Madonna, dir vi voglio,*"[24] and "*Per fino amore vo sì letamente.*"[25]

Wherefore it should become clear to those who mark what has been said above, that neither the Sicilian nor the Apulian dialect is that vulgar tongue which is the most beautiful in Italy, for we have shown that eloquent natives of those parts have diverged from their own dialect.

XIII

Next let us come to the Tuscans, who, infatuated through their frenzy, seem to arrogate to themselves the title of the illustrious vernacular; and in this matter not only the minds of the common people are crazed, but we find that many distinguished men have embraced the delusion; for instance Guittone of Arezzo, who never aimed at the curial vernacular, Bonagiunta of Lucca, Gallo of Pisa, Mino Mocato of Siena, and Brunetto of Florence, whose works, if there be leisure to examine them, will be found to be not curial but merely municipal. And since the Tuscans exceed the rest in this frenzied intoxication, it seems right and profitable to deal with the dialects of the Tuscan towns one by one, and to take off somewhat of their vain glory. The Florentines open their mouths and say, "*Manichiamo introque—Noi non facciano atro*";[26] the Pisans, "*Bene andonno li fanti De Fiorensa per Pisa*";[27] the people of Lucca, "*Fo voto a Dio che in gassarra eie lo comuno de Lucca*";[28] the Sienese, "*Onche renegata avesse io Siena!*"[29] "*Ch'ee chesto?*"[30] the Aretines, "*Vo tu venire ovelle?*"[31] (We do not intend to deal with Perugia, Orvieto, and Città Castellana at all, because of their close connection with the Romans and Spoletans.) But obtuse as almost all the Tuscans are in their degraded dialect, we notice that some have recognized wherein the excellence of the vernacular consists, namely, Guido, Lapo, and another, all Florentines, and Cino of Pistoja, whom we now undeservedly put last, having been not undeservedly driven to do so. Therefore if we examine the Tuscan dialects, reflecting how the writers commended above have deviated from their own dialect, it does not remain doubtful that the vernacular we are in search of is different from that which the people of Tuscany attain to.

But if any one thinks that what we say of the Tuscans may not also be said of the Genoese, let him but bear this in mind, that if the Genoese were through forgetfulness to lose the letter *z*, they would have either to be dumb altogether, or to discover some new kind of speech, for *z* forms the greatest part of their dialect, and this letter is not uttered without great harshness.

XIV

Let us now cross the leaf-clad shoulders of the Apennines, and hunt inquiringly, as we are wont, over the left side of Italy, beginning from the east.

Entering Romagna, then, we remark that we have found in Italy two alternating types of dialect with certain opposite characteristics in which they respectively agree. One of these, on account of the softness of its words and pronunciation, seems so feminine that it causes a man, even when speaking like a man, to be believed to be a woman. This type of dialect prevails among all the people of Romagna, and especially those of Forli, whose city, though the newest, seems to be the centre of all the province. These people say *deuscì* in affirmation, and use *"Oclo meo"*[32] and *"Corada mea"*[33] as terms of endearment. We have heard that some of them have diverged in poetry from their own dialect, namely the Faentines Thomas and Ugolino Bucciola.

There is also, as we have said, another type of dialect, so bristling and shaggy in its words and accents that, owing to its rough harshness, it not only distorts a woman's speech, but makes one doubt whether she is not a man. This type of dialect prevails among all those who say *magara*,[34] namely the Brescians, Veronese, and Vicentines, as well as the Paduans, with their ugly syncopations of all the participles in *tus* and denominatives in *tas*, as *mercò* and *bontè*. With these we also class the Trevisans, who, like the Brescians and their neighbors, pronounce *f* for consonantal *u*, cutting off the final syllable of the word, as *nof* for *novem*,[35] *vif* for *vivo*, which we disapprove as a gross barbarism.

Nor do the Venetians also deem themselves worthy of possessing that vernacular language which we have been searching for; and if any of them, trusting in error, should cherish any delusion on this point, let him remember whether he has ever said *"Per le plage de Dio tu non veràs."*[36]

Among all these we have noticed one man striving to depart from his mother-tongue, and to apply himself to the *curial* vernacular language, namely Ildebrandino of Padua.

Wherefore, on all the dialects mentioned in the present chapter coming up for judgment, our decision is that neither that of Romagna nor its opposite (as we have mentioned), nor that of Venice is that illustrious vernacular which we are seeking.

XV

Let us now endeavor to clear the way by tracking out what remains of the Italian wood.

We say, then, that perhaps those are not far wrong who assert that the people of Bologna use a more beautiful speech [than the others], since they receive into their own dialect something borrowed from their neighbors of Imola, Ferrara, and Modena, just as we conjecture that all borrow from their neighbors, as Sordello showed with respect to his own Mantua, which is adjacent to Cremona, Brescia, and Verona; and he who was so distinguished by his eloquence, not only in poetry but in every other form of utterance forsook his native vulgar tongue. Accordingly the above-mentioned citizens [of Bologna] get from those of Imola their smoothness and softness [of speech], and from those of Ferrara and Modena a spice of sharpness characteristic of the Lombards. This we believe has remained with the natives of that district as a relic of the admixture of the immigrant Longobards with them: and this is the reason why we find that there has been no poet among the people of Ferrara, Modena, or Reggio; for from being accustomed to their own sharpness they cannot adopt the courtly vulgar tongue without a kind of roughness; and this we must consider to be much more the case with the people of Parma, who say *monto* instead of *multo*. If, therefore, the people of Bologna borrow from both these kinds of dialect, as has been said, it seems reasonable that their speech should by this mixture of opposites remain tempered to a praiseworthy sweetness; and this we without hesitation judge to be the case. Therefore if those who place the people of Bologna first in the matter of the vernacular merely have regard in their comparison to the municipal dialects of the Italians, we are disposed to agree with them; but if they consider that the dialect of Bologna is, taken absolutely, worthy of preference, we disagree with them altogether; for this dialect is not that language which we term courtly and illustrious, since if it had been so, the greatest Guido Guinizelli, Guido Ghisilieri, Fabruzzo, and Onesto, and other poets of Bologna would never have departed from their own dialect; and these were illustrious writers, competent judges of dialects. The greatest Guido, wrote: *"Madonna lo fermo core"*;[37] Fabruzzo, *"Lo meo lontano gire"*;[38] Onesto, *"Più non attendo il tuo secorso, Amore"*;[39] and these words are altogether different from the dialect of the citizens of Bologna.

And since we consider that no one feels any doubt as to the remaining towns at the extremities of Italy (and if any one does, we do not deem him worthy of any answer from us), little remains to be mentioned in our discussion. Wherefore being eager to put down our sieve so that we may quickly see what is left in it, we say that the towns of Trent and Turin, as well as Alessandria, are situated so near the frontiers of Italy that they cannot possess pure languages, so that even if their vernaculars were as lovely as they are hideous, we should still say that they were not truly Italian, because of their foreign ingredients. Wherefore if we are hunting for an illustrious Italian language, what we are hunting for cannot be found in them.

XVI

After having scoured the heights and pastures of Italy, without having found that panther which we are in pursuit of, in order that we may be able to find her, let us now track her out in a more rational manner, so that we may with skillful efforts completely enclose within our toils her who is fragrant everywhere but nowhere apparent.

Resuming, then, our hunting-spears, we say that in every kind of things there must be one thing by which all the things of that kind may be compared and weighed, and which we may take as the measure of all the others; just as in numbers all are measured by unity and are said to be more or fewer according as they are distant from or near to unity; so also in colors all are measured by white, for they are said to be more or less visible according as they approach or recede from it. And what we say of the predicaments which indicate quantity and quality, we think may also be said of any of the predicaments and even of substance; namely, that everything considered as belonging to a kind becomes measurable by that which is simplest in that kind. Wherefore in our actions, however many the species into which they are divided may be, we have to discover this standard by which they may be measured. Thus, in what concerns our actions as human beings simply, we have virtue, understanding it generally; for according to it we judge a man to be good or bad; in what concerns our actions as citizens, we have the law, according to which a citizen is said to be good or bad; in what concerns our actions as Italians, we have certain very simple standards of manners, customs, and language, by which our actions as Italians are weighed and measured. Now the supreme standards of those activities which are generically Italian are not peculiar to any one town in Italy, but are common to all; and among these can now be discerned that vernacular language which we were hunting for above, whose fragrance is in every town, but whose lair is in none. It may, however, be more perceptible in one than in another, just as the simplest of substances, which is God, is more perceptible in a man than in a brute, in an animal than in a plant, in a plant than in a mineral, in a mineral than in an element, in fire than in earth. And the simplest quantity, which is unity, is more perceptible in an odd than in an even number; and the simplest color, which is white, is more perceptible in orange than in green.

Having therefore found what we were searching for, we declare the illustrious, cardinal, courtly, and curial vernacular language in Italy to be that which belongs to all the towns in Italy but does not appear to belong to any one of them, and by which all the municipal dialects of the Italians are measured, weighed, and compared.

XVII

We must now set forth why it is that we call this language we have found by the epithets illustrious, cardinal, courtly, and curial; and by doing this we disclose the nature of the language itself more clearly. First, then, let us lay bare what we mean by the epithet illustrious, and why we call the language illustrious. Now we understand by this term "illustrious" something which shines forth illuminating and illuminated. And in this way we call men illustrious either because, being illuminated by power, they illuminate others by justice and charity; or else because, having been excellently trained, they in turn give excellent training, like Seneca and Numa Pompilius. And the vernacular of which we are speaking has both been exalted by training and power, and also exalts its followers by honor and glory.

Now it appears to have been exalted by training, inasmuch as from amid so many rude Italian words, involved constructions, faulty expressions, and rustic accents we see that it has been chosen out in such a degree of excellence, clearness, completeness, and polish as is displayed by Cino of Pistoja and his friend in their canzoni.

And that it has been exalted by power is plain; for what is of greater power than that which can sway the hearts of men, so as to make an unwilling man willing, and a willing man unwilling, just as this language has done and is doing?

Now that it exalts by honor is evident. Do not they of its household surpass in renown kings, marquises, counts, and all other magnates? This has no need at all of proof.

But how glorious it makes its familiar friends we ourselves know, who for the sweetness of this glory cast [even] our exile behind our back. Wherefore we ought deservedly to proclaim this language illustrious.

XVIII

Nor is it without reason that we adorn this illustrious vernacular language with a second epithet, that is, that we call it cardinal: for as the whole door follows its hinge, so that whither the hinge turns the door also may turn, whether it be moved inward or outward, in like manner also the whole herd of municipal dialects turns and returns, moves and pauses according as this illustrious language does, which really seems to be the father of the family. Does it not daily root out the thorny bushes from the Italian wood? Does it not daily insert grafts or plant young trees? What else have its foresters to do but to take away and bring in, as has been said? Wherefore it surely deserves to be adorned with so great a name as this.

Now the reason why we call it "courtly" is that if we Italians had a court it would be spoken at court. For if a court is a common home of all the realm and an august ruler of all parts of the realm, it is fitting that whatever is of such a character as to be common to all [parts] without being peculiar to any, should frequent this court and dwell there; nor is any other abode worthy of so great an inmate. Such in fact seems to be that vernacular language of which we are speaking; and hence it is that those who frequent all royal palaces always speak the illustrious vernacular. Hence also it is that our illustrious language wanders about like a wayfarer, and is welcomed in humble shelters, seeing we have no court.

This language is also deservedly to be styled "curial," because "curiality" is nothing else but the justly balanced rule of things which have to be done; and because the scales required for this kind of balancing are only wont to be found in the most excellent courts of justice, it follows that whatever in our actions has been well balanced is called curial. Wherefore since this illustrious language has been weighed in the balances of the most excellent court of justice of the Italians, it deserves to be called curial. But it seems mere trifling to say that it has been weighed in the balances of the most excellent court of justice of the Italians, because we have no [Imperial] court of justice. To this the answer is easy. For though there is no court of justice of Italy in the sense of a single [supreme] court, like the court of the king of Germany, still the members of such a court are not wanting. And just as the members of the German court are united under one prince, so the members of ours have been united by the gracious light of reason. Wherefore, though we have no prince, it would be false to assert that the Italians have no [such] court of justice, because we have a court, though in the body it is scattered.

XIX

Now we declare that this vernacular language, which we have shown to be illustrious, cardinal, courtly, and curial, is that which is called the Italian vernacular. For just as a vernacular can be found peculiar to Cremona, so can one be found peculiar to Lombardy; and just as one can be found peculiar to Lombardy, [so] can one be found peculiar to the whole of the left side of Italy. And just as all these can be found, so also can that which belongs to the whole of Italy. And just as the first is called Cremonese, the second Lombard, and the third Semi-Italian, so that which belongs to the whole of Italy is called the Italian vernacular language. For this has been used by the illustrious writers who have written poetry in the vernacular throughout Italy, as Sicilians, Apulians, Tuscans, natives of Romagna, and men of both the Marches. And because our intention is, as we promised in the beginning of this work, to give instruction concerning the vernacular speech, we will begin with this illustrious Italian as being the most excellent, and treat in the books immediately following of those whom we think worthy to use it; and for what, and how, and also where, when, and to whom, it ought to be used. And after making all this clear, we will make it our business to throw light on the lower vernaculars, gradually coming down to that which belongs to a single family.

BOOK II

I

Urging on once more the nimbleness of our wit, which is returning to the pen of useful work, we declare in the first place that the illustrious Italian vernacular is equally fit for use in prose and in verse. But because prose writers rather get this language from poets, and because poetry seems to remain a pattern to prose writers, and not the converse, which things appear to confer a certain supremacy, let us first disentangle this language as to its use in meter, treating of it in the order we set forth at the end of the first book.

Let us then first inquire whether all those who write verse in the vernacular should use this illustrious language; and so far as a superficial consideration of the matter goes, it would seem that they should, because every one who writes verse ought to adorn his verse as far as he is able. Wherefore, since nothing affords so great an adornment as the illustrious vernacular does, it would seem that every writer of verse ought to employ it. Besides, if that which is best in its kind be mixed with things inferior to itself, it not only appears not to detract anything from them but even to improve them. Wherefore if any writer of verse, even though his verse be rude in matter, mixes the illustrious vernacular with his rudeness of matter, he not only appears to do well, but to be actually obliged to take this course. Those who can do little need help much more than those who can do much, and thus it appears that all writers of verse are at liberty to use this illustrious language. But this is quite false, because not even poets of the highest order ought always to assume it, as will appear from a consideration of what is discussed farther on. This illustrious language, then, just like our behavior in other matters and our dress, demands men of like quality to its own; for munificence demands men of great resources, and the purple, men of noble character, and in the same way this illustrious language seeks for men who excel in genius and knowledge, and despises others, as will appear from what is said below. For everything which is suited to us is so either in respect of the genus, or of the species, or of the individual, as sensation, laughter, war; but this illustrious language is not suited to us in respect of our genus, for then it would also be suited to the brutes; nor in respect of our species, for then it would be suited to all men; and as to this there is no question; for no one will say that this language is suited to dwellers in the mountains dealing with rustic concerns: therefore it is suited in respect of the individual. But nothing is suited to an individual except on account of his particular worth, as for instance commerce, war, and government. Wherefore if things are suitable according to worth, that is the worthy (and some men may be worthy, others worthier and others worthiest), it is plain that good things will be suited to the worthy, better things to the worthier, and the best things to the worthiest. And since language is as necessary an instrument of our thought as a horse is of a knight, and since the best horses are suited to the best knights, as has been said, the best language will be suited to the best thoughts. But the best thoughts cannot exist except where knowledge and genius are found; therefore the best language is only suitable in those in whom knowledge and genius are found; and so the best language is not suited to all who write verse, since a great many write without knowledge and genius; and consequently neither is the best vernacular [suited to all who write verse]. Wherefore, if it is not suited to all, all ought not to use it, because no one ought to act in an unsuitable manner. And as to the statement that every one ought to adorn his verse as far as he can, we declare that it is true; but we should not describe an ox with trappings or a swine with a belt as adorned, nay rather we laugh at them as disfigured; for adornment is the addition of some suitable thing.

As to the statement that superior things mixed with inferior effect an improvement [in the latter], we say that it is true if the blending is complete, for instance when we mix gold and silver together; but if it is not, the inferior things appear worse, for instance when beautiful women are mixed with ugly ones. Wherefore, since the theme of those who write verse always persists as an ingredient distinct from the words, it will not, unless of the highest quality, appear better when associated with the best vernacular, but worse; like an ugly woman if dressed out in gold or silk.

II

After having proved that not all those who write verse, but only those of the highest excellence, ought to use the illustrious vernacular, we must in the next place establish whether every subject ought to be handled in it, or not; and if not, we must set out by themselves those subjects that are worthy of it. And in reference to this we must first find out what we understand by that which we call *worthy*. We say that a thing which has worthiness is worthy, just as we say that a thing which has nobility is noble; and if when that which confers the habit is known, that on which the habit is conferred is [also] known, as such, then if we know what worthiness is, we shall know also what *worthy* is. Now worthiness is an effect or end of deserts; so that when any one has deserved well we say that he has arrived at worthiness of good; but when he has deserved ill, at worthiness of evil. Thus we say that a soldier who has fought well has arrived at worthiness of victory; one who has ruled well, at worthiness of a kingdom; also that a liar has arrived at worthiness of shame, and a robber at worthiness of death.

But inasmuch as [further] comparisons are made among those who deserve well, and also among those who deserve ill, so that some deserve well, some better, and some best; some badly, some worse, and some worst; while such comparisons are only made with respect to the end of deserts, which (as has been mentioned before) we call *worthiness*, it is plain that worthinesses are compared together according as they are greater or less, so that some are great, some greater, and some greatest; and, consequently, it is obvious that one thing is worthy, another worthier, and another worthiest. And whereas there can be no such comparison of worthinesses with regard to the same object [of desert] but [only] with regard to different objects, so that we call *worthier* that which is worthy of greater objects, and *worthiest* that which is worthy of the greatest, because no thing can be more worthy [than another] in virtue of the same quali-fication, it is evident that the best things are worthy of the best [objects of desert], according to the requirement of the things. Whence it follows that, since the language we call illustrious is the best of all the other forms of the vernacular, the best subjects alone are worthy of being handled in it, and these we call the *worthiest* of those subjects which can be handled; and now let us hunt out what they are. And, in order to make this clear, it must be observed that, as man has been endowed with a threefold life, namely, vegetable, animal, and rational, he journeys along a threefold road; for in so far as he is vegetable he seeks for what is useful, wherein he is of like nature with plants; in so far as he is animal he seeks for that which is pleasurable, wherein he is of like nature with the brutes; in so far as he is rational he seeks for what is right—and in this he stands alone, or is a partaker of the nature of the angels. It is by these three kinds of life that we appear to carry out whatever we do; and because in each one of them some things are greater, some greatest, within the range of their kind, it follows that those which are greatest appear the ones which ought to be treated of supremely, and consequently, in the greatest vernacular.

But we must discuss what things are greatest; and first in respect of what is useful. Now in this matter, if we carefully consider the object of all those who are in search of what is useful, we shall find that it is nothing else but safety. Secondly, in respect of what is pleasurable; and here we say that that is most pleasurable which gives pleasure by the most exquisite object of appetite, and this is love. Thirdly, in respect of what is right; and here no one doubts that virtue has the first place. Wherefore these three things, namely, safety, love, and virtue, appear to be those capital matters which ought to be treated of supremely, I mean the things which are most important in respect of them, as prowess in arms, the fire of love, and the direction of the will. And if we duly consider, we shall find that the illustrious writers have written poetry in the vulgar tongue on these subjects exclusively; namely, Bertran de Born on Arms, Arnaut Daniel on Love, Giraut de Borneil on Righteousness, Cino of Pistoja on Love, his friend on Righteousness. For Bertan says: *"Non posc mudar c'un cantar non exparja."*[40] Arnaut: *"L'aura amara fals bruols brancuz clairir."*[41] Giraut: *"Per solaz reveillar / que s'es trop endormitz."*[42] Cino: *"Digno sono eo de morte."*[43] His friend: *"Doglia mi reca nello core ardire."*[44] I do not find, however, that any Italian has as yet written poetry on the subject of Arms.

Having then arrived at this point, we know what are the proper subjects to be sung in the highest vernacular language.

III

But now let us endeavor carefully to examine how those matters which are worthy of so excellent a vernacular language are to be restricted. As we wish, then, to set forth the form by which these matters are worthy to be bound, we say that it must first be borne in mind that those who have written poetry in the vernacular have uttered their poems in many different forms, some in that of canzoni, some in that of ballate, some in that of sonnets, some in other illegitimate and irregular forms, as will be shown farther on. Now we consider that of these forms that of canzoni is the most excellent; and therefore, if the most excellent things are worthy of the most excellent, as has been proved above, those subjects which are worthy of the most excellent vernacular are worthy of the most excellent form, and consequently ought to be handled in canzoni. Now we may discover by several reasons that the form of canzoni is such as has been said. The first reason is that though whatever we write in verse is a canzone, the canzoni [technically so called] have alone acquired this name; and this has never happened apart from ancient provision.

Moreover, whatever produces by itself the effect for which it was made, appears nobler than that which requires external assistance. But canzoni produce by themselves the whole effect they ought to produce; which ballate do not, for they require the assistance of the performers for whom they are written; it therefore follows that canzoni are to be deemed nobler than ballate, and therefore that their form is the noblest of any, for no one doubts that ballate excel sonnets in nobility of form.

Besides, those things appear to be nobler which bring more honor to their author; but canzoni bring more [honor] to their authors than ballate; therefore they are nobler [than these], and consequently their form is the noblest of any.

Furthermore, the noblest things are the most fondly preserved; but among poems canzoni are the most fondly preserved, as is evident to those who look into books; therefore canzoni are the noblest [poems], and consequently their form is the noblest.

Also, in works of art, that is noblest which embraces the whole art. Since, therefore, poems are works of art, and the whole of the art is embraced in canzoni alone, canzoni are the noblest poems, and so their form is the noblest of any. Now, that the whole of the art of poetic song is embraced in canzoni is proved by the fact that whatever is found to belong to the art is found in them; but the converse is not true. But the proof of what we are saying is at once apparent; for all that has flowed from the tops of the heads of illustrious poets down to their lips is found in canzoni alone. Wherefore, in reference to the sub-

ject before us, it is clear that the matters which are worthy of the highest vulgar
tongue ought to be handled in canzoni.

IV

Having then labored by a process of disentangling [to show] what persons and things are worthy of the courtly vernacular, as well as the form of
verse which we deem worthy of such honor that it alone is fitted for the highest
vernacular, before going off to other topics, let us explain the form of the
canzone, which many appear to adopt rather at haphazard than with art; and let
us unlock the workshop of the art of that form which has hitherto been adopted
in a casual way, omitting the form of ballate and sonnets, because we intend
to explain this in the fourth book of this work, when we shall treat of the middle
vernacular language.

Reviewing, therefore, what has been said, we remember that we have
frequently called those who write verse in the vernacular poets; and this we
have doubtless ventured to say with good reason, because they are in fact poets,
if we take a right view of poetry, which is nothing else but a rhetorical composition set to music. But these poets differ from the great poets, that is, the
regular ones, for the language of the great poets was regulated by art, whereas
these, as has been said, write at haphazard. It therefore happens that the more
closely we copy the great poets, the more correct is the poetry we write; whence
it behooves us, by devoting some trouble to the work of teaching, to emulate
their poetic teaching.

Before all things therefore we say that each one ought to adjust the
weight of the subject to his own shoulders, so that their strength may not be
too heavily taxed, and he be forced to tumble into the mud. This is the advice
our master Horace gives us when he says in the beginning of his "Art of Poetry"
["Ye who write] take up a subject [suited to your strength"].

Next we ought to possess a discernment as to those things which suggest
themselves to us as fit to be uttered, so as to decide whether they ought to be
sung in the way of tragedy, comedy, or elegy. By tragedy we bring in (*sic*)
the higher style, by comedy the lower style, by elegy we understand the style
of the wretched. If our subject appears fit to be sung in the tragic style, we
must then assume the illustrious vernacular language, and consequently we must
bind up a canzone. If, however, it appears fit to be sung in the comic style,
sometimes the middle and sometimes the lowly vernacular should be used; and
the discernment to be exercised in this case we reserve for treatment in the fourth
book. But if our subject appears fit to be sung in the elegiac style, we must adopt
the lowly vernacular alone.

But let us omit the other styles and now, as is fitting, let us treat of the
tragic style. We appear then to make use of the tragic style when the stateliness

of the lines as well as the loftiness of the construction and the excellence of the words agree with the weight of the subject. And because, if we remember rightly, it has already been proved that the highest things are worthy of the highest, and because the style which we call tragic appears to be the highest style, those things which we have distinguished as being worthy of the highest song are to be sung in that style alone, namely, Safety, Love, and Virtue, and those other things, our conceptions of which arise from these; provided that they be not degraded by any accident.

Let every one therefore beware and discern what we say; and when he purposes to sing of these three subjects simply, or of those things which directly and simply follow after them, let him first drink of Helicon, and then, after adjusting the strings, boldly take up his *plectrum*[45] and begin to ply it. But it is in the exercise of the needful caution and discernment that the real difficulty lies; for this can never be attained to without strenuous efforts of genius, constant practice in the art, and the habit of the sciences. And it is those [so equipped] whom the poet in the sixth book of the *Æneid* describes as beloved of God, raised by glowing virtue to the sky, and sons of the Gods, though he is speaking figuratively. And therefore let those who, innocent of art and science, and trusting to genius alone, rush forward to sing of the highest subjects in the highest style, confess their folly and cease from such presumption; and if in their natural sluggishness they are but geese, let them abstain from imitating the eagle soaring to the stars.

V

We seem to have said enough, or at least as much as our work requires, about the weight of the subjects. Wherefore let us hasten on to the stateliness of the lines, in respect of which it is to be observed that our predecessors made use of different lines in their canzoni, as the moderns also do; but we do not find that any one has hitherto used a line of more than eleven or less than three syllables. And though the Italian poets have used the lines of three and of eleven syllables and all the intermediate ones, those of five, seven, and eleven syllables are more frequently used [than the others], and next to them, that of three syllables in preference to the others. But of all these the line of eleven syllables seems the stateliest, as well by reason of the length of time it occupies as of its capacity in regard to subject, construction, and words: and the beauty of all these things is more multiplied in this line [than in the others], as is plainly apparent; for wherever things that weigh are multiplied so also is weight. And all the teachers seem to have given heed to this, beginning their illustrious canzoni with a line of eleven syllables, as Giraut de Borneil: *"Ara auzirez encabalitz cantars."*[46]

And though this line appears to be of ten syllables, it is in reality of eleven, for the last two consonants do not belong to the preceding syllable. And though they have no vowel belonging to them, still they do not lose the force of a syllable; and the proof of this is that the rhyme is in this instance completed by one vowel, which could not be the case except by virtue of another understood there. The king of Navarre writes: *"De fine Amor si vient sen et bonté,"*[47] where, if the accent and its cause be considered the line will be found to have eleven syllables. Guido Guinizelli writes: *"Al cor gentil repara sempre Amure."*[48] The Judge [Guido] delle Colonne of Messina: *"Amor che lungiamente m' ài menato."*[49] Rinaldo d'Aquino: *"Per fino amore vo sì letamente."*[50] Cino of Pistoja: *"Non spero che già mai per mia salute."*[51] His friend: *"Amor che movi tua vertù da cielo."*[52] And though this line which has been mentioned appears, as is worthy, the most celebrated of all, yet, if it be associated in some slight degree with the line of seven syllables (provided only it retain its supremacy), it seems to rise still more clearly and loftily in its stateliness. But this must be left for further explanation.

We say also that the line of seven syllables follows next after that which is greatest in celebrity. After this we place the line of five, and then that of three syllables. But the line of nine syllables, because it appeared to consist of the line of three taken three times, was either never held in honor or fell into disuse on account of its being disliked. As for the lines of an even number of syllables, we use them but rarely, because of their rudeness; for they retain the nature of their numbers, which are subject to the odd numbers as matter to form. And so, summing up what has been said, the line of eleven syllables appears to be the stateliest line, and this is what we were in search of. But now it remains for us to investigate concerning exalted constructions and pre-eminent words; and at length, after having got ready our sticks and ropes, we will teach how we ought to bind together the promised faggot, that is the canzone.

VI

Inasmuch as our intention has reference to the illustrious vernacular, which is the noblest of all, and we have distinguished the things which are worthy of being sung in it, which are the three noblest subjects, as has been established above, and have chosen the form of canzoni for them, as being the highest form of any, and have also (in order that we may be able more perfectly to give thorough instruction in this form) already settled certain points, namely the style and the line, let us now deal with the construction.

Now it must be observed that we call construction a regulated arrangement of words, as "Aristotle philosophised in Alexander's time," for here there are five words arranged by rule, and they form one construction. Now in reference to this we must first bear in mind that one construction is congruous, while another is incongruous; and inasmuch as, if we recollect the beginning of our distinction, we are only pursuing the highest things, the incongruous construction finds no place in our pursuit, because it has not even proved deserving of a lower degree of goodness. Let therefore illiterate persons be ashamed—I say, let them be ashamed of being henceforth so bold as to burst forth into canzoni, for we laugh at them as at a blind man making distinctions between colors.

It is, then, it seems, the congruous construction after which we are following. But here we come to a distinction of not less difficulty before we can reach that construction which we are in search of, the construction, I mean, which is most full of refinement. For there are a great many degrees of constructions; namely, [first] the insipid, which is that of uncultivated people; as, "Peter is very fond of Mistress Bertha." [Then] there is that which has flavor but nothing else, which belongs to rigid scholars or masters; as, "I, greater in pity than all, am sorry for all those who, languishing in exile, only revisit their native land in their dreams." There is also that which has flavor and grace, which belongs to some who have taken a shallow draught of rhetoric; as, "The praiseworthy discernment of the Marquis of Este and his munificence prepared for all makes him beloved." Then there is that which has flavor and grace and also elevation, which belongs to illustrious writers; as, "Having cast the greatest part of the flowers out of thy bosom, O Florence, the second Totila went fruitlessly to Trinacria." This degree of construction we call the most excellent, and this is the one we are seeking for, since, as has been said, we are in pursuit of the highest things. Of this alone are illustrious canzoni found to be made up as [that by] Giraut de Borneil,

> *Si per mon Sobre-totz no fos.*[53]
> [that by] Folquet of Marseilles,
>   *Tan m' abellis l'amoros pensamens.*[54]
> [that by] Arnaut Daniel,
>   *Sols sui qui sai lo sobraffan quem sortz.*[55]
> [that by] Aimeric de Belenoi,
>   *Nuls hom non pot complir addreciamen.*[56]
> [that by] Aimeric de Pegulhan,
>   *Si com l'arbres que per sobrecarcar.*[57]
> [that by] the King of Navarre,
>   *Ire d'amor qui en mon cor repaire.* [58]
> [that by] Guido Guinizelli,
>   *Tegno de folle 'mpresa a lo ver dire.*[59]
> [that by] Guido Cavalcanti,
>   *Poi che di doglia cor conven ch'io porti.*[60]
> [that by] Cino of Pistoja,
>   *Avegna che io aggia più per tempo.*[61]
> [that by] his friend,
>   *Amor che nella mente mi ragiona.*[62]

Nor, reader, must you be surprised at our calling to memory so many poets; for we cannot point out that construction which we call the highest except by examples of this kind. And it would possibly be very useful in order to the full acquirement of this construction if we had surveyed the regular poets, I mean Virgil, Ovid in his *Metamorphoses*, Statius, and Lucan, as well as other writers who have employed the most lofty prose, as Titus Livius, Pliny, Frontinus, Paulus Orosius, and many others whom friendly solitude invites us to consult. Let, then, those followers of ignorance hold their peace who praise up Guittone of Arezzo and some others who have never got out of the habit of being plebeian in ·vords and in construction.

VII

The next division of our progress now demands that an explanation be given as to those words which are of such grandeur as to be worthy of being admitted into that style to which we have awarded the first place. We declare therefore to begin with that the exercise of discernment as to words involves by no means the smallest labor of our reason, since we see that a great many sorts of them can be found. For some words are *childish*, some *feminine*, and some *manly*; and of these last some are *sylvan*, others *urban*; and of those we call urban we feel that some are *combed-out* and *glossy*, some *shaggy* and *rumpled*. Now among these urban words the combed-out and the shaggy are those which we call *grand*; whilst we call the glossy and the rumpled those whose sound tends to superfluity, just as among great works some are works of magnanimity, others of smoke; and as to these last, although when superficially looked at there may be thought to be a kind of ascent, to sound reason no ascent, but rather a headlong fall down giddy precipices will be manifest, because the marked-out path of virtue is departed from. Therefore look carefully, Reader, consider how much it behooves thee to use the sieve in selecting noble words; for if thou hast regard to the illustrious vulgar tongue which (as has been said above) poets ought to use when writing in the tragic style in the vernacular (and these are the persons whom we intend to fashion), thou wilt take care that the noblest words alone are left in thy sieve. And among the number of these thou wilt not be able in any wise to place childish words, because of their simplicity, as *mamma* and *babbo, mate* and *pate*; nor feminine words, because of their softness, as *dolciada* and *placevole*; nor sylvan words, because of their roughness, as *greggia* and *cetra*; nor the glossy nor the rumpled urban words, as *femina* and *corpo*. Therefore thou wilt see that only the combed-out and the shaggy urban words will be left to thee, which are the noblest, and members of the illustrious vulgar tongue. Now we call those words *combed-out* which have three, or as nearly as possible three syllables; which are without aspirate, without acute or circumflex accent, without the double letters *z* or *x*, without double liquids, or a liquid placed immediately after a mute, and which, having been planed (so to say), leave the speaker with a certain sweetness, like *amore, donna, disio, vertute, donare, letitia, salute, securitate, defesa.*

We call *shaggy* all words besides these which appear either necessary or ornamental to the illustrious vulgar tongue. We call *necessary* those which we cannot avoid, as certain monosyllables like *sì, no, me, te, se, a, e, i, o, u,* the interjections, and many more. We describe as *ornamental* all polysyllables which when mixed with combed-out words produce a fair harmony of structure, though they may have the roughness of aspirate, accent, double letters, liquids, and length; as *terra, honore, speranza, gravitate, alleviato, impossibilità, impossibilitate, benaventuratissimo, inanimatissimamente, disaventuratissimamente, sovramagnificentissimamente,* which last has eleven syllables. A word might yet be found with more syllables still; but as it would exceed the capacity of all our lines it does not appear to fall into the present discussion; such is that word *honorificabilitudinitate,* which runs in the vernacular to twelve syllables, and in grammar to thirteen, in two oblique cases.

In what way shaggy words of this kind are to be harmonised in the lines with combed-out words, we leave to be taught farther on. And what has been said [here] on the pre-eminent nature of the words to be used may suffice for every one of inborn discernment.

VIII

Having prepared the sticks and cords for our faggot, the time is now come to bind it up. But inasmuch as knowledge of every work should precede performance, just as there must be a mark to aim at, before we let fly an arrow or javelin, let us first and principally see what that faggot is which we intend to bind up. That faggot, then (if we bear well in mind all that has been said before), is the canzone. Wherefore let us see what a canzone is, and what we mean when we speak of a canzone. Now canzone, according to the true meaning of the name, is the action or passion itself of singing, just as *lectio*[63] is the passion or action of reading. But let us examine what has been said, I mean whether a canzone is so called as being an action or as being a passion. In reference to this we must bear in mind that a canzone may be taken in two ways. In the first way, as its author's composition, and thus it is an action; and it is in this way that Virgil says in the first book of the *Æneid,* "I sing of arms and the man." In another way, when, after having been composed it is uttered either by the author or by some one else, whether with or without modulation of sound; and thus it is a passion. For in the first case it is acted, but in the second it appears to act on some one else; and so in the first case it appears to be the action of some one, and in the second it also appears to be the passion of some one. And because it is acted on before it acts, it appears rather, nay, altogether, to get its name from its being acted and being the act of some one than from its acting on others. Now the proof of this is, that we never say "This is Peter's canzone," meaning that he utters it, but meaning that he has composed it.

Moreover, we must discuss the question whether we call a canzone the composition of the words which are set to music, or the music itself; and, with regard to this, we say that no music [alone] is ever called a canzone, but a sound, or tone, or note, or melody. For no trumpeter, or organist, or lute-player calls his melody a canzone, except in so far as it has been wedded to some canzone; but those who write the words for music call their words canzoni. And such words, even when written down on paper without any one to utter them, we call carzoni; and therefore a canzone appears to be nothing else but the completed action of one writing words to be set to music. Wherefore we shall call canzoni not only the canzoni of which we are now treating, but also ballate and sonnets, and all words of whatever kind written for music, both in the vulgar tongue and in Latin. But, inasmuch as we are only discussing works in the vulgar tongue, setting aside those in Latin, we say that of poems in the vulgar tongue there is one supreme which we call canzone by super-excellence. Now the supremacy of the canzone has been proved in the third chapter of this book. And since the term which has been defined appears to be common to many things, let us take up again the common term which has been defined, and distinguish by means of certain differences that thing which alone we are in search of. We declare therefore that the canzone as so called by super-excellence which we are in search of is a joining together in the tragic style of equal stanzas without a *ripresa*,[64] referring to one subject, as we have shown in our composition "*Donne che avete intellecto d'amore.*"[65] Now the reason why we call it "a joining together in the tragic style" is because when such a composition is made in the comic style we call it diminutively *cantilena*, of which we intend to treat in the fourth book of this work. And thus it appears what a canzone is, both as it is taken generally, and as we call it in a super-excellent sense. It also appears sufficiently plain what we mean when we speak of a canzone, and consequently what that faggot is which we are endeavoring to bind up.

IX

Inasmuch as the canzone is a joining together of stanzas, as has been said, we must necessarily be ignorant of the canzone if we do not know what a stanza is, for knowledge of the thing defined results from knowledge of the things defining; and it therefore follows that we must treat of the stanza, in order, that is, that we may discover what it is, and what we mean to understand by it. And in reference to this matter we must observe that this word has been invented solely with respect to the art [of the canzone]; namely, in order that that in which the whole art of the canzone is contained should be called stanza, that is a *room* able to hold, or a receptacle for the whole art. For just as the canzone embosoms the whole theme, so the stanza embosoms the whole art; nor is it lawful for the subsequent stanzas to call in any additional scrap of the art, but only to clothe themselves with the art of the first stanza; from which it is plain that the stanza of which we are speaking will be the delimitation or putting together of all those things which the canzone takes from the art; and if we explain them, the description we are in search of will become clear. The whole art, therefore, of the canzone appears to depend on three things: first, on the division of the musical setting; second, on the arrangement of the parts; third, on the number of the lines and syllables. But we make no mention of rhyme, because it does not concern the peculiar art of the canzone, for it is allowable in any stanza to introduce new rhymes and to repeat the same at pleasure, but this would by no means be allowed if rhyme belonged to the peculiar art of the canzone, as has been said. Anything, however, relating to rhyme which the art, as such, is concerned to observe will be comprised under the heading "Arrangement of the Parts."

Wherefore we may thus collect the defining terms from what has been said, and declare that a stanza is a structure of lines and syllables limited by reference to a certain musical setting, and to the arrangement [of its parts].

X

If we know that man is a rational animal, and that an animal consists of a sensible soul and a body, but are ignorant concerning what this soul is or concerning the body itself, we cannot have a perfect knowledge of man, because the perfect knowledge of every single thing extends to its ultimate elements, as the master of the wise[66] testifies in the beginning of the *Physics*. Therefore in order to have that knowledge of the canzone which we are panting for, let us now compendiously examine the things which define its defining term[67]; and first let us inquire concerning the musical setting, next concerning the arrangement [of the parts], and afterwards concerning the lines and syllables.

We say, therefore, that every stanza is set for the reception of a certain ode; but they appear to differ in the modes [in which this is done]; for some proceed throughout to one continuous ode, that is, without the repetition of any musical phrase, and without any diesis: and we understand by diesis a transition from one ode to another. (This when speaking to the common people we call *volta*). And this kind of stanza was used by Arnaut Daniel in almost all his canzoni, and we have followed him in ours beginning, "*Al poco giorno e al gran cerchio d'ombra.*"[68]

But there are some stanzas, which admit of a diesis: and there can be no diesis in our sense of the word unless a repetition of one ode be made either before the diesis, or after, or both. If the repetition be made before [the diesis] we say that the stanza has feet; and it ought to have two, though sometimes there are three; very rarely, however. If the repetition be made after the diesis, then we say that the stanza has verses. If no repetition be made before [the diesis] we say that the stanza has a *Fronte*; if none be made after, we say that it has a *Sirma* or Coda. See, therefore, Reader, how much license has been given to poets who write canzoni, and consider on what account custom has claimed so wide a choice; and if reason shall have guided thee by a straight path, thou wilt see that this license of which we are speaking has been granted by worthiness of authority alone.

Hence it may become sufficiently plain how the art of the canzone depends on the division of the musical setting; and therefore let us go on to the arrangement [of the parts].

XI

It appears to us that what we call the arrangement [of the parts of the stanza] is the most important section of what belongs to the art [of the canzone], for this depends on the division of the musical setting, the putting together of the lines, and the relation of the rhymes; wherefore it seems to require to be most diligently treated of.

We therefore begin by saying that the *fronte* with the verses, and the feet with the coda or *sirma*, and also the feet with the verses, may be differently arranged in the stanza. For sometimes the *fronte* exceeds or may exceed the verses in syllables and in lines; and we say "may exceed" because we have never yet met with this arrangement. Sometimes [the *fronte*] may exceed [the verses] in lines, and be exceeded by them in syllables; as, if the *fronte* had five lines, and each verse had two lines, while the lines of the *fronte* were of seven syllables and those of the verses of eleven syllables. Sometimes the verses exceed the *fronte* in syllables and in lines, as in our canzone *"Traggemi de la mente Amor la stiva."*[69] Here the *fronte* was composed of four lines, three of eleven syllables and one of seven syllables; for it could not be divided into feet, since an equality of lines and syllables is required in the feet with respect to one another, and also in the verses with respect to one another. And what we say of the *fronte* we might also say of the verses; for the verses might exceed the *fronte* in lines and be exceeded by it in syllables; for instance, if each verse had three lines of seven syllables and the *fronte* were made up of five lines, two of eleven syllables and three of seven syllables.

And sometimes the feet exceed the coda in lines and syllables as in our canzone, *"Amore che movi tua vertù da cielo."*[70] Sometimes the feet are exceeded by the sirma both in lines and syllables, as in our canzone, *"Donna pietosa e di novella etate."*[71] And just as we have said that the *fronte*, [though] exceeded [by the verses] in syllables may exceed them in lines, and conversely, so we say of the *sirma* [in relation to the feet].

The feet likewise may exceed the verses in number, and be exceeded by them; for there may be in a stanza three feet and two verses, or three verses and two feet; nor are we limited by that number so as not to be able to combine more feet as well as verses in like manner.

And just as we have spoken of the victory of lines and syllables in comparing the other parts of the stanza together, we now also say the same as regards the feet and verses [compared together]: for these can be conquered and conquer in the same way.

Nor must we omit to mention that we take feet in a sense contrary to that of the regular poets, because they said that a line consisted of feet, but we say that a foot consists of lines, as appears plainly enough.

Nor must we also omit to state again that the feet necessarily receive from one another an equality of lines and syllables, and their arrangement, for otherwise the repetition of the melodic section could not take place. And we declare that the same rule is to be observed in the verses.

XII

There is also, as has been said above, a certain arrangement which we ought to consider in putting the lines together; and therefore let us deal with this, repeating what we have said above respecting the lines.

In our practice three lines especially appear to have the prerogative of frequent use, namely, the line of eleven syllables, that of seven syllables, and that of five syllables, and we have shown that the line of three syllables follows them, in preference to the others. Of these, when we are attempting poetry in the tragic style, the line of eleven syllables deserves, on account of a certain excellence, the privilege of predominance in the structure [of the stanza]. For there is a certain stanza which rejoices in being made up of lines of eleven syllables alone, as this one of Guido of Florence: "*Donna me prega, perch' io voglio dire.*"[72] And we also say: "*Donne ch' avete intellecto d'amore.*"[73] The Spaniards have also used this line, and I mean by Spaniards those who have written poetry in the vernacular of *oc*. Aimeric de Belenoi [has written] "*Nuls hom non pot complir adrechamen.*"[74]

There is a stanza where a single line of seven syllables is woven in, and this cannot be except where there is a *fronte* or a coda, since (as has been said) in the feet and verses an equality of lines and syllables is observed. Wherefore also neither can there be an odd number of lines where there is no *fronte* or no coda, but where these occur, or one of them alone, we may freely use an even or an odd number of lines. And just as there is a certain stanza formed containing a single line of seven syllables, so it appears that a stanza may be woven together with two, three, four, or five such lines, provided only that in the tragic style the lines of eleven syllables predominate in number, and one such line begin. We do indeed find that some writers have begun with a line of seven syllables in the tragic style, namely, Guido dei Ghisilieri and Fabruzzo, both of Bologna, as thus: "*Di fermo sofferire,*"[75] and, "*Donna, lo fermo core,*"[76] and, "*Lo meo lontano gire,*" and some others also. But if we go carefully into the sense of these writers, their tragedy will not appear to have proceeded without a certain faint shadow of elegy.

With regard to the line of five syllables also, we are not so liberal in our concessions; in a great poem it is sufficient for a single line of five syllables to be inserted in the whole stanza, or two at most in the feet: and I say "in the feet," because of the requirements of the musical setting in the feet and verses.

But it by no means appears that the line of three syllables existing on its own account should be adopted in the tragic style; and I say, "existing on its own account," because it often appears to have been adopted by way of a certain echoing of rhymes, as may be discovered in that canzone of Guido of Florence, "*Donna me prega*," and in the following of ours: "*Poscia ch' Amor del tutto m' ha lasciato.*"[77] And there the line of three syllables does not appear at all on its own account, but only as a part of a line of eleven syllables, answering like an echo to the rhyme of the line before.

This further point also must be specially attended to with regard to the arrangement of the lines, [namely] that if a line of seven syllables be inserted in the first foot, it must take up the same position in the second that it receives in the first. For insance, if a foot of three lines has the first and last of eleven syllables, and the middle one—that is the second—of seven syllables, so the second foot must have the second line of seven syllables and the first and last of eleven syllables, otherwise the repetition of the melodic section, with reference to which the feet are constructed, as has been said, could not take place; and consequently there could be no feet.

And what we have said of the feet we say of the verses also; for we see that the feet and the verses differ in nothing but position, the former term being used before the diesis of the stanza, and the latter after it.

And we declare also that what has been said of the foot of three lines is to be observed in all other feet. And what we have said of one line of seven syllables we also say of more than one, and of the line of five syllables, and of every other line.

Hence, Reader, you are sufficiently able to choose how your stanza is to be arranged as regards the arrangement which it appears should be considered with reference to the lines.

XIII

Let us apply ourselves to the relation of the rhymes, not [however] in any way treating of rhyme in itself; for we put off the special treatment of them (*sic*) till afterwards, when we shall deal with poems in the middle vulgar tongue.

At the beginning of this chapter it seems advisable to exclude certain things: one is the unrhymed stanza, in which no attention is given to arrangement of rhymes; and Arnaut Daniel very often made use of this kind of stanza, as here: *"Sim fos Amors de joi donar";*[78] and we say: *"Al poco giorno."* Another is the stanza all of whose lines give the same rhyme; and here it is plainly unnecessary to seek for any arrangement [of rhymes].

And so it remains for us only to dwell upon the mixed rhymes. And first it must be remarked that in this matter almost all writers take the fullest license; and this is what is chiefly relied on for the sweetness of the whole harmony. There are, then, some poets who sometimes do not make all the endings of the lines rhyme in the same stanza, but repeat the same endings, or make rhymes to them, in the other stanzas: as Gotto of Mantua, who recited to us many good canzoni of his own. He always wove into his stanza one line unaccompanied by a rhyme, which he called the key. And as one such line is allowable, so also are two and perhaps more.

There are also some other poets, and almost all the authors of canzoni, who never leave any line unaccompanied in the stanza without answering it by the consonance of one or more rhymes.

Some poets also make the rhymes of the lines following the diesis different from the rhymes of the lines preceding it; while some do not do this, but bring back the endings of the former [part of the] stanza, and weave them into the lines of the latter part. But this occurs oftenest in the ending of the first line of the latter part of the stanza, which very many poets make to rhyme with the ending of the last line of the former part; and this appears to be nothing else but a kind of beautiful linking together of the whole stanza.

Also with regard to the arrangement of the rhymes, according as they are in the *fronte* or coda, every wished-for license should, it seems be conceded; but still the endings of the last lines are most beautifully disposed if they fall with a rhyme into silence.

But in the feet we must be careful; and [here] we find that a particular arrangement has been observed; and, making a distinction, we say that a foot is completed with either an even or odd number of lines, and in both cases there may be rhymed and unrhymed endings. In [the foot of] an even number of lines, no one feels any doubt [as to this]; but in the other, if any one is doubtful let him remember what was said in the next preceding chapter about the line of three syllables, when, as forming part of a line of eleven syllables, it answers like an echo. And if there happens to be an unrhymed ending in one of the feet, it must by all means be answered by a rhyme in the other. But if all the endings in one of the feet are rhymed, it is allowable in the other either to repeat the endings, or to put new ones, either wholly, or in part, at pleasure, provided, however, that the order of the preceding endings be observed in its entirety; for instance, if in a first foot of three lines, the extreme endings, that is, the first and last, rhyme together, so the extreme endings of the second foot must rhyme together; and according as the middle line in the first foot sees itself accompanied or unaccompanied by a rhyme, so let it rise up again in the second; and the same rule is to be observed with regard to the other kinds of feet. In the verses also we almost always obey this law; and we say "almost," because on account of the above-mentioned linking together [of the two parts of the stanza], and combination of the final endings, it sometimes happens that the order now stated is upset.

Moreover, it seems suitable for us to add to this chapter what things are to be avoided with regard to the rhymes, because we do not intend to deal any further in this book with the learning relating to rhyme. There are, then, three things, which with regard to the placing of rhymes it is unbecoming for a courtly poet to use, namely, [first], excessive repetition of the same rhyme, unless perchance something new and before unattempted in the art claim this for itself; just like the day of incipient knighthood, which disdains to let the period of initiation pass without any special distinction. And this we have striven to accomplish in the canzone, *"Amor, tu vedi ben che questa donna."*[79]

The second of the things to be avoided is that useless equivocation which always seems to detract somewhat from the theme; and the third is roughness of rhymes, unless it be mingled with smoothness; for from a mixture of smooth and rough rhymes the tragedy itself gains in brilliancy.

And let this suffice concerning the art [of the canzone] so far as it relates to the arrangement [of the parts of the stanza].

XIV

Having sufficiently treated of two things belonging to the art in the canzone, it now appears that we ought to treat of the third, namely, the number of the lines and syllables. And in the first place we must make some observations with regard to the stanza as a whole; then we will make some observations as to its parts.

It concerns us therefore first to make a distinction between those subjects which fall to be sung of, because some stanzas seem to desire prolixity, and others do not. For whereas we sing of all the subjects we are speaking of either with reference to something favorable or else to something unfavorable, so that it happens that we sing sometimes persuasively, sometimes dissuasively, sometimes in congratulation, sometimes in irony, sometimes in praise, sometimes in contempt, let those words whose tendency is unfavorable always hasten to the end, and the others gradually advance to the end with a becoming prolixity. . . .

GIOVANNI BOCCACCIO

(1313–1375)

INTRODUCTION

From the point of view of the history of criticism, Giovanni Boccaccio is the foremost spokesman of the humanism that appeared (or reappeared) in Italy in the fourteenth century. The *Genealogy of the Gentile Gods*, while indebted to Boccaccio's friend and mentor Francis Petrarch, is the fullest summary we have of the early phase of the humanistic defense of secular literature.

In his preface Boccaccio tells us that he was in some sense commissioned to write the *Genealogy* by Donino of Parma, acting on behalf of Hugo IV, King of Cyprus from 1324–58. The commission was given during the 1340's. In 1350 Boccaccio met Bechino Bellincioni. He tells us near the end of Book XV that Bellincioni "began with wonderfully urgent importunity to rouse my mind from the drowsiness into which it had fallen over the work; and this he said he did at [King Hugo's] command." The task, however, was immense. Although Boccaccio addresses King Hugo in his conclusion as though the King, who died in 1359, is alive, the *Genealogy* continued to evolve during the 1360's; and, in fact, when Boccaccio heard in 1371 that the manuscript had been copied, he protested on the grounds that it was still incomplete. Evidently, the *Genealogy* was a life work extending from around 1343 to after 1370.

Boccaccio explains the method of the book in his preface:

> Before each book I plan to set a tree; at the root sits the father of the line, and on the branches, in genealogical order, all his progeny, so that you may have an index of what you are looking for in the book that follows. These Books you will find divided into chapters with proper and fuller rubrics corresponding to the mere name which you have already noted on the tree.
>
> I shall conclude with two books, in the first of which I shall reply to certain objections that have been raised against poetry and poets. In the second—and last of all—I shall endeavor to remove such criticisms as may possibly be leveled at me.

187

The result of this plan is an enormous compendium of classical mythology, arranged in terms of a genealogical scheme, followed by a two-book defense of poetry. If the size and rather wooden organization are typically medieval, the purpose and the range of scholarship are new. The *Genealogy* is a textbook for humanist poets. As we know from Bercorius, Christine de Pisan, John de Ridevall and others, classical mythology fascinated secular writers during the later Middle Ages. Knowledge of the myths, however, was limited, being based chiefly on Ovid, Servius, Fulgentius, and a few other classical and late classical authorities. In addition, there was the question of whether the pagan myths were idolotrous or obscene or both. The task that Boccaccio set himself was twofold. First, he had to collect and rationalize the enormous body of material waiting to be drawn from classical sources unknown or neglected during the Middle Ages. This meant not only the considerable number of Latin writers directly available to Boccaccio, but also a sampling of Greek writers whose work Boccaccio could consult with the aid of his friend Leontius Pilatus, a pupil of the famous Barlaam of Calabria. Second, he had to show, both specifically and in terms of general theory, that reference to and use of this material is entirely fitting a Christian poet.

Like most of his predecessors in the defense of pagan mythology, Boccaccio regarded the ancient myths as storehouses of wisdom concealed under the veil of fable. We must know the inner meaning as well as the story if we are properly to appreciate the achievement of the ancients. This leads to allegorical interpretation. Boccaccio knew several methods of allegorical interpretation and used them all as they seemed appropriate. Euhemerism and etymological interpretation are common in the *Genealogy*. So, also, is the classification of myth in terms of natural, ethical, and theological allegory. And so is the interpretation of myth according to the literal, allegorical, tropological (moral), and anagogical (spiritual) "levels" of scriptural interpretation. Sometimes the methods are used separately, sometimes in combination. The reader who is not overly concerned with consistency can end the mythological section of the work (through Book XIII) comfortably reassured that pagan myths almost always contain natural and moral truths, and, on occasion, adumbrations of the truths of Christian revelation embodied in their definitive form in the Bible.

The defenses of poetry contained in Books XIV and XV of the *Genealogy* have no obvious medieval precedent. The twelfth-century Renaissance had produced apologies for the liberal arts by men like John of Salisbury and Richard of Bury but no full-scale defenses of poetry. Moreover, the humanists of the twelfth century were all but eclipsed for some two centuries by the scholastics of Paris. Although it is becoming increasingly clear that there is much greater continuity than we formerly recognized between the French humanism of the twelfth century and the Italian variety of the fourteenth, the most obvious and primary influences on Boccaccio are classical and contemporary. The idea of a formal defense of poetry may have come originally via Cicero's *Pro Archia Poeta*, a spirited oration defending a minor Roman poet, which Boccaccio quotes at the end of Book XIV as a last, crushing rejoinder to the "enemies of poetry."

Two more recent authorities undoubtedly supplemented whatever influence Cicero may have had. Albertino Mussato (1261–1329) had already become involved in a much-publicized dispute with the Dominican Giovannino of Padua over the value of reading the poets, and his arguments outline the main topics later covered by Boccaccio. Above all, Boccaccio writes under the shadow of his friend Francis Petrarch. Petrarch's ideas about poetry are scattered throughout his letters and prose works. The oration which he delivered when crowned laureate in Rome in 1341 summarizes several of them. His fullest statement of these ideas, however, is his *Invective Against a Physician*. This work is not a defense of poetry so much as a defense of humane learning, but particularly at the end of Book I and the beginning of Book III, Petrarch lists most of the objections to poetry cited by Boccaccio and offers refutations much like those in the *Genealogy*. The *Invective* is thus not the source for the idea of a formal defense of poetry but it is a store-house of arguments, topics, and citations of authority on which Boccaccio leaned heavily.

The argument of the *Genealogy* opens with an attack on poetry's enemies, the dilettantes, the materialistic lawyers, and "other cavillers" (XIV.5). The "other cavillers" are associated with "sacred studies" and "mask themselves with sanctity." They are fond of quoting the line from Psalm 69 "The zeal of God's house hath eaten me up." They pretend to great knowledge but are really ignorant. The portrait reminds one of Erasmus' *Praise of Folly*. Although the "cavillers" are not specifically identified, it is obvious that they are clerics and an open secret that they are Dominicans of the same ilk as Giovannino of Padua. Boccaccio lists their objections to poetry, and the list provides the topics for the remainder of Book XIV. It testifies to the hostility and suspicion with which the dominant party of scholasticism greeted a rising (or reviving) humanism. In one way or another the controversy can be traced throughout the fifteenth century, down to the open warfare between Savonarola and the Florentine humanists during the 1490's.

The main charges against poetry are (1) that it is trivial, (2) that poets lie, (3) that poems are "false, lewd, and obscure," (4) that they corrupt readers, (5) that poets ape philosophers, (6) that it is a sin to read them, and (7) that Plato and Boethius rejected poetry. Boccaccio answers each charge in one or more chapters. Most of the charges are as old as "the ancient quarrel between the philosophers and the poets" mentioned by Socrates at the end of Republic X, but they appear here in a specifically Christian and late medieval guise.

Chapter 6 asserts that poetry is a divine gift, cites the *poesis, poeta, poema* triad inherited with modifications from Alexandrian criticism, and defends the utility of poetry with the claim that it is a "science." As is clear from an earlier chapter (XIV.4) Boccaccio has in mind the distinction between a "faculty" having no content and a "science" which does have content. The analysis of poetry's place in the scheme of knowledge was a central feature of scholastic poetic theory, and the typical scholastic position was that it belongs with the instrumental disciplines of the *Organon*—i.e., it is a part of logic and a faculty to be used on any "content" rather than depending on a content. This justified rejection of the claims of the poets to teaching wisdom, goodness, and higher truth. By claiming that poetry is a science rather than a faculty, Boccaccio is inverting the argument. For him and for later humanists, poetry contains a whole range of truths, from the most arcane verities of revelation to the useful truths of ethics and political science. The fact that it teaches these truths delightfully, according to the Horatian formula, gives it unique social utility.

Chapter 7 is a tissue of humanistic commonplaces. Poetry came from the "bosom of God." It is a gift possessed by a few men and not a skill to be learned, although writing good poetry demands familiarity with the lore of grammar, rhetoric, and moral philosophy. It is the result of inspiration, bringing forth "strange and unheard-of creations of the mind," and it "veils truth in a fair and fitting garment of fiction." The tone is Platonic. We are closer here to Macrobius and Proclus than to Horace. The chapter illustrates the nexus in humanist theory between inspiration, fondness for the marvelous ("unheard-of creations") at the expense of verisimilitude, and allegory. Naturally, poetry that meets these criteria will be obscure, a point that Boccaccio repeats in Chapter 12.

In Chapter 8 Boccaccio adds that poets were the first theologians. His claim is supported by a much-quoted sentence in Aristotle's *Metaphysics* (1000a9) and by the fact that in the earlier books of the *Genealogy* Boccaccio has demonstrated that ancient myths are frequently adumbrations of Christian truths. In the *Life of Dante* Boccaccio argues that "theology and poetry are in agreement as to their form of working, but in subject . . . they are not merely wholly diverse, but in some parts contradictory." Theology treats divine virtue, poets, the pagan gods and mortal men; theology (that is, scripture) is true in all four of the standard senses, poetry is false on the literal level and even "against the Christian religion." Boccaccio adds that when critics "foolishly blame the poets for this they rashly stumble into blaming that Spirit that is none other than the way, the truth, and the life." The *Genealogy* is more circumspect in that it does not claim that the Holy Spirit directly inspires secular poetry, but it tends in the same direction: poetry originated in "the bosom of God," and Dante (XV.6) was "a sacred theologian rather than a mere mythographer."

Taken together, Boccaccio's arguments are a daring assertion of the value of secular poetry. If they are valid, poetry must in some sense be a form of revelation and thus complementary—if not an alternative—to scripture. Here we have the fundamental reason for the hostility of the scholastic tradition to poetry. From the scholastic point of view, the humanist position is nothing less than a challenge to the unique authority of scripture.

The following chapters of Book XIV elaborate arguments already presented. The difficulty of relating Hebrew to Greek chronology makes it difficult (XIV.8) to decide where poetry originated. Boccaccio favors the Greeks. If the Hebrews bear the palm, the first poet was Moses "who wrote the largest part of Pentateuch not in prose but in heroic verse." Moses may, in fact, be the same person as Musaeus! If the Greeks invented poetry, the first poets were Musaeus, Linus, and Orpheus, who "under the prompting stimulus of the divine mind, invented strange songs in regular times and measure, designed for the praise of God." Fables (XIV.9) are exemplary (Aesop), mixed, historical, and fictional. All kinds except the last are found in the Bible, and "the writings of the Old Testament and the writings of the poets seem as it were to keep in step with each other." To reject fables is to reject the Bible; to call them lies is "to call the Holy Spirit, or Christ, the very God, liars." Wherever they are found their power "pleases the unlearned by its exterior appearance, and exercises the minds of the learned with its hidden truth." The latter point is illustrated in Chapter 10 by Vergil, Dante, and Petrarch; i.e., by both the ancients and the moderns. As for the "cavillers," "When they have made themselves clean, let them purify the tales of others, mindful of Christ's commandment to the accusers of the woman taken in adultery, that he who was without sin should cast the first stone."

Chapter 12 is of interest because of its treatment of poetic obscurity. Obscurity is inevitable in poetry that bodies forth truths unavailable to the reason, and biblical obscurity had long been explained by various doctrines including the idea of accommodation, the theory of allegory, and the notion that the highest truths should be clothed in the most elaborate (hence the most involuted) images. As Boccaccio remarks, scripture proceeds from the Holy Spirit and is "full to overflowing with obscurities and ambiguities." The function of poets is to write, not to "rip up and lay bare the meaning which lies hidden in his inventions." In the *Life of Dante* Boccaccio remarked that "anything gained with fatigue seems sweeter than what is understood without effort. The plain truth, since it is understood easily, delights us and passes from the mind. But, in order that it may be more pleasing because acquired with labor, and therefore better valued, the poets hide the truth beneath things appearing quite contrary to it." Here, he is content to quote Petrarch's *Invectives*: "What we acquire with difficulty and keep with care is always the dearer to us."

What stands out here, as elsewhere in Boccaccio's defense of poetry, is the habit of comparing the inspiration of the Muses with the inspiration of the Holy Spirit, the insights of the poets to the wisdom of the theologians, the obscurity of poetic fables to the difficulty of scripture.

In what ways, we might ask, is Christian revelation unique? What is special about the Bible if pagan poetry contains the same levels of meaning, the same literary devices, and the same truths? Of course, Boccaccio's contemporaries did not ask this. Instead, the "cavillers" attacked the pretensions of the poets, and the vehemence of their onslaught is a measure of the threat they felt to their own concept of the Christian tradition. Boccaccio, on his side, did not feel that he was undermining or betraying Christian tradition any more than Petrarch or Ficino or Erasmus. Literature for him, as for later humanists, should supplement and broaden Christianity, not replace it. From this point of view the "cavillers" are not true Christians but bigots. It is they, not Boccaccio, who would be forced if consistent to call the Holy Spirit a liar for using fables in scripture.

This is most of the story but not all of it. If any one, says Boccaccio, should confuse the old poets with "sacred" [i.e. Christian] theologians, "the veriest fool would detect the falsehood." At the same time "the old theology can sometimes be employed in the sense of Catholic truth if the fashioner of the myth should choose." After all the explanations, there is an ambivalence in Boccaccio's defense that is not present—or at least not nearly so obvious—in Petrarch. It is the ambivalence of a Platonizing Christianity, whether in Alexandria, in twelfth-century France, or Ficino's fifteenth-century academy. If Boccaccio's defense of poetry looks back, in this respect to Bernard Silvestris, it looks forward to Ficino, Landino, and a host of later humanistic defenders of art and poetry.

The translation, here slightly modernized, and the notes have been taken from Charles G. Osgood, *Boccaccio on Poetry* (Princeton: Princeton University Press, 1930). For bibliography, see especially pp. 489–90.

GENEALOGY OF THE GENTILE GODS

from BOOK XIV
V. Other Cavillers at the Poets and Their Imputations

There is also, O most serene of rulers, as you know far better than I, a kind of house established in this world by God's gift, in the image of a celestial council, and devoted only to sacred studies. Within, on a lofty throne, sits philosophy, messenger from the very bosom of God, mistress of all knowledge. Noble is her mien and radiant with godlike splendor. There she sits arrayed in royal robes and adorned with a golden crown, like the empress of all the world. In her left hand she holds several books, with her right hand she wields a royal sceptre, and in clear and fluent discourse she shows forth to such as will listen the truly praiseworthy ideals of human character, the forces of our Mother Nature, the true good, and the secrets of heaven. If you enter you do not doubt that it is a sanctuary full worthy of all reverence; and if you look about, you will clearly see there every opportunity for the higher pursuits of the human mind, both speculation and knowledge, and will gaze with wonder till you regard it not merely as one all-inclusive household, but almost the very image of the divine mind. Among other objects of great veneration there, behind the mistress of the household, are certain men seated in high places, few in number, of gentle aspect and utterance, who are so distinguished by their seriousness, honesty, and true humility, that you take them for gods not mortals. These men abound in the faith and doctrine of their mistress, and give freely to others of the fullness of their knowledge.

But there is also another group—a noisy crowd—of all sorts and conditions. Some of these have resigned all pride, and live in watchful obedience to the injunctions of their superiors, in hopes that their obsequious zeal may gain them promotion. But others there are who grow so elated with what is virtually elementary knowledge, that they fall upon their great mistress' robes as it were with their talons, and in violent haste tear away a few shreds as samples; then don various titles which they often pick up for a price; and, as puffed up as if they knew the whole subject of divinity, they rush forth from the sacred house, setting such mischief afoot among ignorant people as only the wise can calculate. Yet these rascals are sworn conspirators against all high arts. First they try to counterfeit a good man; they exchange their natural expression for an anxious, careful one. They go about with downcast eye to appear inseparable from their thoughts. Their pace is slow to make the uneducated think that they stagger under an excessive weight of high speculation. They dress unpretentiously, not because they are really modest, but only to mask themselves with sanctity. Their talk is little and serious. If you ask them a question they heave a sigh, pause a moment, raise their eyes to heaven, and at length deign to answer. They hope the bystanders will infer from this that their words rise slowly to their lips, not from any lack of eloquence, but because they are fetched from the remote sanctuary of heavenly secrets. They profess piety, sanctity, and justice, and often utter the words of the prophet, "The zeal of God's house hath eaten me up."[1]

Then they proceed to display their wonderful knowledge, and whatever they don't know they damn—to good effect too. This they do to avoid inquiry about subjects of which they are ignorant, or else to affect scorn and indifference in such matters as cheap, trivial, and obvious, while they have devoted themselves to things of greater importance. When they have caught inexperienced minds in traps of this sort, they proceed boldly to range about town, dabble in business, give advice, arrange marriages, appear at big dinners, dictate wills, act as executors of estates, and otherwise display arrogance unbecoming to a philosopher. Thus they blow up a huge cloud of popular reputation, and thereby so strut with vanity that, when they walk abroad, they want to have everybody's finger pointing them out, to overhear people saying that they are great masters of their subjects, and see how the grand folk rise to meet them in the squares of the city and call them "Rabbi," speak to them, invite them, give place, and defer to them. Straightway they throw off all restraint and become bold enough for anything; they are not afraid to lay their own sickles to the harvest of another; and, while they are basely defiling other people's business, the talk may fall upon poetry and poets. At the sound of the word they blaze up in such a sudden fury that you would say their eyes were afire. They cannot stop; they go raging on by the very momentum of their wrath. Finally, like conspirators against a deadly enemy, in the schools, in public squares, in pulpits, with a lazy crowd, as a rule, for an audience, they break out into such mad denunciation of poets that the bystanders are afraid of the speakers themselves, let alone the harmless objects of attack.

They say poetry is absolutely of no account, and the making of poetry a useless and absurd craft; that poets are tale-mongers, or, in lower terms, liars; that they live in the country among the woods and mountains because they lack manners and polish. They say, besides, that their poems are false, obscure, lewd, and replete with absurd and silly tales of pagan gods, and that they make Jove, who was, in point of fact, an obscene and adulterous man, now the father of gods, now king of heaven, now fire, or air, or man, or bull, or eagle, or similar irrelevant things; in like manner poets exalt to fame Juno and infinite others under various names. Again and again they cry out that poets are seducers of the mind, prompters of crime, and, to make their foul charge fouler, if possible, they say they are philosophers' apes, that it is a heinous crime to read or possess the books of poets; and then, without making any distinction, they prop themselves up, as they say, with Plato's authority to the effect that poets ought to be turned out-of-doors—nay, out of town, and that the Muses, their mumming mistresses, as Boethius says, being sweet with deadly sweetness, are detestable, and should be driven out with them and utterly rejected. But it would take too long to cite everything that their irritable spite and deadly hatred prompt these madmen to say. It is also before judges like these—so eminent, indeed, so fair, so merciful, so well-inclined—that my work will appear, O glorious Prince; and I know full well they will gather about it like famished lions, to seek what they may devour. Since my book has entirely to do with poetic material, I cannot look for a milder sentence from them than in their rage they thunder down upon poets. I am well aware that I offer my breast to the same missiles that their hatred has already employed; but I shall endeavor to ward them off.

O merciful God, meet now this foolish and ill-considered clamor of mad men, and oppose their rage. And thou, O best of kings, as I advance upon their line, support me with the strength of thy noble soul, and help me in my fight for thee; for courage and a stout heart must now be mine. Sharp and poisonous are their weapons, but weak withal. Foolish judges though they be, they are strong in other ways, and I tremble with fear before them, unless God, who deserteth not them that trust in Him, and thou, also, favor me. Slender is my strength and my mind weak, but great is my expectation of help; borne up by such hope, I shall rush upon them with justice at my right hand.

VI. Poetry Is a Useful Art

I am about to enter the arena, a manikin against these giant hulks—who have armed themselves with authority to say that poetry is either no art at all or a useless one. In the circumstances, for me first to discuss the definition and function of poetry would be hunting a mare's nest. But since the fight must be fought I wish these past masters of all the arts would declare upon what particular point they desire the contest to bear. Yet I know full well that with a sneer and a brazen front they will unblushingly utter the same ineptitudes as before. Come, O merciful God, give ear to their foolish objections and guide their steps into a better way.

They say, then, in condemnation of poetry, that it is naught. If such is the case, I should like to know why, through generation after generation, so many great men have sought the name of poet. Whence come so many volumes of poems? If poetry is naught, whence came this word poetry? Whatever answer they make, they are going out of their way, I think, since they can give no rational answer that is not directly against their present vain contention. It is absolutely certain, as I shall show later,[2] that poetry, like other studies, is derived from God, Author of all wisdom; like the rest it got its name from its effect. From this name "poetry" at length comes the glorious name of "poet"; and from "poet," "poem." In that case poetry apparently is not wholly naught, as they said.

If then it prove a science, what more will those noisy sophists have to say? They will either retract a little, or rather, I think, flit lightly over the gap thus opening in their argument to the second point of their objection, and say that if poetry *is* a mere art, it is a useless one. How rank! How silly! Better to have kept quiet than hurl themselves with their frivolous words into deeper error. Why, do not the fools see that the very meaning of this word "art" or "faculty" always implies a certain plenitude? But of this elsewhere. Just now I wish that these accomplished gentlemen would show how poetry can reasonably be called futile when it has, by God's grace, given birth to so many famous books, so many memorable poems, clearly conceived, and dealing with strange marvels. They will keep quiet at this, I think, if their vain itch for display will let them.

Keep quiet, did I say? Why they would rather die than confess the truth in silence, not to say with the tip of their tongues. They will dart off on another tack, and by their own arbitrary interpretation, will say, with slight addition, that poetry must be regarded a futile and empty thing, nay, damnable, detestable, because the poems which come of it sing the adulteries of the gods they celebrate, and beguile the reader into unspeakable practices. Though this interpretation is easy to refute—since nothing can be empty that is filled with adulteries—in any case it may be borne with a calm mind; nay their contention based upon it may be granted in all reason, since I readily acknowledge that there are poems of the kind they describe, and if the bad kind were to corrupt the good, then the victory would be theirs. But, I protest; if Praxiteles or Phidias, both experts in their art, should choose for a statue the immodest subject of Priapus on his way to Iole[3] by night, instead of Diana glorified in her chastity; or if Apelles, or our own Giotto—whom Apelles in his time did not excel—should represent Venus in the embrace of Mars[4] instead of the enthroned Jove dispensing laws unto the gods, shall we therefore condemn these arts? Downright stupidity, I should call it!

The fault for such corruption lies in the licentious mind of the artist. Thus for a long time there have been "poets," if such deserve the name, who, either to get money or popularity, study contemporary fashions, pander to a licentious taste, and at the cost of all self-respect, the loss of all honor, abandon themselves to these literary fooleries. Their works certainly should be condemned, hated, and spurned, as I shall show later.[5] Yet if a few writers of fiction erred thus, poetry does not therefore deserve universal condemnation, since it offers us so many inducements to virtue, in the monitions and teaching of poets whose care it has been to set forth with lofty intelligence, and utmost candor, in exquisite style and diction, men's thoughts on things of heaven.

But enough! Not only is poetry more than naught, but it is a science worthy of veneration; and, as often appears in the foregoing as well as in suc-ceeding pages, it is an art or skill, not empty, but full of the sap of natural vigor for those who would through fiction subdue the senses with the mind. So, not to be tedious, it would seem that at the first onset of this conflict, these leaders have turned tail, and, with slight effort on my part, have abandoned the arena. But it is my present duty to define Poetry, that they may see for themselves how stupid they are in their opinion that poetry is an empty art.

VII. The Definition of Poetry, Its Origin, and Function

This poetry, which ignorant triflers cast aside, is a sort of fervid and exquisite invention, with fervid expression, in speech or writing, of that which the mind has invented. It proceeds from the bosom of God, and few, I find, are the souls in whom this gift is born; indeed so wonderful a gift it is that true poets have always been the rarest of men. This fervor of poesy is sublime in its effects: it impels the soul to a longing for utterance; it brings forth strange and unheard-of creations of the mind; it arranges these meditations in a fixed order, adorns the whole composition with unusual interweaving of words and thoughts;

and thus it veils truth in a fair and fitting garment of fiction. Further, if in any case the invention so requires, it can arm kings, marshal them for war, launch whole fleets from their docks, nay, counterfeit sky, land, sea, adorn young maidens with flowery garlands, portray human character in its various phases, awake the idle, stimulate the dull, restrain the rash, subdue the criminal, and distinguish excellent men with their proper reward of praise: these, and many other such, are the effects of poetry. Yet if any man who has received the gift of poetic fervor shall imperfectly fulfill its function here described, he is not, in my opinion, a laudable poet. For, however deeply the poetic impulse stirs the mind to which it is granted, it very rarely accomplishes anything commendable if the instruments by which its concepts are to be wrought out are wanting—I mean, for example, the precepts of grammar and rhetoric, an abundant knowledge of which is opportune. I grant that many a man already writes his mother tongue admirably, and indeed has performed each of the various duties of poetry as such; yet over and above this, it is necessary to know at least the principles of the other liberal arts, both moral and natural, to possess a strong and abundant vocabulary, to behold the monuments and relics of the ancients, to have in one's memory the histories of the nations, and to be familiar with the geography of various lands, of seas, rivers, and mountains.

Furthermore, places of retirement, the lovely handiwork of nature herself, are favorable to poetry, as well as peace of mind and desire for worldly glory; the ardent period of life also has very often been of great advantage. If these conditions fail, the power of creative genius frequently grows dull and sluggish.

Now since nothing proceeds from this poetic fervor, which sharpens and illumines the powers of the mind, except what is wrought out by art, poetry is generally called an art. Indeed the word poetry has not the origin that many carelessly suppose, namely *poio, pois,* which is but Latin *fingo, fingis;* rather it is derived from a very ancient Greek word *poetes,* which means in Latin exquisite discourse (*exquisita locutio*). For the first men who, thus inspired, began to employ an exquisite style of speech, such, for example, as song in an age hitherto unpolished, to render this unheard-of discourse sonorous to their hearers, let it fall in measured periods; and lest by its brevity it fail to please, or, on the other hand, become prolix and tedious, they applied to it the standard of fixed rules, and restrained it within a definite number of feet and syllables. Now the product of this studied method of speech they no longer called by the more general term poesy, but poem. Thus as I said above, the name of the art, as well as its artificial product, is derived from its effect.

Now though I allege that this science of poetry has ever streamed forth from the bosom of God upon souls while even yet in their tenderest years, these enlightened cavillers will perhaps say that they cannot trust my words. To any fair-minded man the fact is valid enough from its constant recurrence. But for these dullards I must cite witnesses to it. If, then, they will read what Cicero, a philosopher rather than a poet, says in his oration delivered before the senate in behalf of Aulus Licinius Archias,[6] perhaps they will come more easily to believe me. He says: "And yet we have it on the highest and most learned authority, that while other arts are matters of science and formula and technique, poetry depends solely upon an inborn faculty, is evoked by a purely mental activity, and is infused with a strange divine inspiration."

But not to protract this argument, it is now sufficiently clear to reverent men, that poetry is a practical art, springing from God's bosom and deriving its name from its effect, and that it has to do with many high and noble matters that constantly occupy even those who deny its existence. If my opponents ask when and in what circumstances, the answer is plain: the poets would declare with their own lips under whose help and guidance they compose their inventions when, for example, they raise flights of symbolic steps to heaven, or make thick-branching trees spring aloft to the very stars, or go winding about mountains to their summits. Perhaps, to disparage this art of poetry now unrecognized by them, these men will say that it is rhetoric which the poets employ. Indeed, I will not deny it in part, for rhetoric has also its own inventions. Yet, in truth, among the disguises of fiction rhetoric has no part, for whatever is composed as under a veil, and thus exquisitely wrought, is poetry and poetry alone.

VIII. Where Poetry First Dawned Upon the World

If you inquire, O King, under what sky, in what period, and by whose agency poetry first came to light, I hardly trust my ability to answer. One group of writers thinks it arose with the holy rites of the ancients, that is, among the Hebrews, since Holy Writ records that they were the first to offer sacrifice to God; for we read that the brothers, Cain and Abel, the first men born on earth, sacrificed to God; so also did Noah when the flood subsided and he went forth from the ark; and so Abraham for victory over his foes, when he offered Melchisedek, the priest, wine and bread. But since these accounts do not yield altogether the desired answer, writers of this opinion—rather by divination than proof, it must be said—insist that these rites were accomplished with some sort of formal discourse. They add that Moses, when, with the people of Israel, he had passed the Red Sea dry-shod, performed a complete sacrifice, since we read that he established rites, priests, and a tabernacle like the temple that was to be, and appointed prayers to placate the Divine Will. So it seems that poetry had its origin among the Hebrews not earlier than Moses, leader of the Israelites; and he led the people forth and performed his rites about the time that King Marathius of the Sicyoni died, which was the three thousand, six hundred and eightieth year of the world.

A second group would give the Babylonians the glory of inventing poetry. Among these the Venetian,[7] bishop of Pozzuolo, a tremendous investigator, was wont to argue at length in bantering fashion, that poetry was far older than Moses, having had its origin about the time of Nembroth. Nimrod, he said, was the founder of idolatry, for when he saw that fire was useful to men, and that he could, to some extent, foretell the future from its various motions and sounds, he averred that it was a god; wherefore he not only worshipped it instead of God, and persuaded the Chaldeans to do likewise, but built temples to it, ordained priests, and even composed prayers. Now, according to the Venetian these prayers showed that he employed formal, polished discourse. Possibly; but the Venetian never clearly showed his authority for his statement. Yet I have read often enough that religious worship, the study of philosophy, and the glory of arms all had their origin among the Assyrians. But I cannot easily believe, without more trustworthy evidence, that an art so sublime as that of poetry arose first among peoples so barbarous and wild.

The Greeks also maintain that poetry originated with them, and Leontius supports this view with all his might. I am a little inclined his way, as I recollect hearing my famous teacher once say that among the primitive Greeks, poetry had some such origin as this: While they were still rude, some of them, above the rest in intellectual power, began to wonder at the works of their Mother Nature; and as they meditated they came gradually to believe in some one Being, by whose operation and command all visible things are governed and ordered. Him they named God. Then, thinking that He sometimes visited earth, and considering Him holy, they raised buildings for Him at enormous expense, that He might on His visits find abiding places consecrated to His name. These we now call temples. Then, to propitiate Him, they devised peculiar honors to be rendered Him at appointed seasons, and called them rites. Finally, in their belief that, as He excelled all others in divinity, so ought He in honor also, they had silver tables made for His rites, and fashioned of gold the drinking-cups, candelabra, and whatever other vessels they used; they also selected men from among the wisest and gentlest of the people, whom they afterwards called priests, and these they would have appear in no common garb at the celebration of rites, but made them resplendent in costly robes with tiaras and crosiers. Then, since it seemed absurd for the priests to perform rites to the Deity in utter silence, they had certain discourses composed to show forth the praise, and great works of the Deity himself, to express the petitions of the people, and offer him the prayers of men in their various needs. And since it would appear inappropriate to address the Deity as you would a farmhand, an underling, or a familiar friend, the wiser among them wanted a polished and artistic manner of speech devised, and they committed this task to the priests. Some of these, though few —and among them, it is thought, were Musaeus, Linus, and Orpheus—under the prompting stimulus of the Divine Mind, invented strange songs in regular time and measure, designed for the praise of God. To strengthen the authority of these songs, they enclosed the high mysteries of things divine in a covering of words, with the intention that the adorable majesty of such things should not become an object of too common knowledge, and thus fall into contempt. Now since the art thus discovered seemed wonderful and wholly new, they named it, as I have said, from its *effect,* and called it poetry or *poetes,* that is, in Latin *exquisita locutio*; and they who had composed the songs were named poets. And, as the name favors the effect, the belief is that both the musical accompaniment of poetry and all its other accoutrements arose among the Greeks.

But the date of its origin is very doubtful. Leontius, for one, used to say that he had heard his teacher, Barlaam of Calabria, and other learned authorities on the subject, more than once assign the date to the time of Phoroneus, King of Argos, who came to the throne in the three thousand, three hundred and eighty-fifth year of the world. They also said that Musaeus, whom I mentioned above as one of the inventors of poetry, was eminent among the Greeks, and that Linus flourished about the same time; their fame, which is still great, bears witness even in our day that they presided over the rites of the ancients. To these is added Orpheus of Thrace; they are therefore considered the earliest theologians.

But Paul of Perugia used to infer from the same ancient authorities, that poetry was much younger, and alleged that Orpheus, who is recorded as one of the earliest poets, flourished in the reign of Laomedon, King of Troy, when Eurystheus ruled Mycenae, about the three thousand, nine hundred and tenth year of the world, that he was the Orpheus of the Argonauts, and not only a successor of Musaeus, but the teacher of the same Musaeus, son of Eumolpus. Such, at least, is the testimony of Eusebius in his *Liber Temporum.* Whence Paul's statement, cited above, that poetry was more recent among the Greeks than his opponents held. Leontius, however, in reply maintained that learned Greeks thought there were several by the name of Orpheus and Musaeus, but that the ancient Orpheus was a Greek contemporary with the ancient Musaeus and Linus, whereas it is a younger one who is called the Thracian. Indeed, since this younger Orpheus invented the rites of Bacchus, and the nocturnal gatherings of the Maenads, and made many innovations in the liturgy of the ancients, and especially had great powers of eloquence—all of which won him high esteem in his generation—he was therefore regarded as the great Orpheus by posterity. Perhaps this is the right view especially since some of the ancients bear witness that there were poets before the birth of the Cretan Jove, and it is known from Eusebius that Orpheus the Thracian flourished after Jove's rape of Europa.

But with scholars thus at variance, and me unable to find reliable evidence in ancient authors to support their theories, I cannot tell which to follow. It is at least evident from all accounts that, if one is to follow Leontius, poetry originated with the Greeks before it did with the Hebrews; if the Venetian, then with the Chaldeans before it did among the Greeks; but if we prefer to believe Paul, it follows that Moses was a master of poetry before either Babylonians or

Greeks. Aristotle,[8] to be sure, perhaps for reasons just urged, asserts that the first poets were theologians, by that meaning Greeks; and herein he favors somewhat the opinion of Leontius. Nevertheless I cannot believe that the sublime effects of this great art were first bestowed upon Musaeus, or Linus, or Orpheus, however ancient, unless, as some say, Moses and Musaeus were one and the same. Of the beast Nimrod I take no account. Rather was it instilled into most sacred prophets, dedicated to God. For we read that Moses, impelled by what I take to be this poetic longing, at dictation of the Holy Ghost, wrote the largest part of the Pentateuch not in prose but in heroic verse. In like manner others have set forth the great works of God in the metrical garment of letters, which we call poetic. And I think the poets of the Gentiles in their poetry—not perhaps without understanding—followed in the steps of these prophets; but whereas the holy men were filled with the Holy Ghost, and wrote under His impulse, the others were prompted by mere energy of mind, whence such a one is called "seer." Under fervor of this impulse they composed their poems. But since I have nothing further to say on the origin of poetry, do thou, O glorious King, choose whichever opinion accords with thy serene judgment.

IX. It Is Rather Useful Than Damnable To Compose Stories

These fine cattle bellow still further to the effect that poets are talemongers, or, to use the lower and more hateful term which they sometimes employ in their resentment—liars. No doubt the ignorant will regard such an imputation as particularly objectionable. But I scorn it. The foul language of some men cannot infect the glorious name of the illustrious. Yet I grieve to see these revilers in a purple rage let themselves loose upon the innocent. If I conceded that poets deal in stories, in that they are composers of fiction, I think I hereby incur no further disgrace than a philosopher would in drawing up a syllogism. For if I show the nature of a fable or story, its various kinds, and which kinds these "liars" employ, I do not think the composers of fiction will appear guilty of so monstrous a crime as these gentlemen maintain. First of all, the word "fable" (*fabula*) has an honorable origin in the verb *for, faris,* hence "conversation" (*confabulatio*), which means only "talking together" (*collocutio*). This is clearly shown by Luke in his Gospel, where he is speaking of the two disciples who went to the village of Emmaus after the Passion. He says: "And they talked together of all these things which had happened. And it came to pass, that, while they communed together, and reasoned, Jesus himself drew near, and went with them."[9]

Hence, if it is a sin to compose stories, it is a sin to converse, which only the veriest fool would admit. For nature has not granted us the power of speech unless for purposes of conversation, and the exchange of ideas.

But, they may object, nature meant this gift for a useful purpose, not for idle nonsense; and fiction is just that—idle nonsense. True enough, if the poet had intended to compose a mere tale. But I have time and time again proved that the meaning of fiction is far from superficial. Wherefore, some writers have framed this definition of fiction (*fabula*): Fiction is a form of discourse, which, under guise of invention, illustrates or proves an idea; and, as its superficial aspect is removed, the meaning of the author is clear. If, then, sense is revealed from under the veil of fiction, the composition of fiction is not idle nonsense. Of fiction I distinguish four kinds:[10] The first superficially lacks all appearance of truth; for example, when brutes or inanimate things converse. Aesop, an ancient Greek, grave and venerable, was past master in this form; and though it is a common and popular form both in city and country, yet Aristotle,[11] chief of the Peripatetics, and a man of divine intellect, did not scorn to use it in his books. The second kind at times superficially mingles fiction with truth, as when we tell of the daughters of Minyas at their spinning, who, when they spurned the orgies of Bacchus, were turned to bats; or the mates of the sailor Acestes,[12] who for contriving the rape of the boy Bacchus, were turned to fish. This form has been employed from the beginning by the most ancient poets, whose object it has been to clothe in fiction divine and human matters alike; they who have followed the sublimer inventions of the poets have improved upon them; while some of the comic writers have perverted them, caring more for the approval of a licentious public than for honesty. The third kind is more like history than fiction, and famous poets have employed it in a variety of ways. For however much the heroic poets seem to be writing history—as Vergil in his description of Aeneas tossed by the storm, or Homer in his account of Ulysses bound to the mast to escape the lure of the Sirens' song—yet their hidden meaning is far other than appears on the surface. The better of the comic poets, Terence and Plautus, for example, have also employed this form, but they intend naught other than the literal meaning of their lines. Yet by their art they portray varieties of human nature and conversation, incidentally teaching the reader and putting him on his guard. If the events they describe have not actually taken place, yet since they are common, they could have occurred, or might at some time. My opponents need not be so squeamish—Christ, who is God, used this sort of fiction again and again in his parables!

The fourth kind contains no truth at all, either superficial or hidden, since it consists only of old wives' tales.

Now, if my eminent opponents condemn the first kind of fiction, then they must include the account in Holy Writ describing the conference of the trees[13] of the forest on choosing a king. If the second, then nearly the whole sacred body of the Old Testament will be rejected. God forbid, since the writings of the Old Testament and the writings of the poets seem as it were to keep step with each other, and that too in respect to the method of their composition. For where history is lacking, neither one concerns itself with the superficial possibility, but what the poet calls fable or fiction our theologians have named figure. The truth of this may be seen by fairer judges than my opponents, if they will but weigh in a true scale the outward literary semblance of the visions of Isaiah, Ezekiel, Daniel, and other sacred writers on the one hand, with the outward literary semblance of the fiction of poets on the other. If they find any real discrepancy in their methods, either of implication or exposition, I will accept their condemnation. If they condemn the third form of fiction, it is the same as condemning the form which our Savior Jesus Christ, the Son of God, often used when He was in the flesh, though Holy Writ does not call it "poetry," but "parable," some call it "exemplum," because it is used as such.

I count as naught their condemnation of the fourth form of fiction, since it proceeds from no consistent principle, nor is fortified by the reinforcement of any of the arts, nor carried logically to a conclusion. Fiction of this kind has nothing in common with the works of the poets, though I imagine these objectors think poetry differs from it in no respect.

I now ask whether they are going to call the Holy Spirit, or Christ, the very God, liars, who both in the same Godhead have uttered fictions. I hardly think so, if they are wise. I might show them, your Majesty, if there were time, that difference of names constitutes no objection where methods agree. But they may see for themselves. Fiction, which they scorn because of its mere name, has been the means, as we often read, of quelling minds aroused to a mad rage, and subduing them to their pristine gentleness. Thus, when the Roman plebs seceded from the senate, they were called back from the sacred mount to the city by Menenius Agrippa, a man of great influence, all by means of a story. By fiction, too, the strength and spirits of great men worn out in the strain of serious crises, have been restored. This appears, not by ancient instance alone, but constantly. One knows of princes who have been deeply engaged in important matters, but after the noble and happy disposal of their affairs of state, obey, as it were, the warning of nature, and revive their spent forces by calling about them such men as will renew their weary minds with diverting stories and conversation. Fiction has, in some cases, sufficed to lift the oppressive weight of adversity and furnish consolation, as appears in Lucius Apuleius; he tells how the highborn maiden Charis, while bewailing her unhappy condition as captive among thieves, was in some degree restored through hearing from an old woman the charming story of Psyche.[14] Through fiction, it is well known, the mind that is slipping into inactivity is recalled to a state of better and more vigorous fruition. Not to mention minor instances, such as my own, I once heard Giacopo Sanseverino, Count of Tricarico and Chiarmonti, say that he had heard his father tell of Robert, son of King Charles,[15]—himself in after time the famous King of Jerusalem and Sicily—how as a boy he was so dull that it took the utmost skill and patience of his master to teach him the mere elements of letters. When all his friends were nearly in despair of his doing anything, his

master, by the most subtle skill, as were, lured his mind with the fables of
Aesop into so grand a passion for study and knowledge, that in a brief time he
not only learned the liberal arts familiar to Italy, but entered with wonderful
keenness of mind into the very inner mysteries of sacred philosophy. In short,
he made of himself a king whose superior in learning men have not seen since
Solomon.

Such then is the power of fiction that it pleases the unlearned by its
external appearance, and exercises the minds of the learned with its hidden
truth; and thus both are edified and delighted[16] with one and the same perusal.
Then let not these disparagers raise their heads to vent their spleen in scornful
words, and spew their ignorance upon poets! If they have any sense at all, let
them look to their own speciousness before they try to dim the splendor of
others with the cloud of their maledictions. Let them see, I pray, how pernicious
are their jeers, fit to rouse the laughter only of girls. When they have made
themselves clean, let them purify the tales of others, mindful of Christ's commandment[17] to the accusers of the woman taken in adultery, that he who was
without sin should cast the first stone.

X. It Is a Fool's Notion That Poets Convey No Meaning Beneath the Surface of Their Fictions

Some of the railers are bold enough to say, on their own authority, that
only an utter fool would imagine the best poets to have hidden any meaning
in their stories; rather, they have invented them just to display the great power
of their eloquence, and show how easily such tales may bring the injudicious
mind to take fiction for truth. O the injustice of men! O what absurd dunces!
What clumsiness! While they are trying to put down others, they imagine in
their ignorance that they are exalting themselves. Who but an ignoramus would
dare to say that poets purposely make their inventions void and empty, trusting
in the superficial appearance of their tales to show their eloquence? As who
should say that truth and eloquence cannot go together. Surely they have missed
Quintilian's saying; it was this great orator's opinion that real power of eloquence is inconsistent with falsehood. But this matter I will postpone that I
may come to the immediate subject of this chapter. Let any man, then, read the
line in Vergil's *Bucolics*: "He sung the secret seeds of Nature's frame,"[18] and
what follows on the same matter: or in the *Georgics*: "That bees have portions
of ethereal thought / Endued with particles of heavenly fires."[19] with the relevant
lines; or in the *Aeneid*: "Know first that heaven and earth's compacted frame, /
And flowing waters, and the starry frame, etc."[20]

This is poetry from which the sap of philosophy runs pure. Then is any
reader so muddled as not to see clearly that Vergil was a philosopher; or mad
enough to think that he, with all his deep learning, would, merely for the sake

of displaying his eloquence—in which his powers were indeed extraordinary—
have led the shepherd Aristeus into his mother Climene's presence in the depths
of the earth, or brought Aeneas to see his father in Hades? Or can anyone
believe he wrote such lines without some meaning or intention hidden beneath
the superficial veil of myth? Again, let any man consider our own poet Dante
as he often unties with amazingly skillful demonstration the hard knots of holy
theology; will such a one be so insensible as not to perceive that Dante was a
great theologian as well as philosopher? And, if this is clear, what intention
does he seem to have had in presenting the picture of the griffon[21] with wings
and legs, drawing the chariot on top of the austere mountain, together with the
seven candlesticks, and the seven nymphs, and the rest of the triumphal proces-
sion? Was it merely to show his dexterity in composing metrical narrative? To
mention another instance: that most distinguished Christian gentleman, Francis
Petrarch, whose life and character we have, with our own eyes, beheld so laudable
in all sanctity—and by God's grace shalll continue to behold for a long time;
no one has saved and employed to better advantage—I will not say, his time,
but every crumb of it, than he. Is there anyone sane enough to suppose that he
devoted all those watches of the night, all those holy seasons of meditation,
all those hours and days and years—which we have a right to assume that he
did, considering the force and dignity of his bucolic verse, the exquisite beauty
of his style and diction—I say, would he have taken such pains merely to represent Gallus begging Tyrrhenus[22] for his reeds, or Pamphilus and Mitio[23] in
a squabble, or other like pastoral nonsense? No man in his right mind will
agree that these were his final object; much less, if he considers his prose treatise
on the solitary life, or the one which he calls *On the Remedies for all Fortunes*,
not to mention many others. Herein all that is clear and holy in the bosom of
moral philosophy is presented in so majestic a style, that nothing could be
uttered for the instruction of mankind more replete, more beautified, more
mature, nay, more holy. I would cite also my own eclogues, of whose meaning
I am, of course, fully aware; but I have decided not to, partly because I am not
great enough to be associated with the most distinguished men, and partly
because the discussion of one's attainments had better be left to others.

Then let the babblers stop their nonsense, and silence their pride if they
can; for one can never escape the conviction that great men, nursed with the
milk of the Muses, brought up in the very home of philosophy, and disciplined
in sacred studies, have laid away the very deepest meaning in their poems; and
not only this, but there was never a grumbling old woman, sitting with others
late of a winter's night at the home fireside, making up tales of Hell, the fates,
ghosts, and the like—much of it pure invention—that she did not feel beneath
the surface of her tale, as far as her limited mind allowed, at least some meaning
—sometimes ridiculous no doubt—with which she tries to scare the little ones,
or divert the young ladies, or amuse the old, or at least show the power of fortune.

XII. The Obscurity of Poetry Is Not Just Cause for Condemning It

These cavillers further object that poetry is often obscure, and that poets are to blame for it, since their end is to make an incomprehensible statement appear to be wrought with exquisite artistry; regardless of the old rule of the orators, that a speech must be simple and clear. Perverse notion! Who but a deceiver himself would have sunk low enough not merely to hate what he could not understand, but incriminate it, if he could? I admit that poets are at times obscure. At the same time will these accusers please answer me? Take those philosophers among whom they shamelessly intrude; do they always find their close reasoning as simple and clear as they say an oration should be? If they say yes, they lie; for the works of Plato and Aristotle, to go no further, abound in difficulties so tangled and involved that from their day to the present, though searched and pondered by many a man of keen insight, they have yielded no clear nor consistent meaning. But why do I talk of philosophers? There is the utterance of Holy Writ, of which they especially like to be thought expounders; though proceeding from the Holy Ghost, is it not full to overflowing with obscurities and ambiguities? It is indeed, and for all their denial, the truth will openly assert itself. Many are the witnesses, of whom let them be pleased to consult Augustine,[24] a man of great sanctity and learning, and of such intellectual power that, without a teacher, as he says himself, he learned many arts, besides all that the philosophers teach of the ten categories. Yet he did not blush to admit that he could not understand the beginning of Isaiah. It seems that obscurities are not confined to poetry. Why then do they not criticize philosophers as well as poets? Why do they not say that the Holy Spirit wove obscure sayings into his works, just to give them an appearance of clever artistry? As if He were not the sublime Artificer of the Universe![25] I have no doubt they are bold enough to say such things, if they were not aware that philosophers already had their defenders, and did not remember the punishment[26] prepared for them that blaspheme against the Holy Ghost. So they pounce upon the poets because they seem defenseless, with the added reason that, where no punishment is imminent, no guilt is involved. They should have realized that when things perfectly clear seem obscure, it is the beholder's fault. To a half-blind man, even when the sun is shining its brightest, the sky looks cloudy. Some things are naturally so profound that not without difficulty can the most exceptional keenness in intellect sound their depths; like the sun's globe, by which, before they can clearly discern it, strong eyes are sometimes repelled. On the other hand, some things, though naturally clear perhaps, are so veiled by the artist's skill that scarcely anyone could by mental effort derive sense from them; as the immense body of the sun when hidden in clouds cannot be exactly located by the eye of the most learned astronomer. That some of the prophetic poems are in this class, I do not deny.

Yet not by this token is it fair to condemn them; for surely it is not one of the poet's various functions to rip up and lay bare the meaning which lies hidden in his inventions. Rather where matters truly solemn and memorable are too much exposed, it is his office by every effort to protect as well as he can and remove them from the gaze of the irreverent, that they cheapen not by too common familiarity. So when he discharges this duty and does it ingeniously, the poet earns commendation, not anathema.

Wherefore I again grant that poets are at times obscure, but invariably explicable if approached by a sane mind; for these cavillers view them with owl eyes, not human. Surely no one can believe that poets invidiously veil the truth with fiction, either to deprive the reader of the hidden sense, or to appear the more clever; but rather to make truths which would otherwise cheapen by exposure the object of strong intellectual effort and various interpretation, that in ultimate discovery they shall be more precious. In a far higher degree is this the method of the Holy Spirit; nay, every right-minded man should be assured of it beyond any doubt. Besides it is established by Augustine in the *City of God*, Book Eleven,[27] when he says: "The obscurity of the divine word has certainly this advantage, that it causes many opinions about the truth to be started and discussed, each reader seeing some fresh meaning in it." Elsewhere he says of Psalm 126: "For perhaps the words are rather obscurely expressed for this reason, that they may call forth many understandings, and that men may go away the richer, because they have found that closed which might be opened in many ways, than if they could open and discover it by one interpretation."

To make further use of Augustine's testimony (which so far is adverse to these recalcitrants), to show them how I apply to the obscurities of poetry his advice on the right attitude toward the obscurities of Holy Writ, I will quote his comment on Psalm 146: "There is nothing in it contradictory: somewhat there is which is obscure, not in order that it may be denied thee, but that it may exercise him that shall afterward receive it," etc.

But enough of the testimony of holy men on this point, I will not bore my opponents by again urging them to regard the obscurities of poetry as Augustine regards the obscurities of Holy Writ. Rather I wish that they would wrinkle their brows a bit, and consider fairly and squarely, how, if this is true of sacred literature addressed to all nations, in far greater measure is it true of poetry, which is addressed to the few.

If by chance in condemning the difficulty of the text, they really mean its figures of diction and rhetorical imagery and the beauty which they fail to recognize in alien words, if on this account they pronounce poetry obscure—my only advice is for them to go back to the grammar schools, bow to the rod, study, and learn what license ancient authority granted the poets in such matters, and give particular attention to such alien terms as are permissible beyond common and homely use. But why dwell so long upon the subject? I could have urged them in a sentence to put off the old mind, and put on the new and noble; then will that which now seems to them obscure look familiar and open. Let them not trust to concealing their gross confusion of mind in the precepts of the old orators; for I am sure the poets were ever mindful of such. But let them observe that oratory is quite different, in arrangement of words, from fiction, and that fiction has been consigned to the discretion of the inventor as being the legitimate work of another art than oratory. "In poetic narrative above all, the poets maintain majesty of style and corresponding dignity." As saith Francis Petrarch in the Third Book of his *Invectives,* contrary to my opponents' supposition, "Such majesty and dignity are not intended to hinder those who wish to understand, but rather propose a delightful task, and are designed to enhance the reader's pleasure and support his memory." "What we acquire with difficulty and keep with care is always the dearer to us"; so continues Petrarch. In fine, if their minds are dull, let them not blame the poets but their own sloth. Let them not keep up a silly howl against those whose lives and actions contrast most favorably with their own. Nay, at the very outset they have taken fright at mere appearances, and bid fair to spend themselves for nothing. Then let them retire in good time, sooner than exhaust their torpid minds with the onset and suffer a violent repulse.

But I repeat my advice to those who would appreciate poetry, and unwind its difficult involutions. You must read, you must persevere, you must sit up nights, you must inquire, and exert the utmost power of your mind. If one way does not lead to the desired meaning, take another; if obstacles arise, then still another; until, if your strength holds out, you will find that clear which at first looked dark. For we are forbidden by divine command to give that which is holy to dogs, or to cast pearls before swine.

XXII. The Author Addresses the Enemies of Poetry in Hope of Their Reform

And now, O men of sense, ye will do wisely to calm your indignation and quiet your swollen hearts. Our contest has grown perhaps too bitter. You began by taking up the cudgel against an innocent class of men, with the intention of exterminating them. I came to their defense, and, with God's help and the merits of the case, did what I could to save deserving men from their deadly enemies. Yet, if the poets in person had fairly taken the field against you, you would see how far their powers surpass both yours and mine, and repent at the eleventh hour. But the fight is over; with some glory of war, and a good deal more sweat, we have reached the point where the lust for victory may be a bit qualified, and we may part company with a fair settlement. Come then, let us freely unite to rest from our labors, for the prizes of the contest have been awarded. You forfeit to me your theory, and I to you a bit of consolation; this leaves ample room for peace. I have no doubt you are willing, since you are sorry to have begun the contest, and by this arrangement we shall both enjoy its benefits. To prove my sincerity, I, who am the first to tire of it, will be the first to resume friendly relations; that you may do likewise, I beg of you to consider with fair and unruffled mind the few words which I, in all charity and friendship, am about to say to you.

You recall, gentlemen, that, as well as I could, I have shown you the nature of poetry, which you had counted as naught, who the poets are, their function, and their manner of life, whom you cried out upon as depraved liars, moral perverters, corrupt with a thousand evils. I have shown also the nature of the Muses, whom you had called whores and consigned to the houses of prostitution. Yet being actually so worthy of regard as I have shown, you should not only cease to condemn them, but should cherish, magnify, love them, and search their books to your improvement. And that old age may not prevent you, or the popularity of other arts, try your best to do what an aged prince was not ashamed to attempt; I refer to that shining example of all virtues, famous King Robert of Sicily and Jerusalem, who besides being king, was a distinguished philosopher, an eminent teacher of medicine, and an exceptional theologian in his day. Yet in his sixty-sixth[28] year he retained a contempt for Vergil, and, like you, called him and the rest mere story-tellers, and of no value at all apart from the ornament of his verse. But as soon as he heard Petrarch unfold the hidden meaning of his poetry, he was struck with amazement, and saw and rejected his own error; and I actually heard him say that he never had supposed such great and lofty meaning could lie hidden under so flimsy a cover of poetic fiction as he now saw revealed through the demonstration of this expert critic. With wonderfully keen regret he began upbraiding his own judgment and his misfortune in recognizing so late the true art of poetry. Neither fear of criticism, nor age, nor the sense of his fast expiring lease of life were enough to prevent him from abandoning his studies in the other great sciences and arts, and devoting himself to the mastery of Vergil's meaning. As it happened, an early end broke off his new pursuit, but if he might have continued in it, without doubt he would have won much glory for the poets, and no little advantage for the Italians engaged in such studies. Will you, then, hold that gift not worth the taking which was holy in the sight of this wise king? Impossible! You are not mere tigers or huge beasts, whose minds, like their ferocity, cannot be turned to better account.

But if my pious expectation is doomed to disappointment, and the heat of your hatred still burns against them who deserve it not, then whenever your tongues itch to be at it again, I beseech you, for the sake of your own decency, mind my words. I adjure you, by the sacred breast of philosophy, which in other days has nourished you, not to rush in headlong fury upon the whole company of poets. Rather, if you have sense enough, you must observe right and timely distinction among them—such distinction as only can bring harmony out of discord, dispel the clouds of ignorance, clear the understanding, and set the mind in the right way. This you must do if you would not confuse the poets we revere—many of them pagans, as I have shown—with the disreputable sort. Let the lewd comic writers feel the stream of your wrath, the fiery blast of your eloquence; but be content to leave the rest in peace. Spare also the Hebrew authors. Them you cannot rend without insulting God's majesty itself. I have already cited Jerome's statement that some of them uttered their prophetic song in poetic style as dictated by the Holy Ghost. By the same token must Christian writers escape injury; for many even of our own tongue have been poets—nay, still survive—who, under cover of their compositions, have expressed the deep and holy meaning of Christianity. One of many instances is our Dante. True, he wrote in his mother tongue, which he adapted to his artistic purpose; yet in the book which he called the *Commedia* he nobly described the threefold condition of departed souls consistently with the sacred teaching of theology. The famous modern poet Petrarch has, in his *Bucolics*,[29] employed the pastoral guise to show forth with marvellous effect both the praise and the blame visited by the true God and the glorious Trinity upon the idle ship of Peter. Many such volumes are there which yield their meaning to any zealous inquirer. Such are the poems of Prudentius, and Sedulius, which express sacred truth in disguise. Arator, who was not merely a Christian, but a priest and cardinal in the church of Rome, gave poetic form to the Acts of the Apostles by recounting them in heroics. Juvencus, the Spaniard, also a Christian, employed the symbolic device of the man, the ox, the lion, and the eagle, to describe all the acts of Christ our Redeemer, Son of the Living God. Without citing further examples, let me say that, if no consideration of gentleness can induce you to spare poets of our own nation, yet be not more severe than our mother the Church; for she, with laudable regard, does not scorn to favor many a writer; but especially hath she honored Origen. So great was his power in composition that his mind seemed inexhaustible and his hand tireless; so much so that the number of his treatises on various subjects is thought to have reached a thousand. But the Church is like the wise maiden who gathered flowers among thorns without tearing her fingers, simply by leaving the thorns untouched; so she has rejected the less trustworthy part of Origen, and retained the deserving part to be laid up among her treasures. Therefore distinguish with care, weigh the words of the poets in a true balance, and put away the unholy part. Neither condemn what is excellent, as if, by raising a sudden hue and cry against poets, you hoped to seem Augustines or Jeromes to an ignorant public. They were men whose wisdom equalled their righteousness; they directed their attack not against poetry, or the art of poetry, but against the pagan errors contained in the poet's works. At these they hurled fearless and outspoken condemnation because it was a time when Catholic truth was surrounded and beset with harassing enemies. At the same time they cherished them and ever recognized in these works so much art, and polish, such seasoning of wisdom and skillful application of ornament, that whoever would acquire any grace of Latin style apparently must derive it from them.

Finally in the words of Cicero pleading for Archias:[30] "These studies may engage the strength of our manhood and divert us in old age; they are the adornment of prosperity, the refuge and solace of adversity; delightful at home, convenient in all places; they are ever with us through the night season; in our travels; in our rural retreats. And if we may not pursue them ourselves nor enjoy them in person, yet should we admire them as seen in others," etc. Poetry, then, and poets too, should be cultivated, not spurned and rejected; and if you are wise enough to realize this there is nothing more to say. On the other hand, if you persevere in your obstinate madness, though I feel sorry for you, contemptible as you are, yet no writing in the world could help you.

from BOOK XV
Proem

I have now steadied and trimmed my little craft, O most clement King, by such means as I could, for fear she be driven ashore by the wash of a stormy sea or the counterforce of the wind, with joints sprung and timbers crushed. And I have spread above her such protection as seemed opportune against lowering clouds that dissolve in rain or deadly flashes of lightning, lest she be either swamped or burned. Finally I have made her fast to the rocks, with ropes and hawsers, that the ebb tide might not drag her into the depths. But mortal precaution avails naught against the wrath of God; and I have therefore resolved that the fate of my venture must be left in His hands without Whose favor naught shall endure. May He in His mercy keep her!

VIII. The Pagan Poets of Mythology Are Theologians

There are certain pietists who, in reading my words, will be moved by holy zeal to charge me with injury to the most sacrosanct Christian religion; for I allege that the pagan poets are theologians—a distinction which Christians grant only to those instructed in sacred literature. These critics I hold in high respect; and I thank them in anticipation for such criticism, for I feel that it implies their concern for my welfare. But the carelessness of their remarks shows clearly the narrow limitations of their reading. If they had read widely, they could not have overlooked that very well-known work on the *City of God*; they might have seen how, in the Sixth Book, Augustine cites the opinion of the learned Varro, who held that theology is threefold in its divisions—mythical, physical, and civil. It is called mythical, from the Greek *mythicon*, a myth, and in this kind, as I have already said, is adapted to the use of the comic stage. But this form of literature is reprobate among better poets on account of its obscenity. Physical theology is, as etymology shows, natural and moral, and being commonly thought a very useful thing, it enjoys much esteem. Civil or political theology, sometimes called the theology of state worship, relates to the commonwealth, but through the foul abominations of its ancient ritual, it was repudiated by them of the true faith and the right worship of God. Now of these three, physical theology is found in the great poets since they clothe many a physical and moral truth in their inventions, including within their scope not only the deeds of great men, but matters relating to their gods. And particularly, as they first composed hymns of praise to the gods, and, as I have said, in a poetic guise, presented their great powers and acts, they won the name of theologians even among the primitive pagans. Indeed Aristotle himself avers that they were the first to ponder theology; and though they got their name from no knowledge or lore of the true God, yet at the advent of true theologians they could not lose it, so great was the natural force of the word derived from the theory of any divinity whatsoever. Aware, I suppose, that the title "theologian" once fairly won, cannot be lost, the present-day theologians call themselves professors of sacred theology to distinguish themselves from theologians of mythological cast or any other. Such distinction admits no possible exception as implying an injury to the name of Christianity. Do we not speak of all mortals who have bodies and rational souls as men? Some may be Gentiles, some Israelites, some Agarenes, some Christians, and some so depraved as to deserve the name of gross beasts not men. Yet we do not wrong our Savior by calling them men, though with His Godhead He is known to have been literally human. No more is there any harm in speaking of the old poets as theologians. Of course, if any one were to call them sacred, the veriest fool would detect the falsehood.

On the other hand there are times, as in this book, when the theology of the ancients will be seen to exhibit what is right and honorable, though in most such cases it should be considered rather physiology or ethology than theology, according as the myths embody the truth concerning physical nature or human. But the old theology can sometimes be employed in the service of Catholic truth, if the fashioner of the myths should choose. I have observed this in the case of more than one orthodox poet in whose investiture of fiction the sacred teachings were clothed. Nor let my pious critics be offended to hear the poets sometimes called even sacred theologians. In like manner sacred theologians turn physical when occasion demands; if in no other way, at least they prove themselves physical theologians as well as sacred when they express truth by the fable of the trees choosing a king.

NOTES

FULGENTIUS: EXPOSITION OF THE CONTENT OF VERGIL

1. He imposed the twelve labors on Hercules.
2. A reference to the theory of the Greek Stoic philosophers about the number of human souls (which remains constant).
3. States of completion or perfection; actuality as contrasted with potentiality.
4. *Virtus*. Alternately, "courage." Here and below, the term "virtue" has been chosen because it fits best in later contexts. The formula anticipates the medieval prescription for the epic virtues of *fortitudo* and *sapientia* (fortitude and wisdom).
5. I Corinthians 7:24.
6. *Materiam laudis*, that is, the formulas of epideictic rhetoric, the rhetorical formulas of praise and blame.
7. Cf. *Corpus Hermeticorum,* ed. A. D. Nock (Paris, 1945), XII.1.
8. Work unknown.
9. Not by Plato. Helm cites Tertullian, *On Modesty* 1.
10. Here and below the Greek readings in brackets are conjecture. Fulgentius does not explain his often bizarre etymologies.
11. The quotation is from *Orestes* 1–3. The error in ascription probably derives from an anthology of quotations used by Fulgentius.
12. The story is told by Donatus in his *Life of Vergil.*
13. A book *On the God of Socrates* was written by Apuleius. The reference by Fulgentius is unclear.
14. Cf. Ezekiel 7:20.
15. Reference unclear.
16. *Epigrams*, ed. Kluge (Leipzig, 1926), p. 37.

AVERROES: THE MIDDLE COMMENTARY ON THE POETICS OF ARISTOTLE

1. Abu Tammam, a "modern." For these and later citations see: W. F. Boggess, "Hermannus Alemanus' Latin Anthology of Arabic Poetry," *Journal of the American Oriental Society* 88 (1968), 657–70.
2. Zuhair, Boggess, pp. 665–67.
3. Normally referred to by Hermannus as Abitaibl (Abi at-Tayyibi), cf. Boggess, p. 669.

4. Meaningless, cf. Boggess, p. 661 for the original and an Italian translation.
5. Quais al-Majnum ben 'Amir.
6. Unknown.
7. Abi ben Zaid.
8. Probably by Kutayyir 'Azza; cf. Boggess, p. 663.
9. For the proper Arabic place names, see Boggess, p. 664.
10. By Samardal ben Sarik; cf. Boggess, p. 664.
11. Laila al-Akyaliya.
12. Harit ben Hisam; Boggess, p. 664.

GEOFFREY OF VINSAUF: POETRIA NOVA

1. Geoffrey makes frequent use of corporal metaphors.
2. For metrical reasons, the author consistently uses the term *ordo* for the more technical term *dispositio*.
3. Limit. (To the Greeks and Romans, Cadiz, the ancient Gades, was long the westernmost point of the known world.)
4. Geoffrey refers, again in a corporal metaphor (head, body, final details) to the three parts of a composition: beginning, middle, end.
5. I.e., natural order or the order of art.
6. That is, amplified or abbreviated treatment, as the dignity of the subject demands.
7. The author understands by the term *proverbium* any general truth drawn from observation or experience.
8. The term *exemplaris imago* (illustrative image) renders more precise what Geoffrey understands by the term exemplum. All the exampla he offers as models in this treatise are exemplary images rather than stories.
9. The topos of *Mater Terra* (mother earth) and *Pater Aether* (father air) appears frequently in classical and medieval times.
10. The story of the snow child was a popular theme in the Middle Ages.
11. Horace, *Ars Poetica* 360ff.
12. The word's "native soil" (*proprium locum*) refers to its literal meaning rather than to its position in the sentence. To "take up an abode on the estate of another" is to assume metaphorical meaning.
13. In his discussion of the tropes, the author follows the treatment in *Ad Herennium* IV.xxxi.42–xxxiv.46. But Goeffrey lists only nine figures (anastrophe and transposition are included under hyperbaton), omitting the tenth, *circumitio* or periphrasis.
14. The reference is to Aulus Gellius' *Noctes Atticae* I.vii.20.
15. The source of this rather obscure line is Sidonius' *Epistles* I.ii.6: "There is more reason for the thirsty to criticize the infrequent filling of goblets than for the intoxicated to refrain from them."

DANTE: DE VULGARI ELOQUENTIA

1. A liquor consisting of honey diluted in water; when fermented, it becomes mead.
2. I.e., "They anticipated the divine solicitude for their well-being." The expression

"divine care" appears to be used as meaning "the time appointed by God's providence."

3. Lines 295–99.

4. *Oc*-Lat. *hoc* (this); *oïl* results from the combination of affirmative *hoc* with *ille* (he). The speakers of the language of *oc* are not inaptly called Spaniards, since a dialect of the language we now call Provençal prevailed over the whole of Aragon and Catalonia.

5. "If a faithful friend heard me, I would make accusation against love."

6. "From pure love proceeds wisdom and goodness."

7. "Before the gentle heart, in nature's scheme / Love was not, nor the gentle heart ere love." (Rossetti's tr.). These are the third and fourth lines of the first stanza of the canzone whose first line is quoted in Book II.v.

8. Dante.

9. "Sir, what are you saying?"

10. Meaning uncertain.

11. "I met a peasant girl (?) from Cascioli; she was slinking off in a great hurry."

12. "At the hour of evening, in the month of October."

13. "What are you doing?"

14. "New house."

15. "My lord."

16. "Even though through fire water forsakes [its great coldness]."

17. "O love, who long has led me." This line and the preceding one are the opening lines of two canzoni by Guido delle Colonne, a judge and notary of Messina (fl. 1257–88). "Weighty poetry" refers to the dignity of its subject matter.

18. Ancient name of Sicily.

19. Frederick II, crowned emperor in 1220.

20. An expression of contempt taken from Matthias 5:22.

21. I.e., Frederick II, king of Sicily from 1296–1337.

22. "Draw me from these fires, if it is thy will." The third line of a poem in the form of a dialogue between a lover and his mistress.

23. Meaning uncertain.

24. "Lady, I will tell you (how love has seized me)." The first line of a canzone by Jacopo da Lentino (fl. first half of 13th century).

25. "For pure love I go so joyfully." The first line of a canzone by Rinaldo d'Aquino, a contemporary of Jacopo.

26. "Let us eat meantime—we do nothing else."

27. "Truly the soldiers of Florence are going through Pisa."

28. "Thank God the commonwealth of Lucca is in a happy state" (?).

29. "Would that I had never forsworn Siena!"

30. "What is this?"

31. "Will you come somewhere?"

32. "My eye."

33. "My heart."

34. "Would it were so."

35. *Novem* is the Latin for "nine" (Ital. *nove*).

36. "By God's wounds thou shalt not come."

37. "Lady, the steadfast heart."

38. "My going afar."
39. "No more do I await thy succor, Love."
40. "I cannot choose but utter a song."
41. "The bitter blast strips bare the leafy woods."
42. "For the awakening of gallantry which is too fast asleep."
43. "Worthy am I of death."
44. "Grief furnishes my heart with daring."
45. A small stick or quill for striking the strings of the lyre.
46. "Now you shall hear perfect songs."
47. See Note 6.
48. "To the gentle heart love ever flies for shelter."
49. See Note 17.
50. See Note 25.
51. "I have no hope that ever for my well-being."
52. "Love who wieldest thy virtue from heaven" (Rossetti's tr.).
53. "Were it not for my all-excelling one."
54. "So pleasing is to me the amorous thought."
55. "I alone am he who knows the excessive grief which rises [in my heart]."
56. "No man can properly fulfill [what he has in his heart]."
57. "Even as the tree which through being overladen."
58. "Sorrow of love which in my heart abides."
59. "To say the truth, I hold his conduct foolish [who yields himself to one too powerful]."
60. "Since I must needs bear a heart of woe."
61. "Albeit my prayers have not so long delayed" (Rossetti's tr.)
62. "Love that discourses to me in my mind."
63. The Latin *lectio* is retained since there is no word in English which expresses at once the "action" and "passion" of reading.
64. The words "without *ripresa*" (*sine responsorio*) are added to distinguish the canzone from the ballata. The *ripresa* was the opening portion of the ballata, and was repeated at its close.
65. "Ladies that have understanding of love." This is the first line of the first canzone in Dante's *Vita Nuova*.
66. Aristotle.
67. The stanza.
68. "To the short day and the great sweep of shadow."
69. "Love drags the plough-pole of my mind."
70. See Note 52.
71. A very pitiful lady, very young" (Rossetti's tr.). The second canzone of the *Vita Nuova*.
72. "A lady prays me, therefore I will speak." The opening line of Guido Cavalcante's celebrated canzone on the nature of love.
73. See Note 65.
74. See Note 56.
75. "Of steadfast endurance."
76. See Notes 37 and 38.

77. "Now that love has entirely forsaken me."
78. "If love were as bountiful in bestowing joy upon me [as I am towards her in purity and sincerity of affection]."
79. "Love, you can well see that this woman."

BOCCACCIO: THE GENEALOGY OF THE GENTILE GODS

1. David, Psalm 69:9.
2. XIV.8.
3. There is no such story. Boccaccio probably means Ovid's obscene tale of Priapus and Lotis, *Fasti* I.415–40.
4. Cf. Homer, *Odyssey* VIII.266–366.
5. XIV.19.
6. *Pro Archias* 18.
7. Paolino, bishop of Pozzuoli, 1324–44.
8. *Metaphysics* II.iv.12. Aristotle, of course, means only authors of theogonies.
9. Luke 24:14–15.
10. Cf. Macrobius, *Somnium Scipionis* I.2., with some suggestion of Cicero's *De Inventione* I.27.
11. *Rhetoric* II.20.
12. Daughters of Minyas . . . Acestes. Ovid, *Metamorphoses* III.582–686; IV.31–415.
13. Judges 9:8–15.
14. *The Golden Ass* IV.21.
15. Charles II. of Anjou.
16. Horace, *Ars Poetica* 333.
17. John 8:7.
18. VI.49 (Dryden's tr., as are the two following quotations).
19. IV.322–23.
20. VI.980–81.
21. Dante, *Purgatory* XXIX.108ff.
22. Petrarch, *Eclogue* 4.
23. Characters in Petrarch's *Eclogue* 6.
24. *Confessions* IV.16.
25. Wisdom 7:21, 22.
26. Mark 3:29.
27. Chapter 19.
28. In fact, it was his sixty-fourth, as he was born in 1278.
29. *Eclogues* 6, 7.
30. *Pro Archia* 16, 17.

BIBLIOGRAPHY

Section I: General; II. Classical and late Classical Sources; III. Christian and Early Medieval; IV. Carolingian; V. The XII Century Renaissance; VI. Scholastic Poetics; VII. Late and Post-Medieval Texts of Importance.

I. GENERAL

Arbusov, Leonid. *Colores Retorici.* Göttingen: Vandenhoeck & Ruprecht, 1948.

Atkins, J. W. H. *English Literary Criticism: The Medieval Phase.* London: Methuen, 1952. Limited to English authors, this volume is rather one-sided in view of the European scope of medieval thought.

Baldwin, Charles S. *Medieval Rhetoric and Poetic.* New York: Macmillan, 1928. The best survey currently available in English, but weakened by its exclusion of non-rhetoric poetic theory and now dated.

Beardsley, Monroe C. *Aesthetics from Classical Greece to the Present.* New York: Macmillan, 1966.

Bolgar, Robert R. *The Classical Heritage and Its Beneficiaries.* London: Cambridge University Press, 1954. Primarily concerned with influences rather than critical theory.

Bruyne, Edgar de. *Etudes d'esthétique médiévale.* 3 vols. Brussels: De Tempel, 1946 and (a 1-volume abridgment) *The Esthetics of the Middle Ages,* tr. by Eileen B. Hennessey. New York: Ungar, 1969. To date the definitive study of medieval aesthetics.

Buck, August. *Italienische Dichtungslehren vom Mittelalter bis zum Ausgang der Renaissance.* Tübingen: Niemeyer, 1952.

Comparetti, Domenico. *Vergil in the Middle Ages,* tr. by E. F. M. Benske. New York: Stechert, 1929. A pioneering work; useful for discussion of Vergilian exegesis.

Curtius, Ernst Robert. *European Literature and the Latin Middle Ages,* tr. Willard Trask. New York: Pantheon, 1953. A brilliant study of poetic themes and *topoi.* Much incisive discussion of rhetorical and literary theory.

Daniélou, Jean. *From Shadows to Reality: Studies in the Biblical Typology of the Fathers,* tr. Dom W. Hibbard. Westminster, Md.: Newman Press, 1960.

Gilson, Etienne. *A History of Christian Philosophy in the Middle Ages.* New York: Random House, 1955.

Glunz, Hans. *Die Literârästhetik des europäischen Mittelalters.* 2nd ed. Frankfurt a. M.: Klostermann, 1963. Emphasis is on stylistics rather than critical theory *per se.*

Halm, Karl. *Rhetores Latini Minores.* Leipzig: Teubner, 1863. Reprinted Dubuque, Iowa: Brown, 1964. A basic collection.

Keil, Heinrich. *Grammatici Latini.* 7 vols. and suppl. Leipzig: Teubner, 1857–80. Definitive collection of texts.

Klibansky, Raymond. *The Continuity of the Platonic Tradition During the Middle Ages.* London: Warburg Institute, 1939. The basic study.

Lubac, Henri de. *Exégèse médiévale.* . . . 4 vols. Paris: Aubier, 1959–64. Standard.

Manitius, Max. *Geschichte der lateinischen Literatur des Mittelalters.* 3 vols. Munich: Beck, 1911–31. The foundation on which much medieval scholarship rests.

Migne, Jacques Paul. *Patrologiae Cursus Completus. Series Graeca.* 161 vols. in 166. Paris, 1857–80.

———. *Patrologiae Cursus Completus. Series Latina.* 221 vols. Paris: Garnier, 1844–64 (see also supplements and indexes). Basic although many texts are now available in superior modern editions.

Montano Rocco. *L'estetica nel pensiero cristiano.* Milan, 1955. A collection of excerpts, with discussion. Emphasizes Neo-platonic aesthetics, esp. those associated with Chartres and its influences.

Monumenta Germaniae Historica, ed. H. G. Pertz and others. Berlin, 1826–   . See esp. *Auctores Antiquissimi* (15 vols.) and *Poetae Latini Medii Aevi* (5 vols.). Like Migne, a magisterial collection.

Norden, Eduard. *Die antike Kunstprosa.* 5th ed. 2 vols. Stuttgart: Teubner, 1958. A standard study, extended to the Renaissance, of "art prose" derived from the Asiatic tradition in rhetoric.

Paetow, Louis J. *The Arts Course at Medieval Universities with Special Reference to Grammar and Rhetoric.* Urbana: University of Illinois Press, 1910.

Raby, F. J. E. *A History of Christian Latin Poetry in the Middle Ages.* 2nd ed. Oxford: Clarendon Press, 1953.

———. *A History of Secular Latin Poetry in the Middle Ages.* 2nd ed. 2 vols. Oxford: Clarendon Press, 1957.

Robertson, D. W. *A Preface to Chaucer: Studies in Medieval Perspectives.* Princeton: Princeton University Press, 1962. Emphasis is on biblical exegesis and allegorical and symbolic interpretation as well as its relation to secular literature.

Robins, Robert H. *Ancient and Medieval Grammatical Theory in Europe.* . . . London: Bell, 1951.

Saintsbury, George. *A History of Criticism and Literary Taste in Europe.* 3 vols. Edinburgh and London: Blackwood, 1900–04. (Vol. I: Classical-Medieval). Dated but the medieval section remains useful. Should be checked regularly against more recent scholarship.

Sandkühler, Bruno. *Die frühen Dantekommentare und ihr Verhältnis zur mittelalterlichen Kommentartradition.* Munich: Hueber, 1967. Discusses the influence of the *accessus* tradition.

Sandys, John E. *A History of Classical Scholarship.* 3 vols. Cambridge: Cambridge University Press, 1920. (Vol. I: Classical-Medieval).

Schanz, Martin, *Geschichte der römischen Literatur.* Vol. I (to Justinian); vol. II (the 4th Century); vol. III (with Carl Hosius and Gustav Krüger: the 5th and 6th Centuries). Munich: Beck, 1904–13. Massive and (for the time of its publication) definitive.

Seznec, Jean. *The Survival of the Pagan Gods,* tr. B. F. Sessions. New York: Pantheon, 1953. Interpretation of classical myth in medieval art and literature.

Smalley, Beryl. *The Study of the Bible in the Middle Ages.* 2nd ed. Oxford: Blackwell, 1962.

Spengel, Leonhard von. *Rhetores Graeci.* 3 vols. Leipzig: Teubner, 1853–56. A collection of basic texts.

Wimsatt, William K. and Brooks, Cleanth. *Literary Criticism: A Short History*. New York: Knopf, 1957.

II. CLASSICAL AND LATE CLASSICAL SOURCES

Atkins, J. W. H. *Literary Criticism in Antiquity*. 2 vols. Cambridge: Cambridge University Press, 1934.

Auerbach, Erich. *Literary Language and Its Public in Late Latin Antiquity and the Middle Ages*, tr. Ralph Manheim. New York: Pantheon, 1965.

Baldwin, Charles C. *Ancient Rhetoric and Poetic*. New York: Macmillan, 1924.

Burgess, Theodore. *Epideictic Literature*. (University of Chicago Studies in Classical Philology, III. Chicago, 1902). Epideictic (or demonstrative) rhetoric was extremely popular in late antiquity and influenced medieval and Renaissance authors.

Clark, D. L. *Rhetoric in Graeco-Roman Education*. New York: Columbia University Press, 1957.

Clark, M. L. *Rhetoric at Rome* [through St. Augustine]. London: Cohen & West, 1953.

Ernesti, Johann Christian. *Lexicon Technologiae Graecorum Rhetoricae*. Leipzig, 1795. Reprinted Hildesheim: Olms, 1962.

———. *Lexicon Technologiae Latinorum Rhetoricae*. Leipzig: Fritsch, 1797.

Fisk, George. *Cicero's de Oratore and Horace's Ars Poetica*. (University of Wisconsin Studies in Language and Literature, XXVII. Madison, 1929).

Grube, G. M. A. *The Greek and Roman Critics*. Toronto: University of Toronto Press, 1965.

Henderson, Charles. "Lexicon of Stylistic Terms Used in Roman Literary Criticism." 3 vols. Unpubl. University of North Carolina dissertation, 1955.

Kennedy, George. *The Art of Persuasion in Greece*. Princeton: Princeton University Press, 1963.

McMahon, A. P. "Seven Questions on Aristotelian Definitions of Tragedy and Comedy." *Harvard Studies in Classical Philology*, XI (1929), 97–198. Shows the continuity of certain definitions throughout the Middle Ages and into the Renaissance.

Quadlbauer, Franz. *Die antike Theorie der Genera Dicendi im lateinischen Mittelalter*. (Sitzungsberichte der Österreichischen Akademie der Wissenschaften. Philosophisch-Historische Klasse, CCXLI.2. Vienna, 1962). The vicissitudes of ancient theory in the Middle Ages.

Survival of Classical Authors

Crossland, Jessie. "Lucan in the Middle Ages." *Modern Language Review*, XXV (1930), 32–51.

Landi, C. "Stazio nel medio evo." *Atti dell' Accademia Padovana*, XXXVII (1921), 201–32.

Manitius, Max. *Analekten zur Geschichte des Horaz im Mittelalter*. Göttingen, 1893.

———. "Beiträge zur Geschichte des Ovidius und anderer römischer Schriftsteller im Mittelalter." *Philologus*. Supplementband VII (1899), 723–68.

Munari, Franco. *Ovid im Mittelalter*. Zurich: Artemis, 1960.

For Vergil, see Comparetti, section I.

Allegory

See Lubac, Daniélou, section I.

Hanson, R. P. C. *Allegory and Event: A Study of the Sources and Significance of Origen's Interpretation of Scripture.* London: S. C. M. Press, 1959.

Heraclitus. *Allégories d'Homère,* ed. and tr. Félix Buffière. Paris, 1962. A little known but important classical interpretation of the *Iliad* and *Odyssey.*

Hersman, A. B. *Studies in Greek Allegorical Interpretation.* Chicago: Blue Sky Press, 1906.

Hollander, Robert. *Allegory in Dante's Commedia.* Princeton: Princeton University Press, 1969.

Pépin, Jean. *Mythe et allégorie.* Paris: Aubier, 1958.

Tate, J. "The Beginnings of Greek Allegory." *Classical Review,* XXXI (1927), 214–15.

———. "Plato and Allegorical Interpretation." *Classical Quarterly,* XXIII (1929), 142–54; XXIV (1930), 1–10.

———. "On the History of Allegorism." *Classical Quarterly,* XXVIII (1934), 105–14.

(For the later tradition of Byzantine allegorism, see Cornutus. *Theologiae Graecae Compendium,* ed. Karl Lang. Leipzig: Teubner, 1881; Psellus. *Allegoriae;* and Tzetzes, *Allegoriae Iliados,* both ed. P. Boissonade. Lyons, 1851).

Neoplatonism

Whittaker, Thomas. *The Neo-Platonists: A Study in the History of Hellenism.* 2nd ed. Cambridge: Cambridge University Press, 1918.

GREEK AUTHORS:

Maximus Tyrius. *Dissertations,* tr. Thomas Taylor. 2 vols. London: Whittingham, 1804.

Plotinus. *Opera,* ed. Paul Henry and Hans-Rudolf Schwyzer. Paris: Desclée de Brouwer, 1951– . This critical edition will be in 4 vols.

———. *Ennéades,* ed. and tr. Emile Bréhier. 6 vols. in 7. Paris: Société d'édition "Les belles lettres," 1924–38.

———. Enneads, tr. Stephen MacKenna. 4th ed., rev. B. S. Page. London: Faber and Faber, 1969.

    Henry, Paul. *Plotin et l'occident: Firmicus Maternus, Marius Victorinus, St. Augustine, et Macrobe.* Dubuque, Iowa: Brown, 1965. (Repr. of Spicilegium Sacrum Lovaniense, études et documents, fasc. XV).

    Keyser, Eugénie de. *La Signification de l'art dans les Ennéades de Plotin.* Louvain: Bibliothèque de l'Université, 1955.

Porphyry. *De Antro Nympharum.* In *Opuscula Selecta,* ed. August Nauck. Leipzig: Teubner, 1886. An example of Neoplatonic exegesis of the "cave of nymphs" episode in Homer.

    Dörrie, Heinrich et al. *Porphyre: Huit exposés suivis de discussions.* Geneva: Foundation Hardt, 1965. (See esp. J. Pépin. "Porphyre exégète d'Homère").

Proclus. *Eis tes Politeias Platonos Hypomnema.* 2 vols. Leipzig: Teubner, 1899–1901.

———. "Proclus on the More Difficult Questions in the *Republic*: The Nature of Poetic Art," tr. Thomas Taylor. In "Preface" to *The Rhetoric, Poetics, and Nico-*

machean Ethics of Aristotle, ed. T. Taylor. 2 vols. London, 1818. Proclus provides
the best exposition of Neoplatonic literary theory.

Friedel, A. J. *Die Homer-Interpretation des Proklos.* Würzburg, 1923.

Rosán, Laurence. *The Philosophy of Proclus: The Final Phase of Ancient
Thought.* New York: Cosmos, 1949.

Late Latin Authors

Arcon. See Porphyrion.

Donatus, Aelius. *Commentum Terenti,* ed. Paul Wessner. 2 vols. Leipzig: Teubner,
1902–5.

———. *Ars Minor* and *Ars Maior* in Keil. *Grammatici Latini,* IV.

———. *The Ars Minor of Donatus,* tr. W. J. Chase. (University of Wisconsin Studies
in the Social Sciences and History, XI. Madison, 1926).

The standard grammarian throughout the Middle Ages.

Donatus, Tiberius Claudius. *Interpretationes Vergilianae,* ed. Heinrich Georges. 2 vols.
Leipzig, 1905–6. A rhetorical exegesis of Vergil.

Evanthius. *De Comoedia et Tragoedia.* In *Commentum Terenti,* ed. Paul Wessner,
vol. I (repr. Teubner, 1969). Often attributed to Aelius Donatus in the Middle
Ages. A basic statement about comedy and tragedy.

Macrobius. *Commentary on the Dream of Scipio,* tr. William H. Stahl. New York:
Columbia University Press, 1952.

———. *The Saturnalia,* tr. Percival V. Davies. New York: Columbia University Press,
1969.

Whittaker, Thomas. *Macrobius, or Philosophy, Science, and Letters in the Year
400.* Cambridge: Cambridge University Press, 1923. Macrobius is a major source
of medieval Neoplatonism, and his influence persists into the Renaissance.

Martianus Capella. *De Nuptiis Philologiae et Mercurii,* ed. Adolf Dick. Stuttgart:
Teubner, 1969. Best edition to date; a new one by James Willis is in preparation.
A favorite medieval allegory, containing much aesthetic and rhetorical lore in a
flamboyant style.

Martianus Capella and the Seven Liberal Arts. Vol. I. The Quadrivium of
Martianus Capella, Latin Traditions in the Mathematical Sciences 50 B.C.–A.D.
1250, by William H. Stahl. With a Study of the Allegory and the Verbal
Disciplines by Richard Johnson with E. L. Burge. New York: Columbia University Press, 1971.

Plutarch. *Moralia,* ed. and tr. Frank C. Babbitt. 15 vols. London: Heinemann, 1927–31
(Loeb Classical Library). See esp. I.2 ("How a Young Man Should Read the
Poets") and V.1 ("On Isis and Osiris").

———. "How a Young Man Should Study Poetry." In *Essays on the Study and Use
of Poetry,* ed. and tr. with an introduction by Frederick M. Padelford. New York:
Holt, 1902. (Yale Studies in English, XV). A treatise emphasizing the didactic function of literature.

Porphyrion. *Arconis et Porphyrionis Commentarii in Q. Horatium Flaccum,* ed. Ferdi-
nand Hauthal. 2 vols. Berlin, 1864–66. Two late classical commentaries on Horace
(useful for *Ars Poetica*).

Servius. *Servii Grammatici qui Feruntur in Vergilii Carmina Commentarii,* ed. Georg
     Thilo and Herman Hagen. 2 vols. Leipzig and Berlin: Teubner, 1923. Reprinted,
     3 vols. Hildesheim: Olms, 1961. A new edition, *Servianorum in Vergilis Carmina
     Commentariorum Editionis Harvardianae Volumen,* ed. Edward K. Rand et al.,
     has been in preparation since 1946 when vol. II (*Aeneid* I–II) appeared (Lancaster,
     Pa.: American Philological Association); vol. III (*Aeneid* III–IV) was published
     in 1965.
        Jones, Julian Ward. "An Analysis of the Allegorical Interpretation in the
          Servian Commentary on the *Aeneid*." Unpub. University of North Carolina
          dissertation, 1959.
        Servius provided the standard commentary-gloss on Vergil from the 4th century
          through the Renaissance.

III. CHRISTIAN AND EARLY MEDIEVAL

Augustine. *Opera.* In Migne. *Patrologiae . . . Latina* XXXII–XLVII. A modern edition
     (Corpus Christianorum. Series Latina) has been in progress since 1954 (Turnhout:
     Brepols).
———. *On Christian Doctrine,* tr. D. W. Robertson, Jr. New York: Liberal Arts Press,
     1958. Basic for its presentation of a "Christian rhetoric."
———. *On Music,* tr. R. C. Taliaferro. Annapolis, Md., 1939. Deals extensively with
     prosody.
        Eskridge, Thomas B. *The Influence of Cicero upon Augustine in the Develop-
          ment of His Oratorical Theory.* Menasha, Wisc. 1912.
        Knight, W. F. *St. Augustine's De Musica: A Synopsis.* London, 1949.
Basil the Great. "On the Right Use of Greek Poetry." In *Essays on the Study and Use
     of Poetry,* ed. and tr. by F. M. Padelford. New York: Holt, 1902. (Yale Studies
     in English, XV). Emphasis on the ethical benefits to be derived from a right use
     of pagan authors.
———. *Exegetic Homilies,* tr. Sister Agnes C. Way. Washington, D.C.: Catholic Uni-
     versity of America Press, 1963. (The Fathers of the Church. A New Translation,
     vol. XXXXVI).
Bede. *De Arte Metrica* and *De Orthographia.* In Keil. *Grammatici Latini* VII.
———. *De Schematibus et Tropis.* In Halm. *Rhetores Latini Minores.* Tr. by G. H.
     Tanenhaus in *Quarterly Journal of Speech,* 48 (1962).
Cassiodorus. *Opera.* In Migne. *Patrologiae . . . Latina* LXIX–LXX. A modern edition
     (Corpus Christianorum. Series Latina) has been in progress since 1958 (Turnhout:
     Brepols).
———. *An Introduction to Divine and Human Readings,* tr. Leslie W. Jones. New
     York: Columbia University Press, 1946. An early attempt to formulate a Christian
     curriculum.
John Cassian. *Opera.* In Migne. *Patrologiae . . . Latina* XLIX–L.
        Translations: In *Select Library of the Nicene and Post-Nicene Fathers of the
          Christian Church.* 2nd series, ed. Henry Wace and Philip Schaff. 14 vols.
          Oxford: Parker, 1891–1905, vol. XI. Cassian was important in the development
          of allegorical exegesis.

Clement of Alexandria. *Stromata.* in Migne. *Patrologiae . . . Graeca* VIII–IX. See esp. I.14, 21 (Greek debt to Hebrew) and VI. 15, 16 (Allegory).

> Translations: In *The Ante-Nicene Christian Library,* ed. A. Roberts and J. Donaldson. London, 1867–72, vols. IV, XII.

> Chadwick, Henry. *Early Christian Thought and the Classical Tradition: Studies in Justin, Clement, and Origen.* New York: Oxford University Press, 1966. Alexandrian and Christian Neoplatonism.

Fulgentius. *De Continentia Vergiliana.* In *Opera,* ed. Rudolf Helm, Leipzig, 1898. For the Middle Ages, the basic allegorical reading of Vergil.

———. *Fulgentius the Mythographer,* tr. Leslie Whitbread. Columbus: Ohio State University Press, 1972.

> Liebeschütz, Hans. *Fulgentius Metaforalis: Ein Beitrag zur Geschichte der antiken Mythologie.* Berlin, 1926. (Studien der Bibliotek Warburg, IV).

Isidore of Seville. *Etymologiarum sive Originum Libri XX,* ed. W. M. Lindsay. 2 vols. Oxford: Clarendon Press, 1911. Contains much literary lore. The standard medieval encyclopedia before Vincent of Beauvais.

Jerome. *Opera.* In Migne. *Patrologiae . . . Latina* XXII–XXV. A modern edition by P. Lagarde et al. (Corpus Christianorum, Series Latina) has been in progress since 1958 (Turnhout: Brepols).

> Translations: In *Select Library of the Nicene and Post-Nicene Fathers of the Christian Church.* 2nd series, vol. VI.

> *The Homilies of Saint Jerome,* tr. by Sister Marie Liguori Ewald. Washington: Catholic University of America Press, 1964–66. (The Fathers of the Church. A New Translation, vols. XLVIII and LVII).

> *Selected Letters,* tr. Paul Carroll. Chicago, 1958. Comments on the theory of translation, the relation of biblical to classical literature, literary style, the value of pagan authors, etc.

Lactantius. *Opera.* In Migne. *Patrologiae . . . Latina* VI–VII; also, ed. by Samuel Brandt and G. Laubmann. 3 vols. Leipzig: Freytag, 1890–97. (Corpus Scriptorum Ecclesiasticorum Latinorum, vols. XIX, XXVII.1, XXVII.2).

> Translations: In *The Ante-Nicene Christian Library,* vols. XX–XXII.

> *The Divine Institutes,* tr. by Sister Mary Francis McDonald. Washington: Catholic University of America Press, 1964. (The Fathers of the Church. A New Translation, vol. XLIX).

Lactantius assimilates much classical tradition to a Christian frame of reference.

Origen. *Opera.* In Migne. *Patrologiae . . . Graeca* XI–XVII.

> Translations: In *The Ante-Nicene Christian Library,* vols. X, XXIII.

Tertullian. *Opera,* ed. E. Dekkers et al. 2 vols. Turnhout: Brepols, 1954 (Corpus Christianorum, Series Latina I–II).

———. *De Spectaculis.* In *Tertullian, Apology, De Spectaculis,* with an English translation, by T. R. Glover. London: Heineman, 1931. (Loeb Classical Library). Arguments against classical drama. Tertullian provides the forerunner of most later attacks on the theatre and related public spectacles.

IV. CAROLINGIAN

Alcuin. *Disputatio de Rhetorica.* In Halm. *Rhetores Latini Minores.*
———. *The Rhetoric of Alcuin and Charlemagne,* tr. W. S. Howell. Princeton: Prince-
ton University Press, 1941.
    A balanced rhetoric influenced by the Ciceronian tradition.
Amalarius of Metz. *Opera,* ed. J. M. Hanssens. 3 vols. Vatican City: Biblioteca Apos-
tolica Vaticana, 1948–50. Allegorical interpretation of Christian liturgy.
Gariépy, Robert J. *Lupus of Ferrières and the Classics.* Darien, Conn., 1967. Con-
tinuity of classical literature.
Rabanus Maurus. *De Clericorum Institutione.* In Migne. *Patrologiae . . . Latina* CVII.
In the tradition of Cassiodorus and Lactantius.
Remigius of Auxerre. *Opera.* In Migne. *Patrologiae . . . Latina* CXXXI.
———. *Commentum in Martianum Capellam,* ed. Cora E. Lutz. 2 vols. Leiden: Brill,
1962–65. Exegesis of *On the Marriage of Philology and Mercury.*
Scholia Vindobonensia ad Horatii Artem Poeticam, ed. Joseph Zechmeister, Vienna,
1877. Extremely important for Carolingian poetic theory. Actually, more of an
extended essay on the *Ars Poetica* than a series of notes in the style of Servius.

V. THE XII CENTURY RENAISSANCE

General

Faral, Edmond, *Les Arts poétiques du XIIe et du XIIIe siècle.* Paris: Champion, 1924.
Reprinted 1958.
Kelly, Douglas. "The Scope of the Treatment of Composition in the Twelfth- and
Thirteenth-Century Arts of Poetry." *Speculum,* XLI (1966), 261–78.
Mari, Giovanni. *I trattati medievali di ritmica latina.* Milan: Hoepli, 1899. Medieval
treatises on accentual prosody.
Murphy, James J., ed. *Three Medieval Rhetorical Arts.* Berkeley: University of Cali-
fornia Press, 1971.

ARTES PRAEDICANDI (Arts of Preaching):

Charland, Th.-M. *Artes Praedicandi.* Paris: Vrim, 1936.

COMMENTARIES:

An Anonymous Medieval Commentary on Juvenal [XII–XIII Century], ed. Robert J.
Barrett. Darien, Conn., 1967.
    Representative examples of a very popular genre.
Commentarius Recentior. In *Scholia Terentiana,* ed. Friedrich Schlee. Leipzig: Teubner,
1893.
Commentum Bernardi Silvestris super Sex Libros Eneidos Vergilii, ed. Wm. Riedel.
Greifswald, 1924.
        Stock, Brian. *Myth and Science in the Twelfth Century: A Study of Bernard
        Silvester.* Princeton: Princeton University Press, 1972.

Wetherbee, Winthrop. *Platonism and Poetry in the Twelfth Century: The Literary Influence of the School of Chartres.* Princeton: Princeton University Press, 1972.

DICTAMINA (LETTER WRITING) AND OTHER FORMS

Breitow, A. *Die Entwicklung mittelalterlicher Briefsteller bis zur Mitte des 12. Jahrhunderts.* Greifswald, 1908.

Haskins, Charles H. "Italian Treatises." In *Mélanges H. Pirenne,* Brussels, 1926, pp. 101–10. Treatises on letter-writing; derived from rhetorical tradition.

——. *The Renaissance of the Twelfth Century.* Cambridge, Mass., 1927. Reprinted New York: Meridian, 1957. Still a basic survey.

Rockinger, Ludwig von. *Briefsteller und Formelbücher des elften bis vierzehnten Jahrhunderts.* Munich, 1863. Reprinted (2 vols.) New York: Franklin, 1961.

Hieronimus, J. P. and Cox, Josiah, eds. *Two Types of XIII Century Grammatical Poem.* Colorado Springs, 1929. (Incl. the paraphrase of the *Ars Minor* of Donatus by Henry of Avranches).

Huygens, R. B. C. *Accessus ad Auctores.* Brussels: Latomus, 1954. The "introduction to the classics" of the later Middle Ages.

Quain, E. A. "The Medieval Accessus ad Auctores." *Traditio,* III (1945), 215–64.

RHETORIC (TO XV CENTURY):

Allen, Judson B. *The Friar as Critic: Literary Attitudes in the later Middle Ages.* Nashville: Vanderbilt, 1971.

Baltzell, Jane. "Rhetorical Amplification and Abbreviation and the Structure of Medieval Narrative." *Pacific Coast Philology,* II (1966), 32–38.

Murphy, James J. "The Earliest Teaching of Rhetoric at Oxford." *Speech Monographs,* XXVII (1960), 345–47.

——. "The Arts of Discourse, 1050–1400." *Mediaeval Studies,* XXIII (1961), 194–205.

——. "The Medieval Arts of Discourse: An Introductory Bibliography." *Speech Monographs,* XXIX (1962), 71–78.

——. "A New Look at Chaucer and the Rhetoricians." *Review of English Studies,* n.s., XV (1964), 1–20.

——. "Rhetoric in Fourteenth-Century Oxford." *Medium Aevum,* XXXIV (1965), 1–20.

——. "A Fifteenth-Century Treatise on Prose Style." *Newberry Library Bulletin,* VI (1966), 205–10.

Authors

For John of Garland, Matthew of Vendôme, Geoffrey of Vinsauf, Everardus, see Faral, V. General.

For treatises on prosody, see Mari, V. General.

Conrad of Hirsau. *Dialogus super Auctores,* ed. R. B. C. Huygens. Brussels: Latomus, 1955. The fullest of the treatises in the *accessus* tradition.

Geoffrey of Vinsauf. *Poetria Nova,* tr. Margaret F. Nims, Toronto: Pontifical Institute of Medieval Studies, 1967.

Gervase of Melcheley. *Ars Poetica,* ed. Hans-Jürgen Gräbener. Münster: Aschendorff,
    1965. (Forschungen der Romanischen Philologie, XVII). Interesting for the
    scholastic influence evident in its classification of figures.
Henri d'Andeli. *The Battle of the Seven Arts,* ed. and tr. L. J. Paetow. Berkeley:
    University of California Press, 1914. The debate between medieval humanism and
    the emergent scholasticism of the universities.
Hugh of St. Victor. *Didascalicon,* tr. Jerome Taylor. New York: Columbia University
    Press, 1961.
John of Salisbury. *Metalogicon* (1929) and *Policraticus* (2 vols., 1909), both ed. C. C. J.
    Webb. Oxford: Clarendon Press. Basic works of medieval humanism.
———. *Metalogicon,* tr. Daniel D. McGarry. Berkeley: University of California Press,
    1955.
———. *Policraticus,* tr., in part, by John Dickinson in *The Stateman's Book of John
    of Salisbury.* New York: Knopf, 1927.
        Liebeschütz, Hans. *Medieval Humanism in the Life and Writings of John of
        Salisbury.* London: Warburg Institute, 1950.
        Ryan, Sister Mary Bride. *John of Salisbury on the Arts of Language in the
        Trivium.* Washington: Catholic University of America Press, 1958.
Richard of Bury, *Philobiblon,* ed. and tr. E. C. Thomas. Oxford: Blackwell, 1960.

VI. SCHOLASTIC POETICS

General

Mandonnet, Pierre. *Siger de Brabant et l'Averroïsme latin au XIIIᵉ siècle.* 2nd ed.
    2 pts. Louvain: Université de Louvain, 1908–11. The context for the translation
    and influence of Averroes' commentaries on Aristotle.
McKeon, Richard. "Rhetoric in the Middle Ages." *Critics and Criticism: Ancient and
    Modern,* ed. R. S. Crane. Chicago: Chicago University Press, 1952, pp. 260–96.
Renan, E. *Averroes et l'Averroïsme.* Paris: Calman Lévy, 1852. Dated and inaccurate,
    but some sections remain useful.

Authors

al-Farabi. *Catálogo de las ciencias,* ed. and tr. Angel González Palencia. 2nd ed. Madrid:
    Consejo Superior de Investigaciones Científicas. . . , 1953. (Incl. tr. into Latin
    by Gerard of Cremona, ca. 1150). Discusses the placement of poetry among the
    sciences.

AVERROES-HERMANNUS ALEMANNUS AND THE POETICS:

    "Averrois Cordubensis Commentarium Medium in Aristotelis Poetriam," ed.
    William F. Boggess. Unpubl. University of North Carolina dissertation, 1965.
    A Latin text based on the manuscripts. Does not use Arabic mss. extensively.
    Lobel, E. "The Medieval Latin Poetics." *Proceedings of the British Academy,*
    XVII (1934), 309–34.

Luquet, G. H. "Hermann l'Allemand." *Revue de l'histoire des religions*, XLIV (1901), 407–22.

Margoliouth, David. *Analecta Orientalia ad Poeticam Aristotelis.* London, 1889. (Incl. fragmentary Latin version of Syriac tr. of the *Poetics*, ca. 900).

——. *The Poetics of Aristotle Translated from Greek into English and from Arabic into Latin.* London, 1911.

Franceschini, E. "La Poetica di Aristotele nel secolo XIII." *Atti del Real Instituto Veneto,* XCIV (1935), 523–48.

Marsa, E. "Ruggero Bacone e la Poetica di Aristotele." *Giornale critico della filosofia italiana,* XXXII (1953), 457–73.

Tkatsch, Jaroslav. *Die arabische Übersetzung der Poetik des Aristoteles.* 2 vols. Vienna and Leipzig, 1928–32. The standard treatment.

Dominicus Gundissalinus. *De Divisione Philosophiae,* ed. with introduction by Ludwig Baur. Münster: Aschendorff, 1903. (Beiträge zur Geschichte der Philosophie des Mittelalters. Texte und Untersuchungen, IV.3–4.). A Latin treatise with discussion of the "placing" of poetry. Arabic influences.

William of Moerbeke. *Aristotelis de Arte Poetica,* ed. E. Valgimigli. Paris, 1953. (Aristoteles Latinus, XXXIII). A translation directly from the Greek which, however, failed to achieve the popularity of the Averroes commentary.

VII. LATE AND POST-MEDIEVAL TEXTS OF IMPORTANCE

General

Trabalza, Ciro. *La critica letteraria del rinascimento.* Milan: Vallardi, 1915.

Vossler, Karl. *Poetische Theorien in der italienischen Frührenaissance.* Berlin: Felber, 1900.

Zabughin, Vladimiro. *Vergilio nel rinascimento italieno da Dante a Torquato Tasso.* 2 vols. Bologna: Zanichelli, 1921–23.

None of these works is as detailed or as comprehensive as the materials require. Zabughin is thorough but limited rather narrowly to Vergil and Italy.

Authors

BERSUIRE, PIERRE (PETER BERCORIUS) AND THE OVIDE MORALISE

Ovide Moralisé, ed. C. de Boer and J. van't Sant. *Verhandelingen der Koninklijke Akademie van Wetenschappen.* 5 vols. Amsterdam: Müller, 1915–38. Ovid with moral allegories. Immensely popular in the late Middle Ages.

Born, L. K. "Ovid and Allegory." *Speculum,* IX (1934), 362–79.

Ghisalberti, F. "L'Ovidius Moralizatus di Pierre Bersuire." *Studi romanzi,* XXII (1933), 5–136.

Tuve, Rosemond. *Allegorical Imagery.* Princeton: Princeton University Press, 1964.

Boccaccio, Giovanni. *Genealogia Deorum Gentilium,* ed. Vincenzo Romano. 2 vols. Bari: Laterza, 1951.

————. *Boccaccio on Poetry,* tr. Charles G. Osgood. Princeton: Princeton University Press, 1930. Books XIV and XV are the first full-scale "defense of poetry" of the Renaissance. Much influenced by Petrarch.

Dante. *De Vulgari Eloquentia,* ed. Aristide Marigo. Florence: Le Monnier, 1968. (English tr. in *A Translation of the Latin Works of Dante Alighieri,* by A. G. F. Howell and P. H. Wicksteed. London: Dent, 1904).

————. *Convivio,* ed. Maria Simonelli. Bologna, 1966. (English tr. by William W. Jackson. Oxford: Clarendon Press, 1909).

————. *La corrispondenza poetica di Dante Alighieri e Giovanni del Virgilio,* ed. E. Bolisani and M. Valgimigli. Florence: Olschki, 1963.

————. *Dante and Giovanni del Virgilio.* Comment and translations by Philip H. Wicksteed. Westminster, 1902.

————. *Epistle to Can Grande della Scala.* In *Opere,* Testo critico della Società dantesca italiana, ed. M. Barbi et al. Florence, 1921. (Epistola XIII). *Epistolae,* ed. and tr. Paget Toynbee. 2nd ed. Oxford: Clarendon Press, 1966.

Imola, Benvenuto de' Rambaldi da. *Commento latino sulla Divina commedia,* tr. (Italian) and ed. Giovanni Tamburini. 3 vols. Imola: Galeati, 1855–56. Influenced by Averroes' commentary on the *Poetics.*

Landino, Christoforo. *Disputationes Camaldulenses.* No modern ed. Allegorical interpretation of Vergil along the lines of Fulgentius.

Mussato, Albertino. See *Dante and Giovanni del Virgilio* under Dante.

    Dazzi, Manlio T. *Il Mussato preumanista (1261–1329): L'Ambiente e l'opera.* Venice: Neri Pozza, 1964. Early humanism.

Petrarch. *Opere.* Edizione nazionale. Florence, 1926–64. (Selected trs. in James H. Robinson and Henry W. Rolfe. *Petrarch: The First Modern Scholar and Man of Letters.* New York, 1898, reprinted Haskell House, 1970, and in Petrarch. *Letters,* sel. and tr. Morris Bishop. Bloomington and London: Indiana University Press, 1966.) Petrarch's critical theory is most evident in his "Invective Against a Physician" and his "Coronation Oration" delivered when he was awarded the laurel crown in 1341.

    Bernardo, Aldo. "Petrarch and the Art of Literature." *Festschrift for Beatrice Corrigan.* Toronto: University of Toronto Press, 1972, pp. 19–43. The best overview of Petrarch's theory of literature.

Politian, Angelo. *Le Selve e la Strega,* ed. Isidoro del Lungo. Florence, 1925.

Pontanus, Iovianus. *I Dialoghi,* ed. Carmelo Previtera. Florence, 1943.

Salutati, Coluccio. *De Laboribus Herculis,* ed. B. L. Ullmann. 2 v. Zurich, 1951.

Savonarola, Girolamo. *De Divisione Scientiarum.* No modern ed. A restatement of the scholastic position concerning the placement of poetry among the sciences.

GLOSSARY AND INDEX
OF PROPER NAMES

I-i

GENERAL INDEX

abusio. See catachresis

accent, 110, 116, 117, 118, 141, 143. *See also* meter.

accessus, 4, 7, 9–10, 13, 14, 31, 32, 33, 35, 125, 147

act division, Evanthius on, 43, 44

action(s) 35–36, 40, 94, 95, 167, 179; Averroes on, 85, 91, 98, 99, 100, 101, 102, 103, 104, 109, 110

actors, 46, 49, 112; costumes of, 43

adornment. *See* style, ornaments of

aesthetics. *See* art

allegory, 64, 65, 66, 137, 188; medieval, 4, 5–6, 14, 15, 16, 17, 18, 19, 21, 22, 33, 34, 35, 36, 51, 53, 58, 64; anagogical (spiritual), 147, 188; biblical, 147, 188; Dante on, 145–46, 147; in Vergil's *Aeneid,* 67–68, 71–80; in Vergil's *Eclogues,* 76, 79; moral, 147, 188; poetics versus theological, 146, 147

ambiguity, 140

amplification (*auxesis*), 5, 124, 125–26, 131–35; Geoffrey of Vinsauf on, 125–26, 131–35

analogy, 90, 116, 141

antonomasia, 137

aposiopesis, 141

apostrophe, 32–32

appearance(s), 17, 50, 52, 55, 59–60, 111. *See also* imitation

appropriateness. *See* decorum

Arab poetry, 83, 84, 86 90–92, 95, 98, 99, 101, 103, 105, 106, 107–11, 115–17, 119–22

Arabic, influence on literature. *See* criticism, Aristotelian; literature, medieval

archetype, 126, 128

architect, artist as, 126, 128–29

argument, 96, 97–98. *See also* rhetoric

ars dictaminis, 36

ars metrica, 8, 10, 15, 84, 87, 148. *See also* meter

ars poetica, 30. *See also artes poeticae*

ars praedicandi, 36

ars rhythmica, 8, 15. *See also* rhythm

art, 147, 173, 174, 175, 180–81, 196, 197; as imitation, 52; as religious experience, 51; Geoffrey of Vinsauf on, 30, 31, 126, 127, 137–38, 141–42; inspiration, and, 56–57; medieval, 3, 10; nature, and, 129, 130, 132; Plato on, 52–53; Plotinus on, 50; truth, and, 50; versus inspiration, 56–57. *See also* artists; arts; imitation; morality; painting; poetry

artes dictaminis, 11

artes metricae, 125, 151

artes poeticae, 4, 13, 22, 28, 30, 31, 34, 36, 127, 152, *See also* poetry

artes praedicandi, 11

artes rhythmicae, 36

articulus, 135

artist(s), as architect, 126, 128; as imitator, 50;
    Plato's low estimate of, 52; Plotinus on, 50.
    See also art; arts
arts, Averroes on, 96, 97
Asianism, 11
asyndeton, 135
auctores, 8, 9, 11, 13, 14, 32, 33, 34, 127
audience, 43, 44, 45, 46, 47, 49, 53; Averroes
    on, 97, 102, 104, 109, 112, 118
authors, lists of. See accessus; auctores
auxesis. See amplification

ballate, 173, 180
beauty, absolute, medieval, and, 3; Plotinus on,
    50; poetry, and, 17, 18; Proclus on, 50, 52, 54
Bible, 4, 6, 7, 8, 9, 16, 17, 18, 20, 21, 25,
    32, 33, 37, 51, 65, 68–69, 71, 76, 79, 103,
    147, 148, 188, 190, 191, 201, 202, 206–
    207; Deuteronomy, 5, 26; Ecclesiastes, 9,
    26; Genesis, 19, 26, 155; Isaiah, 26; Job, 9,
    25, 26; Pentateuch, 9, 191, 201; Psalms, 9,
    20, 26, 72, 75, 189, 207; Songs of Songs,
    9, 25, 26
blame, poetry as the art of, 35, 83, 84–85, 86–
    87, 122; in rhetoric, 125, 126. See also
    poetry as praise and blame
books, 9
brevity (brevitas), 126, 140

canzone, Dante on, 147, 148, 151, 163, 168,
    173, 174, 175–76, 177, 179–86
catachresis, 138
catastrophe, 45, 47, 48
catharsis, 82
cathedral schools, 7, 13, 14, 32, 33, 34
change, 102. See also reversal
character(s), 19, 40, 41, 42, 43, 44, 82; Averroes
    on, 85, 91, 95, 96, 102, 104, 105, 107,
    108; in comedy, 48; Evanthius on, 42–43
chorus, 47; Evanthius on, 40, 41, 42, 43, 44
circuitio. See periphrasis
circumlocutio. See periphrasis
coda, 181, 182, 183, 185
coherence, internal. See probability (to eikos)
collatio, 132
colors of rhetoric. See rhetoric; imagery
comedy, Averroes on, 85; characters in, 48;
    contrasted to tragedy, by Donatus, 46, by

Evanthius, 40–41, 44, 45, Dante on, 147,
    151, 174; definition, 39, by Cicero, 41, 45;
    Donatus on, 41, 45, 46, 47, 48, 49;
    Evanthius on, 40–41, 42–43, 44, 45; history
    of, 40, 41, 42, 43; music for, 49; new, 40,
    43, 44; old, 42–43, 47; origin and develop-
    ment, 40–41, 42, 46; parts of, 45, 47;
    Roman, 40, 47; types and forms, 45, 47.
    See also drama
commentary, 7, 10, 14, 21, 24, 25, 27, 29, 30,
    33, 34, 35, 39–40, 51, 64, 65, 66, 82, 83,
    89, 127, 145, 146
commoratio, 139–40
comparison, 132
compassion. See pity and fear
composition, 5, 7, 8, 142
conformatio, 140
contentio, 140
conversions, 125
copying, 5
craftsmanship, 50, Geoffrey of Vinsauf on, 126,
    127, 128, 135
creativity, 50, 127
criticism, allegorical, 4, 27, 33, 87, 188, ancient
    tradition, 16–22, medieval, 16–22, 64–65;
    Aristotelian, 81, 82–88; classical, 3, 4–5, 6,
    7, 10, 11, 12, 13–15, 16–20, 22, 51, 64–
    65; grammatical, 128; medieval, 3–4, 5, 6–
    10, 10–13, 13–15, 16–22, 51, 64–65, 83,
    86–87, 127, 145–48, 151, 152, Carolingian,
    27–29, high middle ages, 29–34, human-
    istic, 36–37, late classical, 23–26, scholastic
    period, 14, 34–36; modern, 3; Neoplatonic,
    17, 51; Platonic, 37; Renaissance, 23;
    rhetorical, 66, 81, 128. See also critics;
    literature
critics, anthropological, 149; humanist, 51, 87–
    88, 187; medieval, 148; Neoplatonic, 17,
    51; psychological, 149; Renaissance, 51,
    87. See also criticism, new critics

death, 76, 147
decorum, 5, 10, 40; Averroes on, 105, 121;
    Geoffrey of Vinsauf on, 127, 133, 136, 141
delivery, Geoffrey of Vinsauf on, 127, 143–44.
    See also rhetoric
demonstratio, 140
denominatio, 137